Failing Universities

ALSO AVAILABLE FROM BLOOMSBURY

How to Mend a University, Ian M. Kinchin
Transforming University Education, Paul Ashwin
Dominant Discourses in Higher Education,
Ian M. Kinchin and Karen Gravett
Academics' International Teaching Journeys, edited by Anesa
Hosein, Namrata Rao, Chloe Shu-Hua Yeh, and Ian M. Kinchin
Early Career Teachers in Higher Education, edited by Jody Crutchley,
Zaki Nahaboo, and Namrata Rao
Class, Race, Disability and Mental Health in Higher Education,
Mike Seal
Utopian Universities, edited by Miles Taylor and Jill Pellew
Changing Higher Education for a Changing World,
edited by Claire Callender, William Locke, and Simon Marginson
Pursuing Teaching Excellence in Higher Education,
Margaret Wood and Feng Su
Locating Social Justice in Higher Education Research,
edited by Jan McArthur and Paul Ashwin
Subjectivity and Social Change in Higher Education,
Liezl Dick and Marguerite Müller
Decolonizing University Teaching and Learning, D. Tran
Social Theory and the Politics of Higher Education, edited by
Mark Murphy, Ciaran Burke, Cristina Costa, and Rille Raaper

Failing Universities

How Higher Education Became a Commodity and What We Can Do About It

HOWARD KARGER AND DAVID STOESZ

BLOOMSBURY ACADEMIC
LONDON • NEW YORK • OXFORD • NEW DELHI • SYDNEY

BLOOMSBURY ACADEMIC
Bloomsbury Publishing Plc
50 Bedford Square, London, WC1B 3DP, UK
1385 Broadway, New York, NY 10018, USA
29 Earlsfort Terrace, Dublin 2, Ireland

BLOOMSBURY, BLOOMSBURY ACADEMIC and the Diana logo are trademarks of Bloomsbury Publishing Plc

First published in Great Britain 2025

Copyright © Howard Karger and David Stoesz, 2025

Howard Karger and David Stoesz have asserted their right under the Copyright, Designs and Patents Act, 1988, to be identified as Authors of this work.

For legal purposes the Acknowledgments on p. xv constitute an extension of this copyright page.

Cover design by Grace Ridge
Cover image © Sean De Burca via Getty Images

All rights reserved. No part of this publication may be reproduced or transmitted in any form or by any means, electronic or mechanical, including photocopying, recording, or any information storage or retrieval system, without prior permission in writing from the publishers.

Bloomsbury Publishing Plc does not have any control over, or responsibility for, any third-party websites referred to or in this book. All internet addresses given in this book were correct at the time of going to press. The author and publisher regret any inconvenience caused if addresses have changed or sites have ceased to exist, but can accept no responsibility for any such changes.

A catalogue record for this book is available from the British Library.

A catalog record for this book is available from the Library of Congress.

Library of Congress Control Number: 2024942954.

ISBN:	HB:	978-1-3503-8381-4
	PB:	978-1-3503-8380-7
	ePDF:	978-1-3503-8382-1
	eBook:	978-1-3503-8383-8

Typeset by Integra Software Services Pvt. Ltd.
Printed and bound in Great Britain

To find out more about our authors and books visit www.bloomsbury.com and sign up for our newsletters.

For my father, Sam Karger, who always believed in higher education, and to Aaron, Saul, Rafi, Aoi, Hikaru, Grayson, Louisa, and Kath, who carry that belief forward

For Roy, a patriot, geologist, and inspiration

Contents

List of Figures viii
List of Tables ix
Preface x
Acknowledgments xv

1 The Price of Admission 1
2 Just Another Commodity 29
3 Driving Up the Cost of Higher Education 49
4 American Universities, Inc. 81
5 The College Sports Industrial Complex 111
6 Inequality and the Corporatization of Higher Education 143

Conclusion: A Framework for Reforming Higher Education 159

Notes 181
Index 221

Figures

1.1 Percent of Undergraduates by Type of Institution, 2023 2

1.2 Weekly Earnings by Educational Level, 25 years and Older, 2021 6

1.3 Average Earnings for High School, Bachelor's, and Advanced Degree Holders, by Race/Ethnicity, Gender, and Education, 2020 11

1.4 Four- and Six-Year Baccalaureate Graduation Rate by Race/Ethnicity, 2010 Entry Class 22

5.1 Revenues (in Billions) for College Sports Based on 2,027 Institutions 115

Tables

1.1 A Simplified Schematic of American Higher Education 3

1.2 Labor Market Outcomes of College Graduates by Major, 2021 7

1.3 Median 2021 Annual Wage (US Dollars) of High School-Only Workers Compared to the $74,000 Median Wage of Bachelor's Degree Holders 12

1.4 Employment Hours Worked by Independent and Dependent Undergraduates Based on Family Poverty Level, 2015–16 19

1.5 Sample of Labor Market Outcomes of College Graduates by Major, 2021 25

3.1 Average Full-Time Faculty Salary in 897 Institutions, by AAUP Category, Affiliation, and Academic Rank, 2022–3 (US Dollars) 52

3.2 Sample of Administrative Costs per College Student, 2012 and 2020 57

3.3 rpk GROUP's Hourly Rates for Services to West Virginia University, 2023 60

3.4 Universities with the Largest Endowments, 2022 66

4.1 List of Administrative Appointments at the University of Virginia, 2023 83

4.2 The $1+ Million Club: Compensation for Presidents at Nonprofit Schools (with revenues of $100+ million), 2020 85

4.3 Highest Paid College Presidents at Public Universities, 2021 90

4.4 Key 2020 Administrative Salaries for Northwestern University 94

5.1 Division I Football Where Revenue Exceeded Expenses 2020 (in millions) 130

5.2 Salaries of Highest-Paid College Coaches Compared to Presidents of Their Universities (2022) 132

5.3 Student Fees Used to Subsidize Athletics 135

Preface

American higher education is in the midst of a profound crisis. The public's trust in the value of a college degree has fallen dramatically, with most Americans now believing that college is a questionable investment. Some skepticism relates to colleges being increasingly out of reach for many working-class families. For instance, tuition rose more than 135 percent between 1963 and 2021, jumping from $14,000 yearly in 2000 for four-year public colleges to $22,000 in 2021. At the same time, enrollment fell more than 7 percent from 2010 to 2023, as student loan debt tripled from 2007 to 2023. Americans owed $1.74 trillion in student loans in 2023, averaging $38,290 per loan. Although student loan default rates have dropped since 2010, roughly 7 percent of student loans are in default.

Tight university budgets due to declining state government support have led to questionable labor practices like hiring inexpensive adjuncts and contract workers and using graduate assistants to teach most first-year courses. Poorly paid part-time faculty now comprise almost 50 percent of the academic workforce. A California State University-San Marcos report found that roughly 70 percent of their first-year courses were taught by adjunct faculty and another 15 percent by graduate students.

While public colleges and universities are facing a plethora of serious problems, conservative state legislatures are taking a renewed interest by trying to end tenure and censoring course content, like critical race theory, that doesn't fit with their worldview. Even elite, well-endowed private universities are facing problems as their carefully crafted reputations are fading in the backlash against "wokeism," DEI (diversity, equity, and inclusion), allegations of antisemitism, suspect admissions policies, and grade inflation. Many Americans view elite universities as too disconnected from mainstream values.

This book obviously cannot address all those issues in depth since it is not a weighty tome on what ails American higher education.

Instead, the book is a critical analysis that uses a broad canvas to examine how commodification and corporatization have permeated higher education. Simply put, this book is about how education became just another commodified and corporatized institution and what we can do about it. The subsequent chapters tease out the areas where the impact of commodification and corporatization is the most obvious and the most keenly felt.

This book is about the radical transformation of American higher education. Tertiary education in the United States has changed in the last forty years. Whereas forty years ago, most college classes were primarily taught by tenured or tenure-eligible faculty, today low-paid adjuncts or contract workers teach many (if not most) classes. Forty years ago, distance learning involved mailing a course packet to students with arrangements for taking exams. A "flipped classroom" meant that the building had overturned. Textbooks were made of paper instead of ones and zeros. High school graduates with poor grades and low college entrance scores were relegated to "junior colleges" rather than open enrollment four-year universities. The average GPA for US students at four-year colleges went from a C to a B average. Since higher education has become a commodity, students and parents balk at low grades, feeling that they are not getting their money's worth. College instructors often have to justify why students did not receive the A grade they think they deserved. Some college instructors inflate grades to give students what they want to avoid potential grievances. For faculty, student evaluations (similar to Amazon product ratings) can mean the difference between having a job, getting tenure, and receiving a merit raise. Some instructors kowtow to student demands by avoiding extensive homework assignments, crafting easy exams, grading student papers liberally, and providing only positive feedback. While this may sound hyperbolic, there is often truth, even in hyperbole.

The most significant change occurred in the attitude of Americans toward college. Most families across the income spectrum from the 1950s to the 1990s wanted their children to be college graduates. Their belief in college as the ticket to a better future was unshakeable. The Pulaskis, a struggling Missouri farm family, somehow sent all seven of their children to college. The Schmidt family of rough-and-tumble Texas tug boaters put all three children through college. Many

Americans were first-in-family to graduate college. Samuel Karger was a Polish immigrant who came to America at age sixteen with no English and nothing in his pockets. At twenty-five years old, he was back in Europe as an American soldier and received an honorary high school diploma. My father's unwavering belief in higher education pushed me to graduate college, even after I had dropped out of high school. These stories are replicated across the United States as post-Depression working-class families and soldiers returning from the Second World War saw college as a ladder to upward mobility. The legislation that provided GI benefits for the Second World War veterans allowed 8 million (almost half of the 16 million veterans) to attend college or receive educational training. As a result, the number of university degree holders doubled between 1940 and 1950. The belief in the economic benefits of a college degree was proven correct, as Raj Chetty and his associates demonstrated that the post-Second World War "baby boom" generation saw dramatic increases in social and economic mobility. Policymakers recognized the importance of a college education and responded to the demand by expanding existing colleges and funding new ones.

But then something changed. Beginning in the 2000s, Americans' belief in higher education plummeted as almost 50 percent of American families did not want their children to attend college. A 2021 Gallup survey found that 46 percent of parents said they would prefer not to send their children to a four-year college, even without financial or other obstacles. Support is even wavering for recent high school graduates.[1] In a 2022 Best Colleges survey of 1,000 prospective undergraduate and graduate students, 69 percent believed they could be successful without a college degree.[2] Legitimate concerns around high tuition, high college dropout rates, and poor job prospects for some disciplines fueled this skepticism.

The widespread resentment toward a college education largely follows political lines, with Republicans being anti-college and Democrats supporting higher education. A 2021 Hechinger Report found that 46 percent of Republicans and 48 percent of independents were skeptical of the value of a college education. Did this shift occur because Americans don't want their children to attend college or believe they can't afford it? This book examines some of the reasons behind the erosion of support and what can be done about it.

Unless Elon Musk's Neuralink company evolves to where it can implant a chip in our brain that contains the world's knowledge or links us to a computer with that knowledge, the future of higher education is safe. The question is not whether higher education will exist but in what form. "What subjects will be taught?" "How will public higher education be funded?" "Will teaching responsibilities in public and private universities be offloaded to for-profit educational corporations?" "Will elite colleges retain in-person classes while public universities will be largely online?" "Will higher education fully adopt an Uber corporate model and use only casual workers and adjuncts to teach classes?" "Will tuition and student loan debt rise even higher and scare away potential students?" "Will college sports programs continue to bleed resources and detract from the educational mission of colleges and universities?" "Will administrative bloat pilfer even more resources from teaching?" The answer to these questions will determine who goes to college, what they will learn, and who will profit.

Since the University of Bologna's founding in 1088, colleges and universities have been places where students come to learn, experts, thinkers, and others come to teach, and where knowledge is created. Unfortunately, much of the American higher education system is being removed from that mission. Too many students attend college only to acquire a degree to earn more money and enhance their social standing. Coping with the high costs of college education, some parents pressure their children into degrees that lead to high incomes despite the child's real interests. Colleges are replacing a liberal arts education with "job-ready" skills employers demand. Public universities are in danger of becoming technical schools for the masses, while traditional liberal arts education will be reserved for those who can afford an elite private university.

Tuition dollars pay for money-losing football and basketball programs that turn universities into entertainment centers. Scrambling for lost governmental funding, good teaching is replaced by good grant-writing skills. Formerly stable university work environments that provided a livable income are being replaced by a gig economy like Uber and Lyft, where low-paid adjunct faculty (in some places, most teaching faculty) are hired on an as-needed basis and have become an academic precariat. Too many universities are run by "bean-counters" with little knowledge or interest in education beyond cutting costs (except administrative positions). As a straw dog in America's culture wars, universities are becoming teaching spaces where instructors are afraid to present arguments or ideas that question the state's political narrative.

Despite these challenges, we believe in the future and the value of a college education, not just for generating income but for producing citizens who value democracy over authoritarian populism. Higher education can survive and thrive only with a radical restructuring that returns it to its fundamental teaching, research, and service roles. Without this radical change, we fear that higher education will become even more of a commodity bought and sold in the marketplace.

Acknowledgments

Many thanks to those people who helped make this book possible. Emeritus Professor Steven Rose gathered and forwarded so much good information that he should be an honorary co-author. The book was conceived in 2018 while I was a Fulbright Research Scholar at OsloMet University in Norway. I'm indebted to the Fulbright Commission for giving me the time to think and write. Thanks to Bernie for the invaluable help in all parts of the book. Shirley Kuma deserves a medal for patiently listening to my kvetching. Professor Emeritus Michael Seltzer was a great support in helping clarify my ideas. Thanks also to Dr. Halaevalu Vakalahi, President of the Council on Social Work Education. As the former dean of the former College of Health and Society at Hawai'i Pacific University, she urged me to move on from my teaching position after completing my Fulbright, which inadvertently gave me the time to finish the book.

Howard Karger

1

The Price of Admission

In conventional wisdom, a college degree is one of the foremost ways to raise one's income and attain a middle- or upper-middle-class lifestyle. The need for higher education has become increasingly important, given that income inequality is at levels not seen since the 1920s.[1] For example, only the incomes of the top 20 percent of US households rose since 1967; by 2020, these households accounted for 52 percent of all US wealth. This wealth accumulation was greater than the combined income of the second, third, and fourth income quintiles.[2] The stark economic data was corroborated by Raj Chetty and his Harvard associates, who investigated the economic mobility of American families across generations. The researchers found that the chance of children earning more than their parents has declined: 90 percent of US children born in 1940 earned more than their parents; by the 2000s, only 50 percent of children did.[3] Given stagnant economic mobility, the pressure to earn a college degree is intense among many low-income families who see it as essential for success. At the same time, the rising costs of a college education have put it out of reach for many of these same families.

American exceptionalism is rooted in the belief that the United States is so different from other nations that it must carve its own unique path. The US higher education system reflects that exceptionalism, which is evident in the large number of private nonprofit and for-profit colleges and universities compared to Europe. In 2021, there were almost 4,000 postsecondary institutions in the United States;

41 percent were public four- or two-year colleges; 42 percent were four- or two-year private nonprofit schools; and 18 percent were for-profit.[4] By contrast, there were 130 public universities in the UK, and only eight were private; Canada had ninety-seven public universities and nine private ones; and Australia had forty-three public and three private universities. Despite the large number of American colleges and universities, the United States fell from second to sixteenth place among OECD countries in conferring bachelor's degrees from 2000 to 2020.[5] Since most nonprofit colleges and universities are small, the vast majority of American students attend public colleges and universities (see Figure 1.1).

The US higher education system can be roughly divided into several categories (see Table 1.1), making it difficult to generalize about educational quality and prestige. Moreover, much of a college or university's reputation is based on word-of-mouth and ranking systems, such as *U.S. News & World Report*'s "Best Colleges," The Center on World University Rankings, Times Higher Education Supplement, QS World University Ranking, and Shanghai's Academic

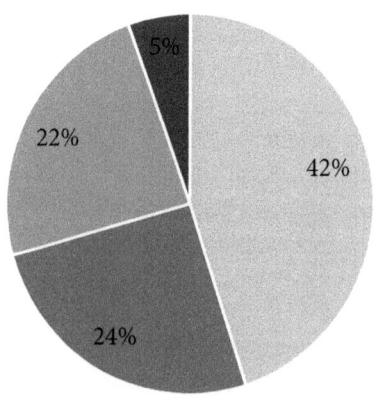

■ 4-year public ■ 2-year public ■ Private nonprofit ■ For-profit

Figure 1.1 *Percent of Undergraduates by Type of Institution, 2023*

Source: "Table 1: Estimated National Enrollment by Institutional Sector: 2019 to 2023" *National Student Clearinghouse* (Spring 2023), https://nscresearchcenter.org/wp-content/uploads/CTEE_Report_Spring_2023.pdf

Table 1.1 A Simplified Schematic of American Higher Education

Categories	Sample Institutions
These 8 Ivy League schools are some of the oldest and most sought-after institutions	Brown, Columbia, Cornell, Dartmouth, Harvard, University of Pennsylvania, Princeton, and Yale
*Ivy Plus schools are private nonprofit universities with similar academic prestige to the traditional eight Ivies	Stanford, Massachusetts Institute of Technology (MIT), University of Chicago, California Institute of Technology (Caltech), Northwestern, Duke, Johns Hopkins, Vanderbilt, Rice, and Washington University
*Little Ivies are prestigious institutions with a competitive admissions policy	Amherst, Bates, Bowdoin, Bucknell, Colby, Colgate, Connecticut College, Hamilton, Haverford, Lafayette, Middlebury, Swarthmore, Trinity, Tufts, Union College, Vassar, Wesleyan, Williams, Davidson, Emory, Wake Forest, Tulane, Barnard Boston, Georgetown, Emory, Skidmore, Case Western Reserve, Notre Dame, Oberlin, Claremont Mckenna, University of Southern California, Kenyon
*Black Ivies are historically Black colleges (HBCUs)	Dillard, Fisk, Hampton, Howard, Morehouse, Spelman, Tuskegee, Clark Atlanta
*Public Ivies are academically strong, have competitive admissions, and are less expensive for in-state students.	University of California campuses in Berkeley, Davis, Irvine, Los Angeles, San Diego, Santa Barbara, Santa Cruz; Miami University of Ohio; University of Michigan at Ann Arbor; University of North Carolina at Chapel Hill; University of Texas at Austin, University of Vermont; University of Virginia; College of William and Mary
Mainstream religious institutions	Brandeis, Yeshiva University, Brigham Young, Notre Dame, Loyola
Evangelical universities and colleges	Liberty, Bob Jones, Oral Roberts, Wheaton, Houston Baptist

(*Continued*)

Categories	Sample Institutions
For-profit colleges and universities	Strayer, Capella, University of Phoenix, Grand Canyon, University of Arizona Global Campus, Walden
Regional colleges, universities, and community colleges	These comprise the vast majority of higher education institutions. Some states, like California, divide universities into research-intensive and teaching-focused state universities.

* These are not officially designated categories, and there is no agreement about which schools properly fit into which category. For space reasons, some institutions were omitted.
Source: Bijal Luhar, "What Are the Ivy Plus Schools?" Collegevine, July 20, 2021, https://blog.collegevine.com/ivy-plus-schools. Genevieve Carlton, "The Public Ivies, Little Ivies, and Other Ivy League Equivalent," Best Colleges, June 27, 2023, www.bestcolleges.com/blog/public-ivy-schools-and-little-ivies/

Ranking of World Universities. One weakness of ranking systems is that they rely on data provided by institutions that cannot be independently verified, and they rely on the opinions of administrators and academics in other institutions. The ranking of US universities is critical since international students constitute an essential revenue source for US colleges. Although American universities dominate the top listings of most international ranking systems, that lead is weakening in the face of growing competition from Chinese, European, and Australian universities. Research in STEM disciplines like math, computer science, and physics is particularly susceptible to competition from Chinese universities. Competition for international students (a vital revenue source for US universities) is also tightening. Twenty years ago, American universities could claim 60 percent of the international students seeking a degree in English-speaking countries. It is now roughly 40 percent.[6]

Since higher rankings translate into more student enrollment and greater revenues, the financial consequences of a low rank can tempt university administrators to embellish or falsify data submitted to ranking entities. One example is how the *U.S. News & World Report* dropped Columbia University's 2022 ranking from second to eighteenth place after the college admitted to falsifying data.[7]

The College Premium

Few countries put as high a premium on a college degree as the United States, and few other countries financially punish people as harshly for not having a college degree.[8] In most capitalist countries, those with the most education generally prosper, while those with the least education are financially disadvantaged. A 2021 Georgetown University study confirmed that more education typically pays off financially.

- High school graduates earn a median of $1.6 million during their lifetimes compared to $1.2 million for non-graduates; the dividend increases with each rung of higher education.

- Those with some college education but no degree earned $1.9 million during their lifetime, or about 19 percent more than high school graduates without college credits.

- Compared to a high school diploma, an associate arts degree will increase lifetime earnings by 25 percent.

- Bachelor degree holders earn $2.8 million over their lifetime, or 75 percent more than those with only a high school diploma.[9]

Accordingly, median lifetime earnings grow with a master's, doctoral, and professional degree.

- Master's degree holders earn $3.2 million over their lifetime, or about 14 percent more than those with only a bachelor's degree.

- Doctoral degree holders earn $4 million over their lifetimes (43 percent more than those with only a bachelor's degree).

- Those with a professional degree earn the highest median lifetime income of $4.7 million, or 68 percent more than those with only a bachelor's degree.[10]

Despite these income advantages, 38 percent of students from very low-income families remain poor after graduating college.[11] In 2014, 4.6 percent of all American college graduates lived below the poverty line.[12] Figure 1.2 illustrates the trajectory of income and educational attainment. Despite the overall benefits of higher education, the Georgetown University study also found that more education does not always guarantee higher lifetime earnings, and less education does not always result in lower earnings.

- At least 25 percent of high school graduates will earn more than an associate arts degree holder over their lifetime.

- At least one-quarter of those with an associate's degree will earn more than half of workers with a bachelor's degree.

- At least one-quarter of those with a bachelor's degree will earn more over their lifetime than half of workers with master's or doctoral degrees.[13]

One perk of higher education often overlooked is the lower risk of unemployment. In 2023, high school-only workers had an unemployment rate of 4.7 percent compared to 3.4 percent for those with an associate arts degree, a 2.2 percent rate for bachelor-degree

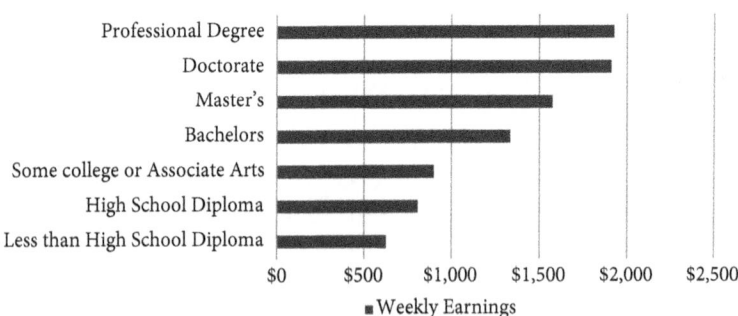

Figure 1.2 *Weekly Earnings by Educational Level, 25 Years and Older, 2021*

Source: "Earnings and Unemployment Rates by Educational Attainment," US Bureau of Labor Statistics 2021, September 8, 2022, https://www.bls.gov/emp/chart-unemployment-earnings-education.htm

workers, and a 1.4 percent unemployment rate for advanced degree holders and professionals.[14]

Whether earning a baccalaureate or a two-year associate arts degree is worth the cost is a nuanced question since the economic value of a degree depends on the field, with disciplines like social work, teaching, and recreation lagging far behind business, engineering, accounting, medicine, and law. In terms of lifetime earnings, undergraduates who major in architecture and engineering are the highest paid ($3.8 million), with computers, statistics, and mathematics ($3.6 million) coming in second and business ranking third at $3 million. In contrast, undergraduate majors in liberal arts, humanities, and recreation are typically on the lower end of the earnings scale. The lowest rungs, however, are reserved for bachelor's degrees in social work and psychology ($2.2 million), with education being the lowest-earning field at $2 million[15] (see Table 1.2).

Table 1.2 Labor Market Outcomes of College Graduates by Major, 2021

Major	Median Wage (Early Career)	Median Wage (Mid-Career)
Agriculture	$45,000	$70,000
Animal and Plant Sciences	$42,000	$67,000
Environmental Studies	$45,000	$68,000
Architecture	$50,000	$85,000
Ethnic Studies	$45,000	$66,000
Communications	$47,000	$75,000
Journalism	$45,000	$75,000
Mass Media	$40,000	$75,000
Advertising and Public Relations	$50,000	$80,000
Information Systems & Management	$54,000	$90,000

(*Continued*)

Major	Median Wage (Early Career)	Median Wage (Mid-Career)
Computer Science	$73,000	$105,000
General Education	$40,200	$51,000
Early Childhood Education	$40,000	$43,000
Elementary Education	$40,000	$48,000
Secondary Education	$40,400	$52,000
Special Education	$40,000	$52,000
Miscellaneous Education	$40,000	$56,000
General Engineering	$60,000	$100,000
Aerospace Engineering	$72,000	$112,000
Chemical Engineering	$75,000	$120,000
Civil Engineering	$65,000	$100,000
Computer Engineering	$74,000	$114,000
Electrical Engineering	$70,000	$109,000
Industrial Engineering	$70,000	$100,000
Mechanical Engineering	$70,000	$105,000
Miscellaneous Engineering	$68,000	$100,000
Foreign Language	$43,000	$65,000
Family and Consumer Sciences	$37,000	$60,000
English Language	$40,000	$65,000
Liberal Arts	$40,000	$63,000
Biology	$40,000	$75,000
Biochemistry	$45,000	$85,000
Miscellaneous Biological Science	$42,000	$70,000
Mathematics	$59,000	$88,000

Major	Median Wage (Early Career)	Median Wage (Mid-Career)
Interdisciplinary Studies	$41,800	$70,000
Nutrition Sciences	$45,000	$60,000
Leisure and Hospitality	$38,000	$60,000
Philosophy	$42,000	$68,000
Theology and Religion	$36,000	$52,000
Chemistry	$47,000	$85,000
Earth Sciences	$40,000	$70,000
Physics	$53,000	$80,000
Miscellaneous Physical Sciences	$52,000	$104,000
Psychology	$37,400	$65,000
Criminal Justice	$43,900	$70,000
Public Policy and Law	$45,000	$70,000
Social Services	$37,000	$52,000
Anthropology	$40,000	$65,000
Economics	$60,000	$100,000
Geography	$48,000	$75,000
Political Science	$50,000	$80,000
Sociology	$40,000	$61,000
General Social Sciences	$43,000	$65,000
Construction Services	$60,000	$100,000
Art History	$48,000	$64,000
Fine Arts	$40,000	$65,000
Performing Arts	$39,000	$62,000

(Continued)

Major	Median Wage (Early Career)	Median Wage (Mid-Career)
Commercial Art & Graphic Design	$43,000	$70,000
Health Services	$40,000	$60,000
Medical Technicians	$51,000	$71,000
Nursing	$55,000	$75,000
Pharmacy	$55,000	$100,000
Treatment Therapy	$48,000	$69,000
General Business	$50,000	$80,000
Accounting	$54,000	$80,000
Business Management	$46,000	$75,000
Business Analytics	$66,000	$99,000
Marketing	$50,000	$85,000
Finance	$60,000	$100,000
International Affairs	$50,000	$86,000
History	$50,000	$70,000
Engineering Technologies	$62,000	$90,000
Miscellaneous Technologies	$48,000	$80,000
Overall	$50,000	$75,000

Source: "Labor Market Outcomes of College Graduates by Major," Federal Reserve Bank of New York, February 10, 2023, https://www.newyorkfed.org/research/college-labor-market/index.html#/outcomes-by-major.

Race and Gender

Income inequality for college-educated women impacts the opportunity costs of higher education.[16] In 2020, women with bachelor's degrees or higher earned 75.4 percent of a male wage with the same educational attainment. That income ratio remained virtually unchanged as women with some college earned 75.9 percent of the wages of men with similar educational credentials.[17] In 2021, white women with a bachelor's degree earned roughly $60,000 a year compared to almost $95,000 for men. This discrepancy exists even with advanced degrees since white women with an advanced degree in 2020 earned $79,000 yearly compared to the average white male's salary of $137,000. An even more significant wage disparity exists for women of color. For example, Hispanic women with advanced degrees earn as much as Hispanic males with baccalaureates.[18] The data illustrates that college-educated women need to earn one degree higher to match the salaries of males with similar education. Income inequality is also racially and ethnically based. As Figure 1.3 illustrates, Black and Hispanic males earn less than white males at every level of education.

Given the income discrepancies based on race and gender, it is not surprising that 38 percent of students from very low-income families remain poor even after graduating college. In 2014, 4.6 percent of all American college graduates lived below the poverty line.[19]

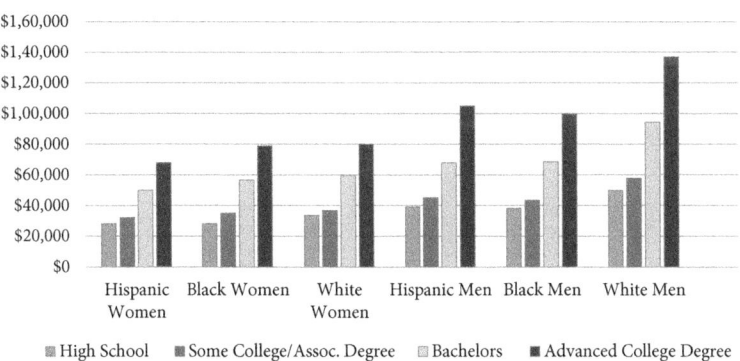

Figure 1.3 *Average Earnings for High School, Bachelor's, and Advanced Degree Holders, by Race/Ethnicity, Gender, and Education, 2020*

Source: "Table A-3. Mean Earnings of Workers 18 Years and Over, by Educational Attainment, Race, Hispanic Origin, and Sex: 1975 to 2020," United States Census Bureau, 2021, www2.census.gov/programs-surveys/demo/tables/educational-attainment/time-series/cps-historical-time-series/taba-2.xlsx

The Questionable Return on Investment (ROI)

Despite the obvious financial benefits of a college degree, questions remain about the return on investment for four to six years of deferred income combined with an average 2023 student loan debt of more than $37,000 for federal student loans and nearly $55,000 for private loans. Since the median income of a twenty- to twenty-four-year-old was roughly $37,000 in 2022, four years of lost wages would total $148,000 or $222,000 for the increasingly common six-year college graduation rate. This figure does not include any raises and promotions in four to six years of full-time employment. While the salary difference between college and high school graduates is significant in the aggregate, it is based on all high school graduates. It does not account for high school graduates in the trades or other relatively well-paying occupations. Table 1.3 illustrates the fairly close income gap between college and high school graduates based on a vocation or job.

Table 1.3 Median 2021 Annual Wage (US Dollars) of High School-Only Workers Compared to the $74,000 Median Wage of Bachelor's Degree Holders

Occupation	Median Annual Wage
Baccalaureate degree holder	$74,000
Elevator installer	$80,000
Boilermaker	$70,000
Electrician	$70,000
Chemical plant systems operator	$70,000
Real estate broker	$70,000
Building Inspector	$70,000
Crane operators	$70,000
Flight attendants	$70,000

Occupation	Median Annual Wage
Police	$70,000
Brick masons	$50,000
Postal workers	$50,000
Machinists	$50,000
Plumbers	$50,000
Sheet metal workers	$50,000
Payroll clerks	$50,000
Welders	$50,000
Auto body repair	$50,000

Source: US Bureau of Labor Statistics, "Office of Occupational Statistics and Employment Projections" in *Occupational Outlook Handbook* (September 28, 2022) https://www.bls.gov/ooh/

How Much Does the Choice of a College Matter?

While the data on college selectivity and economic mobility is complex and somewhat confusing, salaries are generally higher for graduates in highly selective institutions. A 2021 study by the Northwestern Center on Law, Business, and Economics found that graduates of more selective colleges or universities earned more money regardless of their major.[20] However, attending a selective college does not necessarily translate into a better return on investment, given the higher tuition costs and student loan debt.[21]

Raj Chetty and his colleagues found that access to selective colleges varies by parental income. Children whose parents are in the top 1 percent of the income distribution are seventy-seven times more likely to attend an Ivy League college than students whose parents are in the bottom income quintile (earning less than $28,000 a year). Only 3.8 percent of students from the bottom quintile of the income distribution attend Ivy-Plus (e.g., Stanford, MIT, the University of Chicago, and Duke) institutions.[22]

Students are channeled into colleges and universities in myriad ways. However, much of that channeling is based on financial costs, influencing whether a student chooses a first-, second-, or third-tier institution. A Pell Institute study found that students from low-income families typically choose educational institutions with lower tuition and status.[23] Only one-third of low-income undergraduates enroll in colleges with selective admissions; 5 percent enroll in the most competitive institutions, 9 percent in very competitive institutions, and 19 percent in competitive institutions. Among students enrolled in the most competitive institutions, only 12 percent come from the bottom half of the income distribution.[24]

The decision to attend a particular college or university is often based on factors such as cost, location, the prestige of the institution, and family connections (e.g., legacy admissions). One study of college choice found that school choice matters most for business majors. Those from top schools earned 12 percent more than those from middle-tier institutions. In turn, graduates from middle-tier schools earned 6 percent more than graduates from the least-selective schools. In lesser measure, social science, education, and humanities majors have also experienced a salary gain by attending a highly ranked school. Interestingly, the sciences showed the weakest earnings differences based on college selectivity.[25]

Stacy Dale and Alan Kreuger analyzed the earnings of 19,000 college graduates admitted to an elite school but who chose instead to attend a middle-tier school. They found that the earnings difference between the two groups twenty years after graduation was essentially non-existent. On the other hand, the economic gains of Black and Hispanic students from less-educated families were significant if they attended more selective institutions.[26]

Despite the complex relationship between college choice and degree choice, it is clear that a disproportionate number of industry and government leaders graduated from Ivy League or equally selective institutions. In *Where You Go Is Not Who You'll Be*, Frank Bruni voiced his skepticism about elite universities and pointed to successful people who attended second- or third-tier universities. Bruni found that only thirty of 100 American-born chief executives of the top 100 Fortune 500 companies attended an Ivy League or equally selective institution.[27] In contrast to Bruni, Jonathan Wai discovered that 44.8 percent of billionaires, 55.9 percent of powerful women, 63.7 percent of Davos attendees, and 85.2 percent of powerful men attended elite schools.[28]

Anthony Carnevale, Ban Cheah, and Martin Van Der Werf ranked the ROI (return on investment) of 4,500 colleges and found that community colleges and some certificate programs had the highest short-term (ten years) ROI. Primarily baccalaureate-based colleges had the highest long-term (forty years) ROI, and public colleges had a better short-term ROI than private colleges, especially for-profit colleges. On the other hand, degrees from private nonprofit colleges generally had a higher long-term ROI than public universities since the median annual earning ten years after graduation was almost $8,000 higher than for graduates of public universities.[29]

The Uneven Playing Field

Once an engine of upward mobility, colleges now contribute to educational inequality due mainly to the meteoric rise in tuition. Using 2020–1 dollars, one year of college tuition cost just over $4,300 in 1963; by 2020, it cost nearly $14,000. This cost does not include fees, room and board, books, and so forth. These costs put colleges out of reach for many low-income minority families. The need for financial assistance for low-income minority students makes them less attractive to colleges. In 2022, seventeen elite universities were charged with price-fixing, and eight agreed to pay $104.5 million to resolve claims they had conspired to limit financial aid for low- and middle-income students. Described as a price-fixing cartel, the class-action lawsuit against Ivy League and other elite schools claimed they had used a shared methodology to calculate financial need, reducing dollars to students from working-class families. Attorneys for the plaintiffs estimated that about 200,000 students had been financially harmed over twenty years.[30]

Most low-income university students can attend college using a mixture of need-based Pell grants, student loans, employment income, and occasionally academic or sports-based scholarships.

The largest federal grant program for low-income undergraduates is the needs-based Pell Grant. In 2022, nearly 60 percent of Black and 50 percent of American Indian and Hispanic students received Pell Grants. About 34 percent of undergraduates (6+ million) received Pell Grants in 2022, with 51 percent going to students whose families earned less than $20,000 annually. Thirty-nine percent of Pell Grant recipients had families with yearly incomes from $20,001 to $50,000. While the maximum Pell Grant was $7,395 in 2023–4, the average grant was only $4,600.[31] Not unexpectedly, only 24 percent of students in the most competitive institutions had received need-based Pell Grants in 2020 compared to 68 percent in the least competitive institutions.[32]

For most low-income students, Pell Grants constitute a significant, albeit declining, part of their income package.[33] In 1980, the maximum Pell Grant covered the total cost of a two-year degree and 77 percent of the cost of attending a four-year public university.[34] By 2023–4, the maximum Pell Grant of $7,395 covered only 28 percent of the average yearly cost ($25,707) for an in-state student living on campus in a public four-year college. For out-of-state students, Pell Grants covered less than 17 percent, and for students in private non-profit colleges, only 13.5 percent of their costs were covered.[35] This shortfall forces low-income students to take out federal or private loans to cover the remaining costs. By 2016, 64 percent of Pell Grant recipients in public four-year institutions also had received federal student loans.[36]

The choice of college significantly impacts the economic mobility of many students, especially those from low-income families. Academic preparation and providing college-related information are essential factors in college selection and acceptance. Students from low-income backgrounds who attend underperforming high schools are 74 percent more likely to drop out of college and often require remediation.[37] By contrast, middle- and upper-income students have an advantage if their parents invest in enrichment and academic readiness activities, further widening the gap in the competition for places in selective colleges.[38]

Knowledge about college choices, financial aid, and other aspects of college selection factor into a student's decision of where to attend college. For first-in-family students, this information is often relayed through high school counselors, often in short supply in many communities. While the American School Counselor Association recommends a ratio of 250 students per school counselor, the national average in 2021–2 was 408 to one. In some states, that ratio was even higher: In Indiana, it was 694 to one; in Arizona, it was 651 to one; and in Michigan, it was 615 to one.[39]

College is a vastly different experience for students from higher-income families compared to those from lower-income families. For instance, college students from well-off families typically do not need an outside income, freeing them up for unpaid internships, volunteer community activities, campus clubs, cultural and social activities, student government, and networking with students and instructors. In contrast, employed students often have to juggle long work hours, class attendance, homework, study time, and family life.

Some students opt to join a national college fraternity or sorority. These "brotherhood" and "sisterhood" organizations usually involve a lifetime commitment to the organization and its members. In return, members build relationships that are helpful in finding jobs, getting investments or loans, and gaining entry into elite social circles.

Members of Greek organizations are typically white and financially secure since the chapters can require hefty membership dues and a significant time commitment to meet social and other obligations. This time commitment excludes working students who cannot devote six to ten weeks to the pledging process or spend their free time attending house meetings, chapter events, fundraisers, and parties.

Despite the negative stereotypes attributed to fraternities and sororities, there are important benefits to joining these organizations. A 2020 national survey found that fraternity and sorority members were significantly more engaged in college life, reported greater gains in learning, and were more satisfied with their college experiences.[40] A Gallup poll found that students in fraternities and sororities were also more likely to have relationships with mentors and professors, were active in extracurricular activities, and engaged in professional internships where they could apply their learning. They were also more likely to graduate than unaffiliated students.[41] Some fraternities and sororities provide academic support to members, such as tutors, study files, and sharing coursework and exam notes. Several chapters have minimum GPA requirements, which pressure members to get good grades.[42] The time commitment required of fraternities and sororities makes it difficult for students to maintain a part-time job, no less a full-time one.[43]

The Working Student

Due to high tuition, fees, and inadequate Pell Grants, 43 percent of full-time and 81 percent of part-time students work while in college.[44] Many of these students, especially lower-income ones, work long hours (see Table 1.4).

Outside employment is not without its drawbacks. In 2019, 51 percent of low-income students employed twenty hours a week or more had a C or lower grade average.[45] Working college students are about 20 percent less likely to complete their degrees than nonworking students.[46] A study of 600,000 Tennessee students from 2001 to 2017 examined the effect of work on a student's chances of graduation. The study also examined the academic progress of students who worked during some semesters to determine whether they were more successful in completing their classes than a cohort who did not work. The authors found negative associations between work and academic success, especially regarding long work hours (twenty hours a week or longer). In particular, working students earned fewer credits, were less likely to complete their degrees, and took longer to graduate.[47]

Working is a hardship for the 6 million low-income students, most of whom are women, Blacks, and Latinos. These students are likelier to work more than fifteen hours a week, leaving less study time as they forego the campus activities and opportunities available to other students. Instead of working in an internship leading to a job offer after graduation, they are often employed in the secondary or tertiary service sector (e.g., food services, security guards, maids, maintenance, and on-call in temporary employment agencies), working long hours for little pay.

Table 1.4 Employment Hours Worked by Independent* and Dependent Undergraduates Based on Family Poverty Level, 2015–16

Hours worked	Independent % very low-income students	Independent % of low-income students	Independent % above the federal poverty line	Dependent % very low-income students	Dependent % of low-income students	Dependent % above federal poverty line
1-20	17.4%	18.2%	11.8%	28.5%	17.4%	11.8%
21-25	14.5%	20.8%	16.4%	21.4%	14.5%	16.4%
36+	21.1%	31.2%	47.9%	10.1%	21.1%	47.9%

*Independent students are those aged twenty-four or over and those under age twenty-four who are married and have dependents. Undergraduates under age twenty-four are considered dependent.

Source: David Radwin et al., "Student Financial Aid Estimates for 2015–16," National Center for Education Statistics (IES) (January 2018), https://nces.ed.gov/pubs2018/2018466.pdf

The New Face of Poverty: Food and Housing Insecurity among College Students

Due to rising tuition, mandatory fees, and inflation, many low-income college students struggle with food and housing insecurity. A survey of 195,000 college students by Temple University's Hope Center found that almost one-third of college students had experienced food insecurity, including 40 percent of students attending two-year colleges.[48] Food insecurity was so prevalent that in 2022, there were food pantries on almost 800 campuses.[49]

One small study in a large public mid-Atlantic university found that 15 percent of students surveyed were food insecure, with another 16 percent at risk of food insecurity. Black and other minority students who received financial aid or experienced housing problems were the most likely to be food insecure or at risk of it.[50] A 2015 Urban Institute study found food insecurity in 11.2 percent of households where students were in four-year colleges and 13.5 percent of homes where they were in vocational education.[51] Moreover, the US Government Accountability Office (GAO) found that in 2016, less than half of the 3.3 million students potentially eligible for the Supplemental Nutrition Assistance Program (SNAP) participated. The lack of participation in SNAP is based on the government's concern that students from financially better-off families would use the food program instead of receiving assistance from their families. Consequently, the normal income rules for SNAP are bypassed for college students.[52]

In addition to food insecurity, many low-income college students face housing insecurity. During the last fifteen years, the growth in college enrollment exceeded the construction of new on-campus housing. Providing safe, inexpensive, and quality student housing is difficult for public institutions facing deep budget cuts. This shortage has led to high on-campus housing costs and high rent for off-campus apartments. These high rents can lead to missing rent payments and eviction, living in severely overcrowded spaces, renting in dangerous neighborhoods, or being forced to couch surf. Sometimes, students camp out in empty classrooms or sleep in school libraries. A survey by the Hope Center for College, Community, and Justice found that

52 percent of students at two-year colleges and 43 percent at four-year colleges experienced housing insecurity in 2020, with 14 percent living in a homeless shelter or non-residential area.[53]

College Is a Risky Proposition for Low-Income Students

College represents a way out of poverty for low-income students.[54] At the same time, financial assistance offered through federal and state loan programs can entice some low-income students into making a bad investment in their future. By 2021, almost 15 percent (39 million) of Americans had earned some college credits without a degree. Many of those former students were saddled with repaying thousands in student loans.[55]

The number of poor and minority undergraduate students has grown in the last twenty years, with much of that growth in public two-year and less selective four-year colleges.[56] As a result, many high-achieving, low-income students fail to apply to high-quality selective colleges that match their academic ability.[57] In general, selective institutions have more resources for student support and better outcomes, even after controlling for student ability.[58]

The choice of college has a significant impact on a student's chance of graduation. In 2020, six-year graduation rates were highest (90 percent) at the most selective institutions (those that accept less than 25 percent of applicants) and lowest (28 percent) at the least selective institutions (those having an open admissions policy). Especially abysmal was the 29 percent graduation rate in 2020 for private for-profit colleges.[59] The six-year graduation rate was low for Hispanics, Pacific Islanders, Blacks, and American Indian/Alaska Native students.[60] (See Figure 1.4.) The dropout risk is greatest for the lowest-income quartile, whose chance of graduation is only 14 percent, rising to 41 percent for academically strong students.[61] Low-income college students face a significant risk given their overrepresentation in for-profit or low selectivity/open admission colleges with high dropout rates and low post-graduation salaries.[62]

22 FAILING UNIVERSITIES

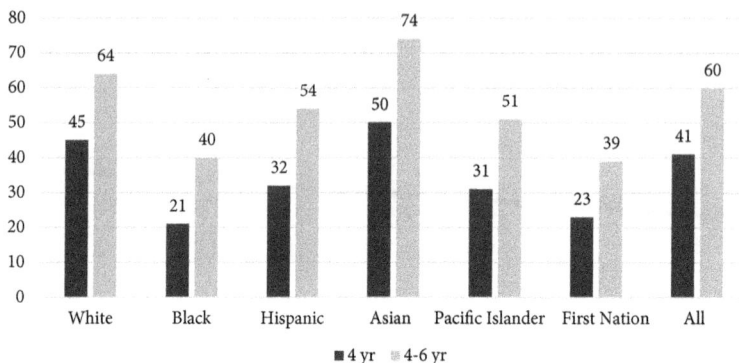

Figure 1.4 *Four- and Six-Year Baccalaureate Graduation Rate by Race/Ethnicity, 2010 Entry Class**

*First Nation includes American Indian and Native Alaskan

Source: "National Center for Education Statistics, Indicator 23: Postsecondary Graduation Rates," U.S. Department of Education, February 2019, https://nces.ed.gov/programs/raceindicators/indicator_red.asp

The decision to enroll in college for low-income students is riskier than gambling in Las Vegas. In Blackjack, Roulette, and Craps, a player has a 40 to 48 percent chance of winning.[63] For Black and American Indian/Native Alaskan students, the odds of betting the amount of their student loans and winning in Las Vegas are higher than the odds of graduating college. The difference is that when you lose money in Las Vegas, you can walk away from the tables; when you drop out of college, you still have to repay your student loans. Until the risks are mitigated, college is not the best choice for many low-income students.

The risks for low-income students are muddied by large data sets highlighting the financial benefits of a college degree while minimizing the risks. Not coincidentally, encouraging low-income students to enroll in college also helps fuel an expensive tertiary education sector marked by too many colleges and stagnant or declining enrollment. Low-income students are fodder for colleges like low-income people were fodder for the housing industry in the early 2000s.

We are not suggesting that low-income students avoid college. On the contrary, the poor need college the most. However, the playing field needs to be leveled, and the long-term financial risks should be minimized for those students who are least able to shoulder the risks.

Any attempt to diminish the risks of attending college must consider factors that impact high dropout rates. For instance, it is unlikely that high college dropout rates can be curbed until the problem of low-performing public schools is addressed. In 2011, achievement scores for both Black and white students were lower in the highest Black density schools (40+ percent Black) compared to the highest-density white schools (80 percent white).[64] Civil rights groups have argued for decades that inadequate funding for schools with large minority student populations plays a significant role in maintaining the achievement gaps.[65] At minimum, colleges should provide comprehensive remediation and support services for students from low-performing high schools.

Another way to mitigate the risks includes automatically linking Pell Grants to the rise in college costs, similar to how Social Security is indexed to inflation. In addition, free or very low-cost tuition could be provided to all college students whose families meet a sliding income guideline. More high school counselors would help steer students into colleges that fit their academic strengths well. Lastly, stricter government regulations are needed for low-performing, for-profit institutions with low graduation rates.

Will a College Degree Become Obsolete?

While a college degree is unnecessary for managing a retail store, some employers hire college graduates based on job-signaling/screening. Employers use education credentials to screen for desirable behavioral traits, such as self-control, self-discipline, reliability, the ability to defer gratification, or a specific social background. This signaling effect eliminates a portion of the workforce who, thirty years ago, would have been qualified for the job with only a high school diploma.[66]

Growing skepticism about the value of a college education is strengthened by more corporations claiming to eliminate a college degree as part of their hiring requirements. This decision is presumably based on mitigating "degree inflation" or the unnecessary degree requirements added to job descriptions. Or, it reflects a kind of virtue signaling. In place of a college degree, companies like Apple, Google, Penguin Random House, Hilton, Costco, Whole Foods, Starbucks, IBM, Home Depot, Bank of America, Lowe's, and Chipotle are focusing on skills-based hiring to widen the applicant pool.[67] While the trend to devalue a college degree portends a sea change, it is unclear whether it will apply across the board, including management positions, or only to a special class of technical workers or others with specialized skills. Moreover, it is hard to imagine a corporate culture where a college degree would not tilt the balance when evaluating two similarly qualified candidates, especially what economists call "revealed preferences" (i.e., what people do rather than what they say).

The shift away from a strict reliance on educational credentials for hiring also impacts the public sector. For instance, Pennsylvania Governor Josh Shapiro eliminated the requirement of a four-year college degree for 92 percent of state government jobs after assuming office in 2023. This change was similar to those enacted in fourteen states, including Maryland, Utah, and Alaska.[68] While lowering the education requirements could reduce state payroll costs and level the job hiring field, the flow-on effects of devaluing a college degree would impact colleges already facing declining or stagnant enrollment.[69]

The "credential inflation" has also impacted underemployment. Overall, almost 40 percent of college graduates are underemployed. These numbers are even higher for specific disciplines where the underemployment rate was more than 50 percent in 2021. (See Table 1.5.)

A pressing question concerning the future of a college degree involves the potential impact of AI on the jobs that traditionally employ college graduates. As AI technology advances, it will perform tasks that have historically involved a high level of education and skill, leading to displaced workers in select industries. Some businesses already use ChatGPT to create website content and promotional materials and respond to customer service inquiries. Lawyers are using AI to produce legal briefs.[70]

Table 1.5 Sample of Labor Market Outcomes of College Graduates by Major, 2021

College Major	Underemployment Rate
Agriculture	52.1%
Animal and Plant Sciences	52.5%
Environmental Studies	50.2%
Ethnic Studies	53.7%
Communications	52.7%
Mass Media	51.7%
Foreign Language	50.1%
Liberal Arts	55.2%
Leisure and Hospitality	58.6%
Philosophy	57.1%
Anthropology	53.3%
Sociology	51.3%
General Social Sciences	50.6%
Fine Arts	55.4%
Performing Arts	64.0%
Medical Technicians	59.5%
General Business	52.4%
Business Management	55.1%
Marketing	52.0%

Source: Federal Reserve Bank of New York, "The Labor Market for Recent College Graduates," May 5, 2023, www.newyorkfed.org/research/college-labor-market/index.html#/unemployment

A University of Pennsylvania and OpenAI study found that some educated white-collar workers earning up to $80,000 a year are the most likely to be affected by AI-driven workforce changes.[71] The jobs most vulnerable to AI are:

- Tech jobs like coders, programmers, software engineers, and data analysts.
- Media jobs in advertising, technical writing, and journalism.
- Legal jobs, including paralegals.
- Market research analysts.
- Teachers (some surmise that AI can already teach classes).
- Finance jobs, including financial analysts, financial advisors, etc.
- Stock traders.
- Graphic designers.
- Accountants.
- Customer service agents.[72]

Despite the prognostications, no one can definitively answer how AI will shape future employment or how slowly or quickly employers will adopt this technology. Nor can we know if or how college curriculums will reflect the new skills required in an AI-dominated work environment.

Conclusion: Is College a Good Investment for Students and Society?

A nuanced question is whether college is a good investment for students and society. On the one hand, a college degree is a great economic and social asset for most middle-class and academically strong students, irrespective of socioeconomic status. On the other hand, the decision to attend college for low-income or academically weak students is a risky proposition that carries grave financial consequences in terms of repaying a student loan without the economic benefit of a college degree.

As public policy, the emphasis on having more people attain a college degree is a two-edged sword. While a society thrives in multiple ways from an educated population and workforce, justifying college costs on purely economic grounds can be misleading. While multiple data sources show that a college degree generally leads to higher earnings, so does a skilled trade and other jobs not requiring a college degree. Moreover, society needs skilled workers and tradespeople as much as those with a college degree. For instance, the Inflation Reduction Act of 2022 includes billions of dollars in tax credits and direct funding for a long list of sustainability projects requiring skilled workers. By 2023, the Act had already created 142,000 new jobs across the United States, a number expected to grow to 1.3 million by 2030. Not coincidentally, the bill's tax credits are only available for projects that pay prevailing wages.[73]

As climate change causes record-breaking high temperatures, an increased supply of electricians will be necessary to maintain power grids and home electrical systems, especially given the increase in electric vehicles. More plumbers will be needed as America's aging water infrastructures need replacement, and rising sea levels threaten access to clean water in many areas. Despite this need, the Associated Builders and Contractors (ABC) trade group complained that the construction industry had a shortage of 546,000 workers in 2023. The ABC claims the reasons for this shortage are: (1) nearly 25 percent of construction workers are fifty-five and older, (2) the number of skilled workers has grown slowly with some occupations declining, and (3) too few young workers are entering the skilled trades.[74]

Students should not have to endure sixteen years of what they perceive as drudgery to get a job with stable hours, benefits, a living wage, and job security. In 2015, Robert Reich argued that a college degree is not the only door into the American middle class. Instead, young people should be offered an alternative that does not require years of lost wages and massive debt. In contrast to the present underfunded system, Reich proposed a robust world-class vocational-technical education system that is well-funded.[75]

Much of the literature is based on viewing higher education as a commodity whose primary value is financial and social mobility. While the raison d'être for pursuing a college education typically focuses on material aspects, this ignores benefits such as enhanced critical thinking, intellectual and personal growth, an appreciation of philosophy and the classics, and an understanding of democratic principles reflected in liberal arts education. The economistic view of higher education also overlooks better health outcomes for college graduates, a longer lifespan, better education for one's children, better working conditions, reduced workplace obsolescence, and high levels of community engagement.[76] Furthermore, college graduates tend to have a more progressive worldview due to exposure to people from diverse geographic, ethnic, racial, social, and cultural backgrounds.

Whether a college degree is worth the investment depends on who asks the question. It is an obvious choice for middle- and upper-class students, while for low-income students, it is less clear.

For many people, the decision on whether to attend college is primarily based on the cost, which is determined by several factors, including the commodification and corporatization of higher education. The next chapter will examine why attending college in America is so expensive compared to European universities.

2

Just Another Commodity

Stein's Law: "If something cannot go on forever, it will stop."

Christopher Newfield points out that no country has a sizeable middle class without mass higher education.[1] However, the numbers look bleak when comparing US higher education to other Organization for Economic Cooperation and Development (OECD) countries, especially considering the high costs. In 2021, the US ranked thirteenth among OECD nations as a percentage of the population with a tertiary degree. This was below Korea, Canada, Japan, Luxemburg, Ireland, the UK, Netherlands, Norway, and Australia. The United States ranked second among OECD countries in national expenditures per tertiary student at $35,736. (Only Luxembourg was higher since tuition is free.) Among OECD nations, US undergraduates paid $9,212 a year compared to Canadian students, who paid $4,923; Japanese students paid $3,717; Australians paid $3,433; New Zealanders paid $4,621; and Israelis paid $2,604.[2]

Between 1963 and 2013, the average college grade point average (GPA) of American students rose from 2.5 to 3.15, while at the same time, the hours spent studying fell by half.[3] Richard Arum and Josipa Roksa used the Collegiate Learning Assessment tool to survey 2,300 undergraduates at twenty-four institutions in their first semester and the end of their second year. They found that 45 percent of students demonstrated no significant improvement in skills like critical thinking, complex reasoning, and writing in their first two years of college.[4] If Arum and Roksa's research is correct,

US students pay a lot for underperforming colleges. In short, American students and taxpayers are far from getting the optimal value for their educational dollars.

The Beginnings of Commodification

Thatcherism and Reaganism marked the halcyon days of neoliberal dominance in public policy in the 1980s. Former British Prime Minister Margaret Thatcher summarized the neoliberal skepticism around the common good when she wrote: "And, you know, there's no such thing as society. There are individual men and women, and there are families ...."[5] Since UK universities are generally viewed as progressive, it is unsurprising that they were hard hit by Thatcher's big spending cuts in the 1980s.[6]

Thatcher's skepticism of higher education was shared by former US President Ronald Reagan, who, as governor of California, punished student activism by increasing tuition at public universities and declaring that "The State should not subsidize intellectual curiosity." After previously supporting Reagan, *The Los Angeles Times* warned that "An anti-intellectual political reactionary now governs California and is determined to bring higher education growth to a grinding halt."[7]

Reagan's antipathy toward higher education continued after he was elected president in 1980. Reagan's budget director David Stockman characterized students as "tax eaters ... [and] a drain and drag on the American economy ... Student aid isn't a proper obligation of the taxpayer."[8] Reagan's budget cuts hit higher education hard, and from 1980 to 1985, student aid was slashed by 25 percent. Many low-income students eligible for Pell Grants were forced to take out student loans. Reagan-era changes effectively shifted the federal government's focus from providing student aid to pushing student loans, a policy continued in later Republican and Democratic administrations.[9] Reagan's landslide reelection in 1984 showed state legislators that there were few electoral consequences in cutting spending on higher education.

The period from 1980 to 1983 ushered in one of the most severe economic downturns since the Second World War. State budgets were in disarray as tax revenues plummeted. In response, states like California and Wisconsin enacted balanced budget amendments linking projected expenditures to projected revenues. Trapped in a fiscal straightjacket and unable to raise taxes, elected state officials diverted funds from discretionary spending programs like higher education to mandatory programs in health care, prisons, and public education. In turn, states cut higher education, and budget shortfalls were expected to be made up through higher tuition and fees. As an example, tuition at the University of California was free for all residents in 1968, but by 1970 undergraduates paid $150 a year. In 1974, tuition and fees were raised to $630; in 1985, it doubled to $1,296.[10] By 2023, in-state undergraduate tuition and fees cost $15,532 a year.[11]

From 2003 to 2023, tuition and fees for in-state students at public universities rose 175 percent, and 141 percent for out-of-state students. This increase was even higher than in private universities, where costs rose 134 percent. By comparison, the overall consumer price index increased by 65 percent from 2002 to 2022.[12] Healthcare costs rose by 96 percent in the same period.[13] Ultimately, state funding cuts forced public universities to become more financially self-sufficient, resulting in higher tuition, increased student debt, and fewer students able or willing to shoulder the costs and defer consumption for four to six years.

Politicizing Higher Education

Higher education in many Republican-led states has become a political and social battleground divided along party lines. For most of the twentieth century, Americans without college degrees were likelier to vote Democratic. For instance, John F. Kennedy won the presidency due to the support of non-college-educated white voters but lost college-educated voters by a two-to-one margin. In contrast, Joe Biden lost non-college-educated white voters by a two-to-one margin while winning 60 percent of the college-educated vote. This "class dealignment" and polarization reversed New Deal politics, where voter income predicted party preference.[14] One consequence of this shift is that the Democratic Party now appeals to college graduates, representing just over one-third of voters. At the same time, the Republican Party attracts the non-college-educated working class, representing two-thirds of voters.[15] In the 2020 presidential election, 67 percent of voters with a postgraduate degree and 56 percent of college graduates voted for Joe Biden, while 56 percent of those with only high school or less voted for Donald Trump.[16]

The successful conservative attack on higher education has fostered skepticism or hostility toward college education. By 2023, Americans' confidence in higher education plummeted to 36 percent, sharply lower than the 57 percent in 2015 and the 48 percent in 2018. Broken down, only 17 percent of US adults had "a great deal" of confidence in higher education; 19 percent had "quite a lot" of confidence; 40 percent had "some confidence," and 22 percent had "very little" confidence. As the attacks on higher education intensified, the percentage of US adults with "a great deal" or "quite a lot" of confidence in higher education plummeted along political lines. From 2015 to 2023, support for higher education dropped by 37 percent among Republicans, 16 percent among Independents, and 25 percent for those without a college degree. Surprisingly, support for higher education also dropped by 9 percent among Democrats, 10 percent for those with a college degree, and 17 percent for those with a postgraduate degree. The loss of support was also noteworthy for those fifty-five and older.[17]

The results of this and similar surveys provide little incentive for Republican state legislatures to increase spending on higher education. Moreover, Republican lawmakers are faced with the prospect that more college graduates translate into fewer Republican votes. However, governors and legislatures also know that simply curbing the number of college graduates would have untoward consequences since Republican voters also send their children to college. To address this conundrum, Republican legislatures and governors shifted their focus to what happens *within* colleges by controlling what liberal college instructors can teach. To cement this control, they crafted legislation to attack "wokeness" and CRT (critical race theory). Conservative columnist George Will added his voice by complaining that "The news from academia is embarrassing—intellectual fads, political hysterias, the hunting of heretics."[18] Pandering to their conservative constituency, some politicians and activists fueled the anti-college resentment with hyperbolic claims that universities offer degrees in zombie studies and that college campuses are "socialism factories."[19]

One of the leaders of the conservative assault on higher education is Florida Governor Ron DeSantis, who promised that "Florida is where woke goes to die."[20] His strategy was to install political allies in top university posts and to change tenure rules while controlling what could be taught in college classes.[21] DeSantis created a template for this transformation through a hostile takeover of the progressive New College of Florida. This coup was executed by appointing six partisan trustees, five of whom lived outside of Florida and were known as right-wing activists. This included the appointment of Chris Rufo, a far-right anti-GLBTQIA+ extremist with no academic experience. The first commencement speaker at the New College was Scott Atlas, a controversial radiologist appointed by Trump who argued for herd immunity over a vaccine. As a protest, students held an alternative commencement.[22]

The goal was to transform the New College from a progressive college into a conservative institution by creating a new core curriculum and eliminating diversity, equity, and inclusion programs. In addition, the goal was to increase the male population (the college was previously two-thirds female) by creating a male-only baseball team whose GPA and standardized tests were below the college norm. The demographic change in Florida's New College was also an attempt to counteract what conservatives called the "feminization of education," which blames the growth of progressive campus politics on the large number of female students and their involvement in college operations.[23]

DeSantis also stacked the governing board of Florida's state university system with his supporters. In 2023, the governing board approved the almost unknown Classic Learning Test (CLT) as an alternative to the SAT and ACT in undergraduate admissions. The CLT emphasizes Western canons and Christian thought and is typically used by home-schooled students and Christian colleges. CLT has a thin research record and no sound empirical evidence of how well it predicts college success, especially for students from non-Christian schools.[24] Fearful of DeSantis' wrath, college administrators throughout Florida's public college system knuckled down in the face of his attack on academic freedom and the banning of discussions on race, gender, and sexual identity.[25]

Conservative governors and legislatures jumped on the DeSantis bandwagon, blaming "wokeness" for contentious issues around transgender athletes, the removal of statues of Confederate war heroes, non-gender designated bathrooms, and the focus on Diversity, Equity, and Inclusion (DEI). By early 2024, the University of Florida, Florida State University, the University of North Florida, and Florida International University shut down their DEI offices.

A particular disdain was reserved for CRT, a little-understood (and misunderstood) theory that examines the history of systemic racism in the United States and its continued impacts. This was taken to the extreme when the Iowa House of Representatives passed a law in 2021 to stem "militant leftwing radicalism" by prohibiting teaching that "the United States of America and the State of Iowa are fundamentally or systemically racist or sexist."[26] Instead of protesting the law, Iowa State University provided written guidance for professors on how to avoid drawing scrutiny under the Act.[27]

Not to be outdone, Texas Governor Greg Abbott signed two bills in 2023 that banned diversity, equity, and inclusion programs for employee hiring and codified restrictions on tenure. Senate Bill 17 banned all public universities from having DEI offices and banned mandatory diversity training for employees. In enforcing the ban, the state plans to audit schools to ensure they do not skirt the aim of the legislation. Kowtowing to the new prohibitions, University of Houston System Chancellor Renu Khator emailed faculty and staff that she expected Texas universities to work together to ensure consistent interpretation of the law.[28] On January 1, 2024, Texas closed its DEI offices at all public universities.

Tom Nichols observes that the current focus of the American right on higher education is driven by cultural resentment rather than CRT (which most Americans don't understand). The disdain toward higher education has become part of America's culture wars and is another grievance in populist resentments. Republican leaders like Ron DeSantis, Ted Cruz, Josh Hawley, Elise Stefanik, and Donald

Trump (all with Ivy League educations) have used this resentment to connect with their non-college-educated base.[29]

Issues around "wokeness" and DEI came to a head during five hours of congressional hearings held on December 5, 2023. New York Republican Congressperson Elise Stefanik pressed the presidents of Harvard, the University of Pennsylvania (Penn), and MIT on the topic of antisemitism by asking whether calling for the genocide of Jews violated their schools' codes of conduct. In varying ways, the leaders stated that the answer would be context-specific and related to whether speech turned into conduct. Both the country and the congress were stunned by the response. The backlash started almost immediately, and within days, Penn President Liz Magill stepped down; plagued by plagiarism allegations, Harvard President Claudine Gay followed less than a month later. MIT president Sally Kornbluth remained on the job.[30]

Even before the December 5th congressional hearing, Harvard was under investigation by the US Education Department following a complaint the university failed to respond to antisemitic harassment on campus after Hamas' attack on October 7, 2023. In addition to Harvard, Tulane University, University of Cincinnati, Montana State University, Temple University, Stanford, University of California at San Diego, UCLA, Cornell, University of Washington, Rutgers University, Columbia University, and the University of Pennsylvania are also under investigation for complaints of campus discrimination.[31]

Behind the Conservative Attack on DEI and CRT

Behind the attacks on DEI and CRT lies the larger goal of ending affirmative action. The argument is that if the United States is neither racist now nor in the past, there is no justification for affirmative action. This argument reached fruition in the US Supreme Court's 2023 decision to reject the policy of race-conscious admissions in higher education, overturning more than forty years of legal precedent. In particular, the plaintiffs in that case argued that Harvard's admissions policies discriminated against Asian applicants. However, even before the Court ruling, nine states (Idaho, Arizona, Florida, Nebraska, New Hampshire, Oklahoma, Washington, California, and Michigan) had already banned affirmative action in college admissions.

The Supreme Court's reversal of affirmative action affects only a small but significant sector of American higher education. Of the roughly 4,000 US colleges and universities, only about 200 have highly selective admissions policies that accept fewer than 50 percent of applicants. It is these elite institutions where race-based affirmative action policies make the most difference since that is where many government and industry leaders graduate from. For example, eight Supreme Court justices in 2023 attended Harvard or Yale law schools.[32] As a classic example of pulling up the ladder behind you, Clarence Thomas, the one Black Justice who voted against affirmative action, acknowledged that he was admitted to Yale law based on their affirmative action policy.[33]

Rejecting race-based admissions decisions as discriminatory also failed to acknowledge forms of discrimination that benefit whites, namely, legacy-based admissions (i.e., giving admissions priority to the children of alumni) and the admissions preference given to the relatives of large donors. The backlash to the Supreme Court decision alleges that legacy admissions discriminate against students of color by providing an unfair advantage to the predominantly white children of alumni.[34] Both wealth and legacy admissions are critical determinants in gaining admission into elite private universities.[35]

How colleges and universities will respond to the Supreme Court ruling is unclear. For instance, a narrow interpretation of the ruling does not explicitly prohibit race-conscious decisions in financial aid. Nor does it forbid substituting other factors for race, such as family income, whether students are the first-in-family to attend college, or where they went to high school.[36]

The Commodification of Higher Education

The view of higher education as a public good is being replaced by the belief that it is a private good like any other market commodity. The view of higher education as just another market commodity is welcomed by a wide range of interests, including neoliberals, libertarians, fiscal conservatives, legislators wanting to cut their state's budgets, college students who view themselves as consumers

JUST ANOTHER COMMODITY

and want a voice, private consultants, education corporations, and a public resentful of paying for services they don't use.

As higher education becomes just another market commodity, universities are adapting by becoming more vocationally oriented and shifting to a "job-ready" or "career-ready" focus.[37] This vocational emphasis is reflected in degree preferences—of the 2 million bachelor's degrees conferred in 2020, 58 percent were in six fields: 19 percent in business, 13 percent in health professions and related programs, and only 8 percent in social sciences and history.[38] Despite the "job ready" branding, professions like nursing, social work, and law do not trust universities to certify competence and require competency-based examinations after a student graduates.

As colleges feel the pressure of increased competition from other universities and stagnant or declining enrollment, their market-based response is to give customers what they want.[39] From 2009 to 2020, undergraduate degrees in computer and information sciences rose 145 percent as colleges chased the burgeoning tech job market. Under "academic prioritization," resources were reallocated from liberal arts and the humanities to high-demand disciplines. In 2020, the University of Vermont eliminated twelve majors and eleven minors in the College of Arts and Sciences. Howard University removed its classics department in favor of strengthening STEM education. The University of Alaska system cut thirty-nine academic departments, including sociology, creative writing, chemistry, and environmental science. Colleges and universities nationwide have made cuts, sometimes deep, to liberal arts programs.

One extreme change occurred at West Virginia University (WVU), the largest university in the state and an R1 school (i.e., in the top tier of US research universities). In response to a $45 million budget shortfall, and based on the recommendations of the rpk GROUP (educational consultants), WVU eliminated 9 percent of its majors and foreign language programs.[40] Some majors included higher education and administration, art history, music, acting, environmental and community planning, communication, creative writing, public administration, linguistics, public health, and all foreign languages. In addition, the university is expected to terminate 7 percent of full-time faculty members (169 in total) on the main campus. Despite these Draconian cuts, the university is not cutting administrative salaries or positions.[41] WVU's president, Gordon Gee, argues that his school is the canary in the coal mine and that other public universities are confronting the same challenges and will respond similarly.[42] As an aside, WVU paid rpk GROUP almost $876,000 for their sage advice in 2023.[43]

The shift to a vocational emphasis also impacts traditional liberal arts colleges. In 2022, St. Mary's University of Minnesota, a traditional liberal arts college, terminated eleven programs, including art, music, and theatre. Their justification was based on declining enrollments and the decision to concentrate on business, technology, and the sciences.[44] In 2023, Marymount University's trustees voted unanimously to eliminate mathematics, art, English, history, and philosophy majors, among other fields. From 2013 to 2016, American universities eliminated 651 foreign language programs.[45]

Liberal arts and the humanities have been especially hard hit. From 2012 to 2020, English and history majors fell nationally by a third, while humanities enrollment declined by more than 17 percent. The number of humanities majors who graduated from Ohio State fell by 46 percent; Tufts, Notre Dame, Vassar, and Bates lost almost 50 percent of their humanities majors; Boston University lost 42 percent; and SUNY Albany lost nearly 75 percent. In 2022, only 7 percent of Harvard's first-year students planned to major in the humanities, down from 30 percent in the 1970s.[46] This trend is international since three-quarters of Organization for Economic Cooperation (OECD) countries reported falling humanities enrollments.[47] The shift to vocationally based degree programs is transforming many liberal arts colleges into technical schools, much to the dismay of scholars who bemoan a generation of college graduates with a narrow education.

Chasing customer interest can take many forms. Despite financial difficulties, the University of Arizona, Livingstone College, Southern New Hampshire University, Hawai'i Pacific University, and Illinois State University have funded Esports (electronic sports competitions using video games) centers to attract students. Some schools like Arcadia University, University of California at Irvine, University of Texas at Dallas, University of Utah, Hawai'i Pacific University, and Valparaiso University even provide Esports scholarships.[48]

The problem with chasing student interests and market trends is that they can (and often do) quickly change. For instance, the demand for high-tech workers has exploded, and colleges have responded by ramping up their offerings. However, the tech bubble deflated by 2022 as more than 21,000 US-based tech workers were laid off in massive job cuts that included 11,000 workers in Alphabet (Google), 10,000 in Microsoft, 18,000 in Amazon, 11,000 in Meta, 8,000 in Salesforce, 4,000–6,000 in Hewlett-Packard, 4,000 in Cisco, and 3,700 in Twitter. All told, 872 technology companies laid off 219,882 employees by mid-2023.[49] Since most tech workers are at-will employees with no contract or a porous one, they can be quickly dismissed through a simple email or video call.[50]

If more hi-tech jobs disappear or workers with families choose more secure employment, students may opt for more traditional professions like human services, teaching, criminal justice, and counseling. Waning student interest will leave universities with expensive, underutilized tech programs and facilities. Moreover, if lower-demand majors are gutted, universities will have to retool to meet new demands, a merry-go-round of expensive catch-up strategies.

Truncating liberal arts and humanities curriculums could lead to a two-tier system of higher education: one system for elite and well-endowed universities that provide a broad classical education and a techno-vocational education for students in state universities who are poor, first-generation, or who have low admissions test scores. Students in elite private schools will benefit from learning a second or third language and being exposed to liberal arts, social sciences, and the humanities. They will develop critical thinking skills and have career opportunities in the arts, higher education, global finance, diplomacy, international law, and other fields.[51] Students at state schools will receive a technical education that may resemble a technical+ high school degree that prepares them for a job rather than leadership.

Creating New Markets

Like any business, a commodified higher education system needs new products to stimulate demand and expand the customer base. This growth is accomplished through credential inflation that devalues the baccalaureate in favor of a master's degree. Once viewed as the consolation prize for failing to complete a doctorate, the master's is now the fastest-growing degree.[52] Between 2011 and 2021, the number of conferred master's degrees rose by 19 percent, from 731,000 to 867,000. By 2023, almost 9 percent of those aged twenty-five and over had a master's degree, roughly the same proportion as had a bachelor's degree in 1960.[53] In many professions (e.g., education, social work, business, and fine arts), the master's degree replaces the bachelor's as the entry-level degree. This trend is a win for colleges and employers: colleges increase enrollment in high-tuition graduate degrees, and employers hire employees with more skills they don't have to pay for. Inevitably, credential inflation costs fall on the backs of students whose debt increases with each degree.[54] Although graduate students represent only 16 percent of all college students, they took out 47 percent of federal student loans ($39 billion) in 2021. In 2016, the average master's student loan debt was $50,290, although that differed widely among disciplines.[55]

It is unclear whether the additional knowledge gained from a master's degree justifies two or more years in a university setting plus thousands of dollars in tuition and student loans. For instance, can master's level content be incorporated into a bachelor's degree? If a master's degree is entry-level in some professions, why not develop a three-year bachelor's degree with a fourth-year master's qualification? To curb credential inflation, professions, and disciplines should be required to demonstrate why a master's degree is essential and the content that differentiates it from a bachelor's degree.

Disgruntled Faculty

The commodification of higher education is leaving many professors disillusioned as their role shifts from educator to skills trainer. Students, in turn, are adapting to this commodification by becoming conscious consumers and demanding to know why, after paying tuition, they are not getting the grades they paid for. Responding to fiscal pressures, university administrators see students as customers and are reluctant to forego tuition. To protect their revenue stream, some college administrators have developed arcane, time-consuming, and complicated student grievance procedures that leave instructors throwing up their hands in resignation and succumbing to student demands. Administrators have also created class satisfaction reviews whereby students rate instructors like customers rate Amazon products. Consistently bad reviews can mean termination, denial of tenure, losing merit pay, and harsh, humiliating warnings. To protect their job and the chance for promotion, some instructors structure classes so that few students fail, grades are inflated, assignments are modest, feedback is positive, and lectures are entertaining. Pedagogical quality inevitably suffers under the twin fears of student grievances and bad reviews.

Publicly funded universities can escape marketplace norms by their monopoly on education and by captive student consumers. Public universities can set prices independent of competition, and where competition in the private sector can drive down prices and increase quality, public universities can raise prices while reducing quality. For instance, while online education can cut costs, it can also impact quality by eliminating face-to-face interaction with faculty. Besides online education, schools can also cut costs by increasing class sizes, filling lecture halls with hundreds of students, employing adjunct and contract workers at low wages, and using underpaid graduate teaching assistants. Rarely are these cost-saving measures reflected in lower tuition.

Commodification and the Student Debt Trap

Every business needs customers, including America's almost 4,000 colleges and universities. While the overall number of US undergraduates has grown over the past twenty years, much of that growth was fueled by an increase in students from low-income families, students of color, and nontraditional students.[56] By 2022, 33 percent of the almost 19 million US college students were age twenty-five and older, and 13 percent were over age thirty-five.[57] The National Center for Education Statistics predicts that college enrollment will increase by roughly 1 percent from 2022 to 2031, representing a steep decline since the US population is expected to grow by 2.7 percent.[58]

The rapid growth in tuition in four-year public universities that grew from $13,000 a year in 2000 to $21,000 in 2020 is reminiscent of the housing bubble of the mid-1990s and early 2000. In 1995, former President Bill Clinton pushed homeownership, especially for low-income families. By 2000, 67 percent of American families owned homes, the highest number ever recorded. Spurred on by the Federal Reserve's policy of keeping interest rates low, the surge in home ownership ignited a housing boom that became a housing bubble. Home prices soared from $138,000 in 1995 to $238,000 in 2007.[59]

There were two major ways for policymakers to address the housing bubble: cool the housing market by raising interest rates or develop "creative" lending instruments to make the unaffordable seem affordable, at least in the short run. The latter option was attractive since banks sold their mortgages to Wall Street financial houses and were not overly concerned about their long-term solvency. This orientation led to a range of dodgy mortgage instruments. While "creative financing" brought more people into the housing market, little concern existed for the lender's ability to repay the loans. By 2007, almost 20 percent of all housing loans were subprime mortgages issued to credit-challenged customers.[60] The predictable collapse of the mortgage and housing market ushered in the global financial crisis of 2007–8. The lessons of the housing debacle went unheeded since the benefits of a college degree are sold in much the same way as homeownership was in the mid-1990s. Both promised a door into the middle class through high-dollar loans.

While former President Obama proclaimed that the United States would once again have the highest proportion of college graduates globally by 2020, state support for higher education fell by roughly $9 billion from 2009 to 2019.[61] Tuition increased to make up the difference, leading to the average student loan debt skyrocketing from $20,467 in 2009 to $37,172 in 2023.[62] By 2023, roughly 55 percent of undergraduates left college with student loan debt, which spiraled to $1.75 trillion, a significant jump from $645 billion in 2008. By the 2000s, student loan debt was greater than auto and credit card debt and only surpassed by mortgage loans.[63]

The response to high college tuition is similar to high housing prices in the mid-1990s to 2000s since both revolved around manipulating the demand side. Using housing policy as an example, policymakers realized that without creative financing, the cost of a college education would be beyond the reach of many—if not most—students and their families. In response, the federal and some state governments developed grant and loan programs to soften higher education costs, if only in appearance. The result is a complex array of government and private market loans using the same flawed logic used in the housing bubble; namely, future income growth will make the debt payable.

Kinds of Student Loans

About 85 percent of all student loans are federal loans that can be roughly broken down into four categories:

- Direct Subsidized Loans are available to undergraduate students based on financial need, with better terms than other loans.

- Direct Unsubsidized Loans are available to undergraduates, graduate students, and professional students. Borrowers are not required to demonstrate financial need.

- Direct PLUS Loans are not based on financial need and require a credit check. There are two categories for these loans: Grad PLUS Loans for graduate students and Parent PLUS Loans for the parents of dependent undergraduate students.

- Direct Consolidation Loans allow borrowers to combine multiple federal student loans into one loan with a fixed interest rate.[64]

Private student loans originate in institutions like banks, credit unions, schools, and some state agencies. These loans usually require a credit check, and interest rates can vary depending on the borrower's credit score. All lending decisions are made at the financial institution's discretion, and these loans may have high or variable interest rates, contain hidden fees, and require borrowers to make payments while they are still in school.[65] Private loans also typically do not offer income-driven repayment or deferment plans, and similar to home mortgages, they are often bundled, securitized, and sold to investors, sometimes multiple times.

Parent PLUS Loans are some of the more pernicious loan instruments since they embroil families in a web of debt. When federally based undergraduate loans prove insufficient to cover actual costs or are maxed out at $57,000, families desperate to help their child's education are roped into Parent PLUS Loans. For parents with a problematic credit history, the debt web is widened even further to a third-party guarantor. The widespread use of parent-based student loans ensures that not only will a student risk default, but their parents will also face aggressive collection efforts, such as wage garnishment, seizure of income tax refunds and Social Security payments, and plummeting credit scores. Like regular student loans, Parent PLUS Loans are not typically discharged in bankruptcy. Instead of leveraging upward mobility, college can become a fiscal albatross around the necks of low-income students, their families, and even extended family members and friends.

Student loan debt has a significant impact on the future of borrowers. An Urban Institute study found that a 1 percent increase in student debt decreases the likelihood of owning a house by 15 percent.[66] Partly as a result of student loan debt, almost 30 percent of borrowers live with their parents after graduation; 34 percent delay starting a family; 47 percent delay buying a new car; 73 percent delay saving for retirement; 63 percent delay buying a home; and 28 percent delay marriage.[67] The impact of student debt is aggravated by starting salaries that are not rising in the same arc as student debt.[68]

Loan Defaults

Not surprisingly, student default rates are relatively high. In the last twenty years, a third of federal student loan borrowers defaulted (i.e., at least 270 days without payment). Within this group, nearly two-thirds have defaulted multiple times.[69] By 2022, 7.1 percent of all student loans were in default, totaling $86 billion. Over a million student loans enter default each year, affecting 9 million borrowers and their families.[70]

The large number of student loan defaults is not surprising since many college graduates are unsuccessfully trying to repay their loans while working in jobs that barely pay a living wage. Roughly 11 percent of college graduates are in low-paying jobs, 6.6 percent in minimum wage jobs, and 4.8 percent are unemployed.[71] Added together, 22.4 percent of college graduates are at risk of default.

While the average wage for a 2023 college graduate was $60,000 a year in 2023, it can be much lower depending on the discipline. For example, according to the NEA, the average starting salary for teachers in 2023 was $42,844.[72] It's tough to repay a student loan at that salary.

A student loan default can result in borrowers having to repay the unpaid balance plus any interest owed. The default is reported to a credit agency, affecting the borrower's ability to purchase a car, rent or buy a home, get a credit card, or even get a job since many employers check credit scores. Borrowers who default may also have their tax refunds and federal benefit payments withheld, have their wages garnished, and be taken to court, where they pay court costs, collection fees, and attorney's fees.[73]

Loan Forgiveness

The federal government has several loan forgiveness programs for borrowers employed in specific settings, including:

- The Teacher Loan Forgiveness program can exempt up to $17,500 in loans if the borrower teaches full-time for five years in a low-income elementary school, secondary school, or educational service agency.

- The Public Service Loan Forgiveness (PSLF) program can forgive the remaining balance on a loan if the borrower has made the equivalent of 120 monthly payments and works full-time in a public or nonprofit qualifying organization in childcare or early childhood. It also covers borrowers employed in some federal, state, local, or tribal governments, doctors, and other medical personnel employed in nonprofit settings.[74] The catch in loan forgiveness programs is that 120 monthly payments are the equivalent of ten years of continuous payments, after which most of a student loan may have already been repaid.

One of President Joe Biden's campaign promises was a student loan forgiveness program. (During the Covid pandemic, student loan payments were suspended.) The Biden administration unveiled a student debt relief plan in 2022 that would have forgiven up to $10,000 in loans for eligible borrowers and up to $20,000 for Pell Grant recipients. The plan would have cost $400 billion over ten years, and an estimated 15 million borrowers would have had their student loan debt forgiven or had reduced payments. The loan forgiveness plan would have only applied to federal student loans and excluded those issued by private financial institutions.[75]

In 2023, the US Supreme Court struck down Biden's plan, and student loan repayments were set to begin in September of that year. The Biden administration countered the Court's ruling with a slimmed-down plan that would impact 804,000 borrowers and cost $39 billion.[76] While the Biden loan forgiveness plan was a step in the right direction, it failed to address the root cause of the problem, namely, an expensive, out-of-control system of higher education that requires comprehensive, far-reaching reforms.

Conclusion

The increasing commodification of higher education is reshaping colleges and universities for students, faculty members, parents, college administrators, and state and federal funders. For instance, high tuition makes it difficult for working-class families to send their children to college, leading to resentment, which impacts voting preferences. Some students and families are so fearful of long-term debt that they reject college—many faculty despair about replacing liberal arts programs with technical training.

The commodification of education led James McWilliams to observe that some students see college education as merely a business decision and the degree as an investment to gain later financial returns.[77] Sadly, this economistic perspective misses the non-material income derived from choosing a challenging and rewarding profession or discipline that contributes to the social good.[78] Rachel Gillette noted that 97 percent of people in moderate-income jobs, such as laboratory technologists, found their jobs meaningful. Similarly, 91 percent of relatively low-paid pastoral ministers found their job meaningful, along with 81 percent of early childhood elementary education teachers and counselors.[79]

Georgetown University's "The College Payoff" almost exclusively focused on occupations and lifetime earnings.[80] Following suit, the Bill and Melinda Gates Foundation's Postsecondary Value Commission focuses on measuring the economic outcomes for higher education students, including post-college wages, the ability to repay debt, earnings premiums for graduates, and economic mobility after college.[81] Overemphasizing the economic benefits of a college degree sidesteps the larger mission of higher education. As Johann Neem observes, it is possible to increase the number of Americans with a college degree without necessarily increasing the number of truly educated Americans.[82]

As universities mold their curriculums to meet student and employer demands, the emphasis is on developing curriculum and degree programs that focus on technological skills. Not coincidentally, this is also where the large donations are found. For example, the Simons Foundation donated $500 million to the State University of New York at Stony Brook in 2023, almost all earmarked for STEM.[83] Despite what students and employers want, narrow STEM-based education has limitations. For instance, Elon Musk is often considered a genius. Yet, despite his technological knowledge, through X (formerly Twitter) he had endorsed (then deleted his tweets) discredited conspiracy theories, such as QAnon's Pizzagate theory about child murder and trafficking.[84]

The impact of the digital age in accessing culture, knowledge, entertainment, travel, and art has bettered life in many ways. However, the potential harm is also evident. Issues abound like corporate and government surveillance, the loss of privacy, degraded public discourse marked by hate and conspiracy theories, social isolation, the rise in populism and the waning belief in democracy, the addictive technologies capturing the attention of the youth, and the fear that AI will provide an opportunity for bad actors to sow discord worldwide. Due to a relatively narrow knowledge base, too many technological innovators have little understanding or interest in where their technologies lead. Without a firm grasp of history, philosophy, humanities, and the social sciences, technology innovators have only limited guideposts to help them understand the implications of their technological achievements.[85] In contrast, Robert Oppenheimer, often considered the father of the atomic bomb, had profound reservations about what he helped create. Two days before the explosion of the first atomic bomb in 1945, he recited a stanza from the Bhagavad Gita: "Now I am become Death, the destroyer of worlds." Oppenheimer demonstrated his humility: "In some sort of crude sense which no vulgarity, no humor, no overstatement can quite extinguish, the physicists have known sin; and this is a knowledge which they cannot lose."[86] One rarely finds that kind of humility or introspection among today's tech leaders like Mark Zuckerberg, Elon Musk, Jeff Bezos, Larry Page, and Sergey Brin.

David Brooks argues that higher education overvalues the technocratic skills universities promote and underappreciates the social and moral skills that any healthy society needs.[87] Commodification that reduces a college degree to a job credential and financial asset misses how education can inculcate values like critical thinking, concern for humanity, and the importance of the common good, traits necessary to navigate the technological waters. This broader knowledge can help society go from accepting technological advancements as a fait accompli to seeing it as a choice we can master. The next chapter will address how the commodification and corporatization of higher education lead to its high costs.

3

Driving Up the Cost of Higher Education

The American higher education system is significantly more expensive than any other Western nation. From 1978 to 2015, tuition in US colleges and universities rose by 1,120 percent, higher than in any other part of the economy, including pharmaceuticals and health care.[1] Following the Covid pandemic, these increases slowed. By 2023, average tuition and fees rose only 1.6 percent at two-year schools, 1.8 percent for in-state students at four-year public colleges, and 3.5 percent for students in four-year nonprofit private institutions. These modest increases were historic since, for the first time, they were below the inflation rate.[2] However, tuition represents only one cost of attending college. During the same period, the cost of on-campus housing rose 72 percent from 2011 to 2021, with the average dorm room in public four-year institutions costing $7,103 for the thirty-week academic year. Food added another $5,403, and textbooks and supplies are still another $1,230.[3]

Why Is Tuition So Expensive?

Several theories have emerged to explain the sharp increases in tuition over the last thirty years. In 1987, former US Secretary of Education William Bennett argued that increases in federal student aid and student loans enabled colleges and universities to raise tuition, believing these initiatives would soften the escalating student costs. After expanded subsidies became available to more students in 1978, college tuition rose year after year above the inflation rate. Bennett argued that while federal student aid did not per se cause inflation in higher education, it did make tuition increases easier for students to manage.[4]

Some critics point to Baumol's cost disease to explain tuition increases.[5] Developed in the 1960s by economist William Baumol, this model maintains that as an economic sector becomes more productive, labor costs are reduced, which results in lower consumer prices. In contrast, workers in industries without productivity increases still receive higher wages, but the costs are passed on to consumers through higher prices.[6] While Baumol's argument could point to the cost-savings and higher productivity in online instruction (e.g., lower brick-and-mortar costs, fewer student activities, and large class sizes irrespective of classroom space), this delivery system does not increase the productivity of full-time faculty since they teach the same number of courses. Because labor costs remain constant, faculty raises are passed on to students through higher tuition. A counter-argument to Baumol's model is that universities can compensate for faculty raises by increasing enrollment and enlarging class sizes, which would increase faculty productivity and justify a raise. This strategy is desirable for universities since only minimal costs are involved in enlarging class sizes. Universities can also raise professors' salaries by replacing retirees with low-paid adjuncts who already teach 50 to 60 percent or more college classes.[7]

Using Baumol's cost disease model, some pundits blame escalating tuition costs on excessive faculty salaries. David Levy argues that college professors are mainly responsible for skyrocketing tuition since most are underworked and overpaid. He argues that faculty work about half the hours of other professionals but earn $80,000 to $150,000 annually, making the system unsustainable.[8]

Are Faculty Salaries Driving Up Tuition?

A 2023 American Association of University Professors (AAUP) faculty survey of nearly 900 US colleges and universities, covering 370,000 full-time and 90,000 part-time faculty members and senior administrators, found that average faculty salaries for all full-time faculty members rose by 4.1 percent in 2022, the most significant one-year increase since 1991. Broken down, average salaries for full-time faculty grew by 4.5 percent in public institutions, 3.8 percent in private-independent institutions, and 2.7 percent in religiously affiliated institutions. The bad news is that real average wages for full-time faculty decreased by 2.4 percent during the third consecutive year when wage growth fell short of inflation. Specifically, the Consumer Price Index for Urban Consumers rose 6.5 percent from 2021 to 2022, on top of a 7 percent increase the previous year. In short, full-time faculty members in 2021–2 saw their average salaries increase by 4.8 percent but decreased by 1.7 percent after adjusting for inflation.[9] The stagnant or reduced salaries for faculty have been consistent. From 2011 to 2021, the nominal faculty salary adjusted for inflation rose 0.8 percent for full professors, 0.4 percent for associate professors, 0.72 percent for assistant professors, and −0.21 percent for instructors.[10] At the same time, inflation rose by 1.7 percent, meaning academic salaries lost roughly 1.3 percent of their value. In contrast, the average US wage rose 2.05 percent after adjusting for inflation from 2011 to 2021.[11] Table 3.1 examines faculty salaries in almost 900 colleges and universities.

There is an important caveat in Table 3.1. In particular, the salaries are strikingly different between flagship and satellite campuses. For example, while a full professor's salary at the University of Wisconsin (UW)-Madison was $169,600 in 2022–3, it dropped to $68,100 at the UW-Superior and $81,200 at UW-Green Bay. A full professor's salary at the University of Michigan-Ann Arbor was $189,100, but $125,900 at the Flint campus. The average full professor salary at the University of Texas (UT)-Austin was $201,900 compared to $93,700 at the UT-Permian Basin and $125,200 at the El Paso campuses. Rural campuses typically have lower salaries; the average full professor's salary at Eastern Kentucky University was $77,600 compared to $138,000 at the University of Kentucky. The average salary for a full professor at the University of Pittsburgh at Greenburg was $90,400 compared to $151,400 at the University of Pittsburg's main campus.[12] Moreover, most US faculty members are employed in AAUP Categories IIA and IIB public institutions, where salaries are considerably lower than in doctoral-granting institutions.

Table 3.1 Average Full-Time Faculty Salary in 897 Institutions, by AAUP Category, Affiliation, and Academic Rank, 2022–3 (US Dollars)

	Combined	Public	Private Independent	Religiously Affiliated
AAUP Category I Doctoral Institutions				
Professor	$169,821	$154,734	$218,005	$177,354
Associate	$110,945	$106,224	$132,203	$114,389
Assistant	$97,050	$92,687	$116,327	$101,545
Instructor	$70,005	$64,887	$83,798	$81,856
Lecturer	$76,107	$70,820	$93,724	$69,641
AAUP Category IIA Master's Institutions				
Professor	$109,866	$108,313	$120,132	$106,895
Associate	$89,061	$89,173	$93,417	$85,396
Assistant	$77,213	$77,791	$79,638	$74,144
Instructor	$61,034	$58,048	$66,217	$64,640
Lecturer	$65,275	$63,907	$77,208	$60,071
AAUP Category IIB Baccalaureate				
Professor	$113,270	$104,295	$131,010	$93,315
Associate	$86,949	$86,022	$97,117	$74,899
Assistant	$73,421	$72,644	$81,594	$64,963
Instructor	$62,619	$62,263	$68,363	$55,969
Lecturer	$67,302	$64,012	$77,401	$47,065

Source: "2022–3 Faculty Compensation Survey Results, Table 1. Average full-time faculty salary by AAUP category, affiliation, and academic rank, 2022–23," American Association of University Professors (AAUP), 2023, www.aaup.org/sites/default/files/AAUP-2023-SurveyAppendices.pdf

The AAUP salary data illustrates that most university faculty members are not living high off the hog. Instructional salaries at almost all levels have not kept up with inflation or overall national wage increases. Consequently, the relatively stagnant faculty salaries suggest that instructors are not the primary culprits responsible for the sharp rise in tuition.

Inadequate State Funding

Public colleges and universities are funded primarily from state and local government tax revenues. While enrollment in public institutions increased by 28 percent from 1999 to 2017 (from 8.6 to 11 million), state and local appropriations to public higher education only grew by 14 percent after adjusting for inflation. All told, there was an 11 percent decline in appropriations per public-sector student.[13] By 2020, thirty-two states had spent less on public colleges and universities than in 2008, with an average decline of nearly $1,500 per student.[14]

State funds make up a relatively modest proportion of the budget of many public universities. In 2022, state funding accounted for only 4.3 percent of the University of Colorado Boulder's budget and 8.6 percent of the University of Virginia's academic budget.[15] State revenues comprised only 15 percent of the University of Wisconsin's budget in 2021, with 21 percent coming from tuition. State funding at the University of Massachusetts-Amherst accounted for less than 28 percent of its budget compared to 29 percent from tuition. In 2023, only 14 percent of the University of Michigan's budget came from state revenues, with student tuition making up 19 percent. While highly touted as a revenue source, sponsored research comprised only 11.6 percent of Michigan's budget.[16]

State cuts to higher education reflect a profound shift in public policy toward having students pay the lion's share of their college costs, supplemented by other sources, such as donations and sponsored research. While not the sole cause of the tuition bubble, state funding cuts are arguably the most crucial variable in driving up the costs of college attendance.

The Institutional Debt Burden

Inadequate state funding has forced institutions to shoulder high debt levels as they turn to the private bond market to fund needed renovations, new buildings, computer hardware, state-of-the-art gyms, and other amenities. Although often overlooked, institutional debt is a critical factor driving up the cost of a college education. Bereft of additional state funds, schools were forced to turn to the municipal bond market and other lending sources. The need to engage private lending sources was especially pressing for some private and public colleges coping with declining enrollment and increased competition from other institutions. To attract more students, especially wealthier ones who paid full tuition, many schools engaged in expensive campus facelifts and capital development projects, including new athletic fields, classroom buildings, and residence halls; upgraded research facilities and equipment; and remodeled student centers. Desperate to maintain enrollment, some colleges offered deep tuition discounts that were rolled into their long-term institutional debt.

According to Moody's bond-rating service, colleges and universities collectively owed $240 billion in 2017. Publicly funded universities owed $145 billion, while private nonprofit universities owed $95 billion. By 2017, half of the infrastructure of public universities was financed by debt. One estimate is that roughly 9 percent of college and university budgets go to debt service, which is rising faster than enrollment growth.[17]

By 2022, the University of California system had a long-term debt of $26.7 billion.[18] The University of Colorado owed almost $2 billion in revenue bonds and other debt in 2022.[19] Private colleges also experience high debt burdens, including Bard College, which owed almost $125 million in 2020; Skidmore College, nearly $94 million; Pacific Lutheran, roughly $55.7 million; and Fordham, almost $500 million.[20]

Students invariably pay a portion of their school's debt.[21] In 2012, a college's interest payment added roughly $750 at a public university and $1,289 at a private university to a student's tuition.[22] A 2022 Campus Debt Reveal report noted that the University of Massachusetts system owed $3 billion in outstanding debt while Massachusetts state colleges owed an additional $1.2 billion. The report found that, on average, each student attending a public college in Massachusetts paid over $2,500 a year in fees to cover the debt, which increased a student's loan debt by about 25 percent.[23]

The increasing commodification of higher education laid the groundwork for institutional debt. State legislatures and governors knew that publicly funded colleges and universities would be forced to turn to the private market for additional capital improvement funds. The more these institutions have to rely on the private lending sector, the more control investors have in their operation. For instance, when universities have to repay matured revenue bonds, they sometimes initiate new bonds to cover the repayment. The interest rate on the new bonds will be contingent on the institution's credit rating. Moody's ranking criteria include the market position, the institution's relationship to the state, the strength of the balance sheet, fundraising success, and endowments, the overall performance of the institution, the management strategy and general aims, and the project's importance to the borrower.[24]

As public universities are increasingly forced to rely on revenue bonds and other loans for expansions or capital projects, they must adopt a debt-financing model that prioritizes credit ratings and debt service above everything else. To placate bondholders (and in the hope of raising their credit ranking), some schools will demonstrate their financial acumen by cutting costs in myriad ways, such as replacing full-time faculty with adjuncts or non-tenurable contract workers, enlarging class sizes, replacing tenure with renewable contracts, cutting the number of courses, paring down library acquisitions, and cutting health and retirement benefits for faculty. Colleges and universities may also be pressed to generate revenue by admitting students they would not have previously considered. Schools may also be pressured to focus on recruiting students who can pay the full price, such as wealthier, international, and out-of-state students. To strengthen their credit position, universities can appoint trustees with strong financial affiliations instead of those with educational experience. For example, about a dozen of the fifty-seven University of Southern California trustees in the early 2000s were billionaires with little or no experience in higher education.[25] In the end, the primary concern of bondholders is the institution's ability to repay the bonds on time. As such, the power of creditors can transform public and private universities into efficient but heartless economic commodities.[26]

Administrative Bloat

Academic faculty are often critical of administrators for many reasons, including the fact that only teaching and grant-funded faculty generate revenue. In particular, faculty resentment is often based on the belief that they are being exploited and controlled by the least productive members of the university community.

Administrative bloat occurs when an increase in administrative positions outpaces the growth in faculty and enrollment. This results in a cost structure whereby fiscal resources are diverted from academic programs to administrative positions, which leads to a diminished educational experience for students as courses and majors are cut to pay for a growing administrative tier.[27]

When former Ohio State University economics professor Richard Vedder started teaching in the 1960s, there were typically about two faculty members for every non-faculty employee; today, there are more administrators than full-time faculty in many schools. Consequently, bureaucrats are usurping more decision-making while the budget allocated to teaching has fallen dramatically. Vedder recounts that budget problems at Ohio State University led to the firing of several hundred faculty, secretarial, janitorial, and related staff. He did not believe that a single highly paid administrator was terminated.[28]

Between 1993 and 2007, administrative costs in higher education grew by 61 percent compared to 39 percent for instructional expenses. The American Council of Trustees and Alumni (ACTA) found that between 2010 and 2018, administrative spending increased by 29 percent compared to 17 percent on instructional staff. From 2016 to 2017, noninstructional spending at American colleges and universities exceeded the gross domestic product of 134 countries.[29] Table 3.2 illustrates the rise in administrative costs related to the cost per student in selected universities.

Table 3.2 Sample of Administrative Costs per College Student, 2012 and 2020

Name of institution	2012 Administrative cost per student	2020 Administrative cost per student
Private Nonprofit		
Harvard University	$16,629	$45,690
Stanford University	$21,601	$39,791
Princeton University	$15,226	$26,624
Yale University	$19,700	$21,571
Swarthmore College	$16,203	$20,106
Notre Dame University	$15,647	$18,348
University of S. California	$9,878	$13,593
University of Valley Forge	$4,968	$10,125
Adelphi University (NY)	$4,304	$5,387
Brigham Young University	$2,675	$3,847
Public University		
U. of N. Carolina Chapel Hill	$3,654	$8,192
U. of California-Berkeley	$4,953	$7,626
University of Minnesota	$4,608	$6,826
University of Washington	$4,036	$5,615
University of Arizona	$3,057	$5,406
SUNY at Albany	$5,565	$4,912
Miami University of Ohio	$2,669	$3,599
University of Alabama	$2,590	$3,371

(Continued)

Name of institution	2012 Administrative cost per student	2020 Administrative cost per student
University of Nebraska	$2,115	$2,359
University of Arkansas	$2,805	$2,283
Florida State University	$1,413	$2,344

Source: "How Colleges Spend Money," American Council of Trustees and Alumni (ACTA), accessed February 2023 from www.howcollegesspendmoney.com/

The Consulting Game

A few of the dozens of consulting companies have higher education divisions. Some larger ones include McKinsey & Company, Deloitte, Boston Consulting Group (BCG), KPMG, Bain & Company, CIL Management Consultants, Credo, and LEK Consulting. Consulting firms like these add to higher education costs while driving the academy toward a corporate business model.

The widespread use of educational consultants is a curious phenomenon since most colleges and universities have business schools and other departments with faculty with expertise in areas that overlap with consulting firms. Given these resources, it is enigmatic why universities look to expensive outside consultants, the cost of which is included in student tuition. One explanation may be the concern that business school and educational administration faculty might oppose administrative priorities.

As they make inroads into the tertiary sector, consulting firms view colleges and universities in dire need of corporate solutions. The rpk GROUP lists forty-six clients, including some well-known universities, such as the University of Texas at Austin and Dallas, the City University of New York, the University of Missouri, the University of South Carolina, and the University of Virginia. Their clients include the Bill and Melinda Gates Foundation, the Lumina Foundation, the William and Flora Hewlett Foundation, and the World Bank.[30] The rpk GROUP is also the consulting firm that recommended the cuts at West Virginia University (WVU) that resulted in eliminating thirty-two majors, all foreign languages, and the firing of 7 percent of the faculty. WVU paid the company more than $875,000 in return for their sage advice.[31]

Management consulting firms advertise their services as indispensable to successful people in successful companies.[32] Some pitches used by consulting firms read like affirmations on wall posters. Bain & Company's tagline is "We champion the bold to achieve the extraordinary." Deloitte promises to transform "What's next into what's now." BCG claims to help leaders "tackle their most important challenges and capture their greatest opportunities." LEK challenges potential clients to "Bring us your intellectual curiosity, your analytical mind, and your appetite for evidence." In addition to generating more business, companies like McKinsey and Company want to reshape higher education: "Over the longer term, a more fundamental reimagining of higher education may be required, rethinking conventional wisdom around value proposition, diversity and inclusion, student experience, business models and delivery channels." The rpk GROUP maintains that traditional business models in higher education are no longer effective and sees their corporation as influencing and defining the future of higher education.[33]

These consulting firms are not burdened by humility. BCG claims, "We've maintained an unwavering commitment to our corporate purpose—to unlock the potential of those who advance the world."[34] Credo's goal is to impact the lives of more than a million learners by 2030 by "empowering your campus and complementing your on-campus talent with external context, strategy, and support."[35] It is frightening to imagine that the future of higher education rests with consulting companies with no in-depth understanding of education and who possess an overblown sense of their self-importance.

Advice is not free; even small educational consulting firms charge $3,500 for a six-hour day and $4,500 for an eight-hour presentation, plus expenses.[36] Table 3.3 lists the fees rpk GROUP quoted to WVU.

McKinsey & Company is one of the most expensive consulting firms, and in 2020, they charged $67,500 a week for a junior consultant, or $3.5 million annually. For $160,000 a week, a client has two consultants, the second being mid-level.[37] In 2023, the University of Florida's (UF) controversial president, Ben Sasse, signed a $4.7

Table 3.3 rpk GROUP's Hourly Rates for Services to West Virginia University, 2023

Position	Hourly Rate
Senior Partner	$500.00
Principal	$450.00
Senior Associate	$350.00
Associate	$300.00
Senior Analyst	$225.00
Analyst	$175.00
Executive Assistant	$100.00

Source: West Virginia University, WVU Procurement Contract and Payment Services, April 18, 2023, https://transformation.wvu.edu/files/d/c25b20f3-cf7a-43b0-a4aa-1fe7cca3ace7/rpk-contract.pdf

million no-bid contract with McKinsey & Company to help develop the university's vision for the future. An additional stipulation was that UF could request other services until February 2025. Interestingly, while Sasse did not list McKinsey as a former employer on his resume to the UF search committee, he did list it on his Senate campaign website.[38]

A public records request by the *Independent Florida Alligator* for the "scope of work" was denied under state public records laws as "trade secrets" and "business proprietary information." Additional requests for materials McKinsey produced, including presentations and reports, yielded no records.[39] Keeping the "secret sauce" under wraps is a modus operandi for McKinsey and other consulting companies that require employees to sign non-disclosure agreements (NDA) prohibiting them from disclosing "trade secrets."[40]

Although McKinsey had relatively little experience in higher education, the University of Arizona (UA) paid them more than $14 million in consultant fees in 2019. Broken down, McKinsey charged UA up to $185,000 weekly for each three-person team, sending at least sixteen consultants to UA over ten months. Like UF, UA

President Robert Robbins hired McKinsey on a no-bid contract. Also similar to UF, the details of McKinsey's work were elusive since it demands secrecy as its methods and strategies are supposedly trade secrets. When an Arizona newspaper made a public records request for McKinsey's contract, UA allowed the firm to redact entire pages the company considered proprietary, making it virtually impossible to identify what the firm did to earn its fees.[41]

The reviews on McKinsey were mixed. UA faculty chair Jessica Summers felt that the university paid too much for what they got. She noted that a McKinsey survey seemed to be written for corporate clients and used terms such as "supervisors" and "reporting to" that were concepts unfamiliar in academic culture. Summers further observed that questions that were supposedly anonymous could identify respondents.[42]

As the world's oldest and largest management consulting firm, McKinsey's flawed ethics are antithetical to the core values that underlie American universities. McKinsey's involvement in various scandals is almost too numerous to document. A few of the more notable ones include OxyContin maker Purdue Pharma. Hired by Purdue, McKinsey advised doctors that "opioids provide freedom and peace of mind" and would make patients "more optimistic and less isolated." In 2021, McKinsey paid $600 million to settle investigations into its role in boosting OxyContin sales and helping to fuel the opioid epidemic.[43]

McKinsey was commissioned by New York City's Rikers Island jail to test an anti-violence strategy named "Restart." The McKinsey report stated that Restart reduced violent crimes by more than 70 percent in Rikers' units. It was later found that McKinsey consultants and jail officials rigged the results by grouping compliant inmates into the studied housing units.[44] In another instance, McKinsey reached a $74 million settlement with South Africa after admitting to overcharging a financially troubled utility.[45]

The *New York Times* reported on McKinsey's efforts to trace the sources of negative Twitter posts about Saudi Arabia. Two of the three Saudis who wrote the posts said they or their family members were subsequently arrested. In a disingenuous apology, McKinsey stated it was "horrified by the possibility, however remote," that its work was used against dissidents. It seems that McKinsey were the only people in the world who didn't know how dissidents were treated in Saudi Arabia.

The *New York Times* and *ProPublica* also reported on McKinsey's work with Immigration and Customs Enforcement (ICE), which involved proposed spending cuts on food and medical care for migrants and speeding up the deportation process that violated due process rights. Former McKinsey managing partner Kevin Sneader lied when he claimed that the company had done no work for ICE. When the discovered documents proved him false, Sneader backtracked and said the contract was not widely known within the company, and it raised concerns. McKinsey subsequently cut ties with ICE.[46] McKinsey's cost-cutting recommendations also minimized safety concerns at U.S. Steel and Disneyland and cost insurance policyholders billions in lower reimbursements for claims.[47] Not surprisingly, McKinsey was also implicated in the Enron scandal.[48]

McKinsey's clients include dictators, despots, autocrats, crooks, former pro-Russian Ukrainian president Viktor Yanukovych, and several Chinese and Russian companies under US sanctions. They also provided consulting services for Rostec, a Russian military manufacturer, and Sberbank, VTB bank, Gazprom, and Rosneft, all of which are tied to the Kremlin. Despite its ethical problems, McKinsey partners earnestly compared the firm to the Marine Corps, the Roman Catholic Church, and the Jesuits as analytically rigorous and principled seekers of knowledge and truth.[49]

McKinsey isn't alone when it comes to flawed ethics. In 2021, the University of Texas signed a $20 million contract with Bain & Company to improve campus diversity. No stranger to controversy, Bain tried to overturn a UK government ban on applying for public sector contracts because of their role in a major corruption scandal in South Africa. In particular, a South African inquiry found that during the presidency of criminally charged former President Jacob Zuma, Bain had helped to undermine the country's revenue service, which impeded its ability to carry out investigations of tax evasion by Zuma.[50] Despite its costs, consultation services often result in little more than the painful (and costly) exposition of the obvious. In the end, it is the students and their parents who foot the bill.

Compensating for Revenue Shortfalls

If tuition and fees were based solely on state appropriations, most higher education tuition and fees would have to be increased by four or five times to be budget neutral. For instance, the budget for the University of Michigan's Ann Arbor campus was almost $11 billion in 2023, with tuition and fees totaling nearly $2 billion. In contrast, state appropriations totaled only $386 million. Since 2023, in-state undergraduate tuition has averaged $17,786 a year. Tuition would have to be increased roughly four-fold for the University of Michigan to become self-funding. Students would have to pay a whopping $71,144 a year or $284,576 for a four-year degree, excluding housing, food, books, supplies, and personal expenses. That would make Michigan's tuition equivalent to an elite private university.

Fundraising

Fundraising has become essential for all public and private colleges and universities. Public universities use it to compensate for cuts in state funding, Ivy League universities use it to raise special purpose revenues, and some struggling private colleges use it to cover bills, salaries, or interest payments. Apart from capital improvements like buildings, gyms, student centers, and dorms, donations can fund student scholarships, endowed chairs, and research activities.

One fundraising strategy is a capital campaign, a targeted fundraising effort with a specific financial goal during a defined period. These campaigns often have two stages: a silent campaign, where individuals or corporations are approached privately for a donation, and a public campaign, where donations from alumni and others are aggressively solicited through phone calls, emails, brochures, text messages, etc.

In some cases, wealthy individuals approach a university and offer funds to dedicate or attach a name to a building, such as the Bloomberg Center for Physics and Astronomy at Johns Hopkins University. Other times, money is used to fund research activities that interest the donor or impact their family. For example, the

Bill & Melinda Gates Foundation pledged $279 million in 2017 to the University of Washington's Institute for Health Metrics and Evaluation (IHME), which focuses on improving population health worldwide.[51]

On the other hand, deep-pocketed donors can influence the direction of a public and private university through targeted donations.[52] In 2009, the ultra-rightwing Charles and David Koch brothers promised $1.5 million to Florida State University's economics department over six years in exchange for influence over appointments and teaching. The conditions included establishing a Koch-appointed review board to scrutinize research funding, hiring five professors, and reviewing professors' work to ensure it followed the board's objectives and purposes. If dissatisfied, the Koch Foundation could terminate the arrangement at any time.[53]

Sometimes fundraising goes awry, as when Harvard admitted it had accepted $8.9 million in donations from convicted pedophile Jeffrey Epstein. Despite having no appropriate academic credentials, Epstein was made a visiting fellow in the school's psychology department after donating $200,000. Epstein was often spotted wearing Harvard-branded shirts despite having never attended the school.[54]

Capital campaigns and other fund-raising efforts are big business. Auburn University raised $1.2 billion from 2008 to 2018, exceeding its goal of $1 billion. Boston University raised $1.85 billion from 2012 to 2019, exceeding its goal. Harvard University's campaign ran from 2013 to 2018, and although its goal was $6.5 billion, it raised $9.6 billion. Catholic University raised $259 million in its campaign. Publicly funded universities also did well. The University of Michigan raised $5.3 billion from 2013 to 2018; the University of Washington raised almost $5 billion from 2016 to 2020; and even less well-known public schools like Central Michigan University raised $101 million from 2019 to 2022.[55]

About 8 to 10 percent of the proceeds of capital campaigns go for overhead. Some estimates suggest that a development effort is cost-effective if it delivers between eight to sixteen cents on the dollar. While some universities use in-house staff for fundraising, others employ outside consultants whose fees range from a few thousand dollars to $30,000 monthly for full-service on-site campaign management. This approach to capital campaigns can amount to a significant expenditure since large campaigns can run from two to three years.[56] Not surprisingly, university fundraising positions are revolving-door jobs with a high turnover rate. According to one study, the average fundraiser stays in their job for only sixteen months before moving on.[57]

Donations and endowment income are important revenue streams for elite universities. For example, 45 percent of Harvard's 2022 revenues came from philanthropy and their $53 billion endowment income. Yale was not far behind with a $42.3 billion endowment, followed by Stanford ($38.7 billion) and Princeton ($38 billion).[58] (See Table 3.4.) Only twenty universities own half of the $800 billion in endowments.[59]

Ensuring a current and future revenue stream can strongly affect enrollment decisions. Students from high-income families or legacy students whose family members previously attended the institution may be seen as large future donors and may get preferential enrollment. A 2020 *Wall Street Journal* report found that 56 percent of America's top 250 institutions considered legacy in their admissions process.[60] An example of a legacy admission was former President George W. Bush, who was accepted at Yale with a low college entrance score (SAT) of 1196, 180 points lower than his classmates. Being the son and grandson of Yale alumni undoubtedly helped.[61]

Research and External Funding

Public universities try to compensate for revenue shortfalls by seeking external research funding through federal, state, or industry grants. The largest portion of the University of Wisconsin's 2022 budget (25 percent) came from competitive federal research grants that helped support research faculty, facilities, staff, and students. The second-largest revenue source (21 percent) was student tuition and fees.[62] At the University of Massachusetts, 18 percent of its 2023 budget came from grants compared to 24 percent from tuition and fees.[63] Federal and other research grants contributed 12 percent to the University of California's revenue stream.[64]

Universities can also increase their revenue from research activities and patents. For example, the University of Queensland (UQ) created a commercialization arm called Uniquest that was responsible for

Table 3.4 Universities with the Largest Endowments, 2022

Institution	Endowment (rounded off in billions)
Harvard University	$49.4
Yale University	$41.2
Stanford University	$37.8
Princeton University	$35.7
Massachusetts Institute of Technology	$24.7
University of Pennsylvania	$20.7
University of Notre Dame	$16.7
Northwestern University	$14.1
Columbia University	$13.2
Washington University in St. Louis	$12.2
Duke University	$12.1
University of Chicago	$10.3
Vanderbilt University	$10.2
Emory University	$9.9
Cornell University	$9.8
University of Oxford	$9.6
John Hopkins University	$8.2
Dartmouth College	$8.1
Rice University	$7.8
University of Southern California	$7.4

Source: Sheryar Siddiq, "20 Most Profitable Universities in the World," *Yahoo Finance*! (June 24, 2023), https://finance.yahoo.com/news/20-most-profitable-universities-world-180929518.html

converting research into revenue. Gardasil, a vaccine against human papillomavirus (HPV), was developed by UQ and licensed to the pharmaceutical industry for hundreds of millions of dollars. Over $700 million was returned to UQ through commercialization from 2010 to 2020, including Inflazome (a potential treatment for a broad range of inflammatory diseases) sold to Roche for $600 million.[65]

Research grants include direct and indirect costs. Direct costs include salary support for those directly on the grant, laboratory supplies, research equipment, and travel and publication costs. Indirect costs are research costs not directly attributable to the grant, such as the depreciation of research equipment and buildings, utilities, hazardous material management, libraries, internet, insurance, administrative services, and compliance with government regulations. Indirect costs can constitute 50 percent or more of the total grant, and it is where universities realize their most direct financial gain. In contrast to government grants, private foundation grants may not fund indirect costs, or if they do, they are reimbursed at a much lower rate (typically only 10 to 20 percent of the grant).

Despite the financial benefits of indirect costs, research universities like Massachusetts Institute of Technology (MIT) claim that they subsidize every research grant, regardless of whether it includes full overhead costs.[66] A study by Karen Holbrook and Paul Sanberg found that most universities lose money on federal and other research grants since they only cover a relatively small portion of the actual indirect costs.[67] On the other hand, whether a research grant represents a financial gain or a loss to the university depends on the accounting measures used. For example, if the indirect research costs are aggressively calculated or overvalued, the grant will appear to be a financial loss. Conversely, the grant will be a financial gain if the indirect costs are calculated more conservatively. Other than for prestige, it makes little sense why a university would engage in sponsored research if it were a monetary loss.

Students pay for funded research in myriad ways. For instance, it is rare for a top-tier research university to hire a tenured full professor based solely on their teaching. A senior faculty member moving to a highly ranked university typically requires a solid record of successful research grants and publications. In many cases, the research portfolio is more important than publications since the faculty member is expected to generate at least the equivalent of their salary (and more) in research funding. Since a lighter teaching load is a perk for securing funded research, professors have little incentive to spend time with undergraduates. Students are, therefore, denied a higher quality educational experience as faculty members scramble to secure research dollars to compensate for the cuts in state funding.

Competition for research faculty can be intense. In 2015, the University of Southern California (USC) lured Paul Aisen's research team from the University of California-San Diego (UCSD). Aisen's research included $340 million in Alzheimer's funding.[68] In response, UCSD filed suit and won a $50 million settlement from USC.[69] From 2010 to 2015, eighty nationally recognized cancer researchers moved their labs from top universities to Texas schools. This move was prompted by $250 million in state money to attract and expand Texas' research capabilities and create more jobs.[70] Since many star faculty see themselves as free agents in the academic marketplace, entire research teams are subject to poaching. The money to pay for these poaching exercises is incorporated into tuition costs.

Premium Tuition

To partially offset state funding cuts, about 60 percent of public research universities charge premium tuition for high-demand undergraduate and graduate majors in business, health sciences, nursing, pharmacy, physical and life sciences, law, chemistry, engineering, and computer science.[71] This premium is often disguised as additional fees rather than higher tuition and is common in high-demand fields in graduate education.

Schools using a premium tuition model base the higher costs on the market value of the degree, student demand, the cost of equipment, and the cost of instruction. For instance, beginning assistant professors in business or engineering can sometimes earn more than full professors in English or other liberal arts. Another justification is that students should shoulder the additional cost since they are expected to secure highly paid positions after graduation.

This assumption is spurious since the choice of a major is often a poor predictor of future income, as many graduates change employment fields during their careers.[72]

Premium tuition encourages low-income students struggling with college costs to cluster in less expensive majors. To counter this, some universities reallocate a portion of the premium tuition toward additional financial aid. Students paying premium tuition may cling to courses in their field to get the maximum value for their tuition dollars, narrowing their educational experience.[73] Charging premium tuition is emblematic of the commodification of education by labeling each item in the education marketplace with a different price tag based on its presumed value. This represents a tacit acknowledgment that a college degree is just an avenue to increase earnings.

Manipulating Tuition and Fees

The decision by colleges and universities to manipulate tuition and fees falls into four categories: (1) Colleges that want to soften the financial blow to students and families and lessen the dependency on student loans; (2) institutions struggling to fill seats; (3) elite universities that want to increase diversity in their student body; and (4) schools that use discounts to compete with other institutions. Tuition discounts can take many forms, such as a "tuition reset," whereby colleges simply lower prices. Schools can also choose a "tuition freeze," where they promise to maintain the same tuition until the student graduates.

A 2021 National Association of College and University Business Officers (NACUBO) study found that among the 359 private nonprofit colleges and universities surveyed, almost 55 percent reported tuition discounts for first-year students and 49 percent for all undergraduates. Tuition discounts differed based on an institution's exclusivity. The NACUBO study found that at selective/highly selective institutions, the discount rate for first-time undergraduates was almost 45 percent, 13 percentage points below the overall 58 percent discount rate for their sample.[74] Despite this, the average tuition discount in dollar terms at private, nonprofit colleges and universities in 2021 was $20,800 compared to $5,200 at public colleges and universities.[75] Not surprisingly, using grants, fellowships, and scholarships cost some colleges more than half the tuition revenue they would have otherwise collected if every student paid the advertised price.[76]

As noted earlier, tuition discounts serve different purposes for different institutions. For elite universities that have no trouble filling seats, these discounts are a lever to increase diversity among the student body, thereby helping to deflect criticism about being elitist and discriminatory. For example, Princeton University provides free tuition, room, and board for students whose family incomes fall below $100,000 annually.[77] They estimate that 25 percent of their undergraduates will receive this benefit. Some public institutions have also taken up the challenge. The University of Michigan-Ann Arbor covers full undergraduate tuition and university fees for up to four years for students eligible for in-state tuition, are eligible for financial aid, have family incomes of less than $65,000 a year, and are pursuing their first bachelor's degree.[78] State university systems like New York, Virginia, Nebraska, Wisconsin, South Carolina, Tennessee, New Hampshire, and Vermont have frozen tuition. Purdue University has kept tuition and fees flat since 2012.[79]

Some colleges and universities with trouble filling seats often use algorithms to determine merit or scholarship awards based on a family's financial condition. The goal is to find a price point that makes attendance seem financially feasible, and students who are less likely to attend due to financial concerns are offered a more considerable discount. As a result of this pricing system, students pay different amounts—those who pay the full price subsidize those with discounts.

Tuition discounts couched as merit-based scholarships are often designed to lower the enrollment price and make the student and their family feel special. Knowing that most students apply to more than one school, tuition discounts function as price competition among private nonprofit institutions. Public universities use discounts to attract international and out-of-state students who pay higher tuition than in-state students.

Other colleges and universities use sports, music, or other scholarships for tuition discounts and enrollment incentives. For example, despite its relatively small size (about 4,000 undergraduates), Hawaii Pacific University (HPU) has fourteen varsity teams with many students on athletic scholarships. It also offers merit, band, orchestra, vocal, and Esports scholarships. Roughly 38 percent of HPU's tuition dollars are funneled into discounted tuition.[80]

Although rising in both numbers and dollars, tuition discounts are unequally distributed, with white and Asian students more likely to receive merit or scholarship aid (and in higher amounts) than Black or Hispanic students. At private nonprofit four-year institutions, 62 percent of Asian, 59 percent of white, 53 percent of Hispanic, and 51 percent of Black students received institutional aid.[81]

Despite its benefits, the loss of tuition dollars through discounts has to be made up somewhere. This can come from cutting the number of low-enrollment majors and courses, replacing tenured and tenure-track faculty with adjuncts or contract workers, and cutting the number of course sections by combining courses and deferring maintenance. Tuition reduction strategies also impact the revenue of public institutions. At the University of Massachusetts, almost $373 million (28.5 percent) of the total $1.3 billion in tuition and fees went toward tuition discounts in 2023.[82] Rarely do the cuts come from reductions in administrative staff.

To compensate for the revenue loss, colleges aggressively recruit wealthier students who can pay the full tuition, resulting in fewer places for lower-income students. Students from more affluent families will cost the university more since they typically expect high-quality housing, wide-ranging food choices, and a well-manicured campus.[83]

In the end, aggressive discounting can lead to a price war with devastating effects on financially fragile institutions. Tuition discounts coupled with shrinking enrollment will ultimately drive struggling colleges into bankruptcy, deeper debt, exhausted endowments, and a desperate attempt to merge with a stronger institution.[84] None of this bodes well for the educational quality a student will receive in these institutions.

The Lack of Transparency

Increased competition and declining enrollment are leading some colleges to employ retail market tactics, including a lack of transparency typical of some retail business models. Many students and their families are confused by the cost of college due to the confusion created by sticker versus discount prices. This experience is similar to buying a new car. Despite wanting to know a car's final driveaway price, consumers often don't find that out until the final paperwork. Using sleight of hand, dealers can increase the cost of the vehicle by adding charges like a "market adjustment" and then drop it after haggling to make the purchase seem like a good deal. Some colleges use a similar tactic by artificially inflating their sticker price to make it seem like they are on par with private elite universities, then offer a discount so the student or family feels they are getting a good deal.[85]

A 2023 Government Accountability Office report found that 91 percent of colleges understate the cost of their degrees, 65 percent omit critical details about aid packages, and 31 percent list loans as grants, leading students to believe they do not have to be repaid. Many financial aid statements omit the price of books, off-campus housing, food, and personal expenses. About a quarter of colleges fail to include any information on tuition and fees.[86]

Chart 3.1 illustrates the lack of transparency in some financial aid offers, while Chart 3.2 defines the terms in Chart 3.1. The offer in Chart 3.1 states that the Cost of Attendance (COA) is $41,725 with the out-of-pocket expenses for the family being only $4,240. These figures obscure the actual cost of attendance by incorporating student and family debt into the aid package. It also omits other costs like books, transportation, and personal expenses. In short, the financial aid offer makes attendance appear feasible using deferred costs rather than actual costs. Chart 3.3 more closely approximates the real costs with the COA at $44,925 and the out-of-pocket family expense shown at $20,940. This is because Chart 3.3 includes consideration for the cost of books, transportation, and personal expenses as well as loans that require repayment.

CHART 3.1 SAMPLE 2023 FINANCIAL AID LETTER FROM SPONGEBOB UNIVERSITY (STUDENT'S ANNUAL FAMILY INCOME IS $40,000)

Dear Student,

Your estimated financial aid award is below, based on the information you provided. This award is for one year only and is subject to change due to various factors, such as federal or state funding changes and subsequent tuition increases.

==
COA= $41,725   *SAI*= $4,240
==

Tuition	$30,600
Activity & Tech Fee	$ 1,615
Room Fee	$ 5,510
Meal Plan	$ 4,000
Total Costs	$41,725

Scholarships, Grants, and Loans	
Pell Grant	$6,485
Merit Scholarship	$8,000
Direct Subsidized Federal Loan	$3,500
Direct Unsubsidized Federal Loan	$2,000
Work Study	$3,000
FSEOG Grant	$ 600
State Grant	$ 900
College Scholarship	$5,000
Parent Plus Loan	$8,000
Total	$37,485

Note: Withdrawal, dismissal, graduation, or a lighter course load will result in a modification or cancellation of the awards. In addition, students must maintain satisfactory academic progress.

CHART 3.2 COMMON TERMS AND CONDITIONS IN FINANCIAL AID OFFERS

COA = Cost of Attendance.

SAI = Student Aid Index or the amount a family must pay out-of-pocket.

Pell Grant = Need-based federal grant that does not require repayment.

Merit Scholarship = Based on a student's grades and test scores.

Federal Subsidized Student Loan = No interest is accrued while a student is in school. Repayment begins six months after graduation.

Federal Direct Student Loans = Unsubsidized federal student loans with interest accruing while a student is in school. Repayment begins six months after graduation

Work-study = Eligible students work 5-10 hours a week at minimum wage on campus.

FSEOG = Federal Supplemental Educational Opportunity Grant has limited funding, is needs-based and administered by the institution.

State Grants = Usually needs-based, and the amount differs by state.

College/Institutional Grant = Needs-based financial aid given by the college.

Parent Plus Loans = Includes higher interest rates than direct student loans.

CHART 3.3 SAMPLE 2023 FINANCIAL AID LETTER FROM SPONGEBOB UNIVERSITY (STUDENT'S ANNUAL FAMILY INCOME IS $40,000)

Dear Student,

Your estimated financial aid award is below, based on the information you provided. This award is for one year only and is subject to change due to various factors, such as federal or state funding changes and subsequent tuition increases.

COA= $44,925   *SAI= $20,940*

Tuition	$30,600
Activity & Tech Fee	$ 1,615
Room Fee	$ 5,510
Meal Plan	$ 4,000
Books, Supplies, Transportation, Personal Expenses	$ 3,200
Total Costs	$44,925

Scholarships, Grants, and Loans	
Pell Grant	$6,485
Merit Scholarship	$8,000
Work Study	$3,000
FSEOG Grant	$ 600
State Grant	$ 900
College Scholarship	$5,000
Total	$23,985

Note: Withdrawal, dismissal, graduation, or a lighter course load will result in a modification or cancellation of the awards. In addition, students must maintain satisfactory academic progress.

To increase transparency, the Ohio House of Representatives passed a bill in 2023 designed to ensure that public universities explain the total cost of their degree and the financial outcomes graduates can expect. To comply, Ohio public colleges and universities are required to include a one-page form for students who qualify for financial aid that breaks down the actual costs of the degree, the duration of the financial aid package, a clear explanation of the difference between grants and loans, and the minimum monthly loan payments after graduation.[87] New Jersey passed a similar law in 2021 that requires public and private institutions to include an itemized breakdown of costs and opportunities relating to financial aid packets. Virginia passed a law in 2022 requiring that similar information be relayed to students while still in high school. While transparency is a positive development, it can also be exploited by conservative state legislatures to discourage college enrollment by emphasizing the cost versus the benefits.[88]

The High Cost of Redundancy

Closing or Merging Low-Enrollment Public Colleges

From 1950 to 1970, colleges grew from small institutions, often teacher's colleges of fewer than 1,000 students, to campuses with 40,000 or more students plus a network of statewide regional campuses. The decision of where to locate a public college was often the result of political wrangling rather than a systematic growth plan.

There are forty public four-year colleges in New York State. Many of these colleges, like Morrisville State College, SUNY at Potsdam, and SUNY at Purchase, have less than 4,000 students, with some having less than 2,000. New York also has thirty community colleges, with a third having less than 2,000 students.[89] New York is not alone in supporting a large number of public colleges. North Carolina has a population of 10 million, sixteen four-year public universities, and fifty-eight community colleges. Of those sixteen colleges, seven have enrollments of under 10,000 students, with three having under 3,000.

Forty-seven community colleges had under 4,000 students, and thirty-eight had about 2,000 or fewer students.[90] While there is no established guideline for the optimal or minimal size of a public college, institutions with small enrollments are costly to maintain and are ultimately not financially viable. The question of the optimal size for efficiency remains unanswered. Also unknown is how much consolidation or closure of low-enrollment institutions will reduce costs and lower tuition. Overall, the policy question is whether more inadequately funded but accessible colleges are preferable to fewer ones with more funding.

Reducing Duplicate Degree Programs

One costly form of redundancy occurs when nearby colleges and universities offer the same degree. For instance, there are thirty-five Masters of Social Work (MSW) programs in New York State, with thirteen in the New York City metropolitan area. Five MSW programs are in public institutions, while eight are in private nonprofit universities. North Carolina has twelve MSW programs and twenty-three Bachelor of Social Work (BSW) programs. Ohio has twenty-seven BSW and eleven MSW programs.[91] Other professions experience a similar oversaturation of degree programs. For instance, California has eighteen law schools, the District of Columbia has six, Florida and Illinois have ten, New York has sixteen, Texas has nine, and Virginia has eight law schools.[92] The Council on Education for Public Health accredits 252 schools and programs: sixty-seven schools of public health, 158 public health programs, and twenty-seven standalone baccalaureate programs.[93] By comparison, fifty UK universities offer undergraduate degrees and courses in public health.[94]

Because only a finite number of students are interested in a specific degree, offering that degree in multiple institutions thins out the applicant pool and reduces the class size, thereby increasing the per-student cost. This duplication weakens the degree program and is reflected in higher tuition. The oversaturation of degree programs eventually leads to an oversupply of graduates, leading to high unemployment and lower wages.

Since accrediting bodies earn money from the fees paid by accredited programs, they have little incentive to calibrate the number of degree programs to the job market. While many accrediting organizations require a needs assessment as part of the application process, accreditors are easily gamed and often minimize it. In short, duplication of degree programs wastes resources and adds to the cost of a college education.

Conclusion

As the chapter demonstrates, no single factor thoroughly explains the rapid growth in college costs. While some pundits blame high faculty salaries for tuition increases, this chapter demonstrates that overall faculty salaries have been flat or contracted during the last ten years. The high faculty salaries pointed to as excessive are not indicative of salaries in rural, religious, and less prestigious colleges and universities that constitute the bulk of America's college system.

While state funding cuts to higher education are arguably the most critical factor in driving up tuition, these cuts are not the sole cause. Nevertheless, the slow but steady offloading of state responsibility for higher education is reflected in universities where state appropriations constitute only 25 percent or less of their total budget, with the rest coming from tuition, research grants, donations, and other activities. Other factors that impact high tuition include high institutional debt and administrative bloat. These factors are tied to the commodification of higher education and its growing subservience to market forces.

The belief that a college degree is a private pursuit and a marketplace commodity is congruent with a corporate business orientation. Consequently, the argument that users should pay the total costs for their education has gained currency as a college degree is being reframed from a social to a private good. This shift in thinking has allowed states to justify funding cuts based on the view that paying for college is the student's responsibility, which can be met by working, student loans (including in the private lending market), and family support. Comedian Lewis Black aptly referred to college as a debtor's prison. The commodification of higher education has formed the basis for corporatization, with its preference for large numbers of well-paid administrative staff and bureaucratic growth. It is this issue that the next chapter will address.

4

American Universities, Inc.

The commodification of higher education represents the shift from a liberal arts education model to a transactional one where students' long-term income growth is the primary goal. It also fits with the goal of state governments to increase their STEM initiatives, with the expectation that it will encourage more tech companies to relocate to the state. Since families and students view college as a financial investment, universities feel pressure to demonstrate positive financial outcomes. This view has forced some universities to shift from liberal arts to a practical "career or job-ready" orientation. This paradigm shift is also occurring internationally. For example, Australia's Queensland University of Technology (QUT) created the tagline "The university for the real world," further stating that "We are transforming the learning experience, embedding work-integrated learning, and focusing on developing entrepreneurial skills."[1] This kind of branding evokes images of a business or vocational school rather than a traditional university.

Bureaucrats and Bureaucracies

In 1895, the typical US university employed roughly four administrators. By 1965, that number grew to more than 225; by 2023, it was closer to 500.[2] The growth in university administrations has eclipsed the growth in faculty and students; America's top fifty colleges now have three times as many administrative and professional staff as faculty.[3] Public colleges and universities are similar to large corporations since both have a sizeable managerial class with multiple layers of bureaucracy. The University of Virginia's organizational structure reflects the top-heavy administrative structures of many, if not most, medium to large universities.

Managerialism has also crossed into the realm of deans and department chairs, formerly time-limited rotating appointments grudgingly taken on by senior faculty. While the traditional role of deans was to shield faculty from cumbersome administrative demands and to fight for departmental resources, nowadays, the deans' loyalty is to university administrators. Instead of acting as a buffer between the faculty and administration, many deans stand with the administration to ensure that policy mandates—even ones that compromise academic norms—are carefully followed. While deanships were once rotating appointments, they have become permanent positions where candidates are hired based on their management experience rather than academic credentials. This shift also impacts the departmental level, where deans hire departmental chairs loyal to them. Unsurprisingly, many faculty have become antagonistic toward deans and departmental chairs, viewing them as little more than apparatchiks.

This antagonism between faculty members, deans, and directors has worsened with the introduction of Responsibility Center Management (RCM), a decentralized management model developed in the 1970s that introduces business principles into academia. RCM gives revenue-generating university units responsibility for managing their revenues and expenditures. In many cases, these academic units are expected to survive on the revenue they generate through enrollment and research. The downside is that RCM (called different names in different schools) pressures deans and directors to make unpopular budget decisions based on cost, not academics. It can also force departments to focus on short-term budget solutions instead of long-term planning. In addition, RCM undermines collaboration between academic units and pits these colleges and department units against each other in the search to maximize scarce revenues.[4]

Table 4.1 List of Administrative Appointments at the University of Virginia, 2023

The Rector and Board of Visitors (Trustees)	Vice Pres. & Chief Human Resources
The President	Vice Pres. for Finance
Executive Vice President and Provost	Vice Pres. & Chief Information Officer
Vice Provost for Academic Affairs	Vice Pres. for Research
Vice Provost for Faculty Affairs	Office of Sponsored Programs
Vice Provost for the Arts & Director of the Virginia Film Festival	Licensing and Ventures Group
Vice Provost for Academic Outreach	Environmental Health and Safety
Vice Provost for Global Affairs	Center for Comparative Medicine
Vice Provost for Administration	Research Compliance
Vice Provost for Planning	Research Development
Vice Provost for Academic Initiatives	Vice Pres. for DEI & Comm. Partnerships
Vice Provost for Enrollment	Vice Pres. for Advancement
Executive Vice Pres. for Health Affairs	Vice Pres. Chief Student Affairs Officer and Dean of Students
CEO, UVA Medical Center	Chief Marketing Officer
CEO, UVA Physicians Group	Vice Pres. for Communications and Chief Marketing Officer
Pres. UVA Physicians Group	Vice Pres. for Strategic Initiatives
Chief Financial Officer, UVA Health	Vice Pres. for Intercollegiate Athletics
Dean, School of Medicine	Office of University Counsel
Dean, School of Nursing	Chief Audit Executive
Director, Moore Health Sciences Library	Chancellor, U. of Virginia's College at Wise
Executive Vice Pres. & Chief Operations	Associate Vice President and Chief of Staff
Senior Vice Pres. Government Relations	

Source: University of Virginia, *Faculty Handbook*, "2.1 University Administrative Structure," 2023, accessed February 2023, from https://provost.virginia.edu/faculty-handbook/university-administrative-structure

The Well-Paid Administrative Class

The corporatization of higher education is evident in the pay scale of administrators in flagship public and nonprofit universities. According to the AAUP's Report on the Economic Status of the Profession, the 2023 median salary of a college president in a public doctoral-granting university was $592,119 compared to $263,865 in a public primarily baccalaureate college. The median wage in private nonprofit institutions ranged from $962,468 in a doctoral-granting university to $467,345 in a primarily baccalaureate college. With an annual salary of $757,246, college presidents in religiously affiliated doctoral universities did almost as well as those in secular nonprofit schools.[5]

Some university administrators receive "other compensation" or perks worth almost as much as their salary.[6] James Finklestein and Judith Wilde examined the bonuses of 115 public university presidents in forty-seven states and identified three basic types of bonuses:

- Performance bonuses were the most common and varied from $13,000 to $200,000, averaging about $80,000 annually.

- A retention or contract completion bonus was included in 13 percent of the contracts and ranged from $50,000 to $1 million, averaging about $97,000.

- About 50 percent of public university presidents received a deferred compensation or a supplemental retirement benefit ranging from $17,000 to $500,000, with an average of $106,000 annually.[7]

Other perks include a car allowance (or a car provided by the university or a foundation) and a housing benefit. Most college presidents live in university-provided homes, some of which are mansions with expensive artwork and service staff, including chefs, groundskeepers, housekeepers, and chauffeurs. Another perk for presidents is business-class or first-class travel while on university business, sometimes extended to accompanying partners or spouses. In contrast, most states prohibit business-class travel for state employees, instead requiring them to book the cheapest fares. In addition, several college presidents were reimbursed for tax and legal services and received complimentary tickets to all athletic games with VIP seating. Many public college presidents are exempt from state regulations stipulating a maximum reimbursable moving amount. Lastly, other perks included paid membership dues for professional organizations, social clubs, and country clubs.[8] In the past, these perks were only afforded to Fortune 500 executives, not public employees.

While only nine private university presidents earned $1 million annually in 2008, by 2016, that number swelled to sixty-one. Compensation seems random and not necessarily based on the size or prestige of the institution.[9] Despite Harvard and Yale being prestigious and well-endowed universities, their presidents earned less than those in lower-ranked schools like High Point University, Macalester College, or Texas Christian University.[10]

Richard Vedder argues that the encroachment of search firms and consultants into academia partially accounts for the staggering growth in presidential salaries. Regardless of the cause, most state and private university presidents earn more than their governors.[11]

The corporatization of higher education is imitating corporate culture whereby some college presidents earn ten to thirty times more than assistant professors. Table 4.2 illustrates how some college presidents' salaries in nonprofit universities rival CEOs in medium to large corporations.

Table 4.2 The $1+ Million Club: Compensation for Presidents at Nonprofit Schools (with revenues of $100+ million), 2020*

$3+ Million Club		
Name	College	Earnings (Rounded off in Millions)
Stephen Klasko	Thomas Jefferson University	$8.43
Charles Monahan	Massachusetts Coll. of Pharmacy & Health Sci.	$4.48
Shirley Ann Jackson	Rensselaer Polytechnic Institute	$4.23

(Continued)

Steven Kaplan	University of New Haven	$3.67
Jerry Falwell Jr.	Liberty University	$3.53
$2+ Million Club		
Paul Klotman	Baylor College of Medicine	$2.79
David Van Zandt	New School	$2.67
Paula Wallace	Savannah College of Art & Design	$2.50
Lee Bollinger	Columbia University	$2.40
Carol Folt	University of Southern California	$2.34
Amy Gutmann	University of Pennsylvania	$2.62
John Fry	Drexel University	$2.05
Robert Zimmer	University of Chicago	$2.03
John Petillo	Sacred Heart University	$2.00
$1.5+ Million Club		
Victor Boschini	Texas Christian	$1.94
Morton Schapiro	Northwestern University	$1.91
Peter Salovey	Yale University	$1.90
Robert Brown	Boston University	$1.84
Ronald Daniels	Johns Hopkins	$1.73
Susan Wente	Vanderbilt University	$1.73
Kathleen Goeppinger	Midwestern University	$1.72
Andrew Hamilton	New York University	$1.71
David Leebron	Rice University	$1.70
Daniele Struppa	Chapman University	$1.61
Nathan Hatch	Wake Forest University	$1.58

R. Gerald Turner	Southern Methodist University	$1.57
Scott Pulsipher	Western Governors University	$1.56
Julio Frenk	University of Miami	$1.52
Jonathan Veitch	Occidental College	$1.51
Vincent Price	Duke University	$1.49
Stuart Rabinowitz	Hofstra University	$1.49
Thomas Rosenbaum	California Institute of Technology	$1.46
Philip Hanlon	Dartmouth College	$1.45
$1.3+ Million Club		
Michael Fitts	Tulane University	$1.39
Jill Tiefenthaler	Colorado College	$1.39
Richard Lifton	Rockefeller University	$1.35
Richard Schneider	Norwich University	$1.34
$1.2+ Million Club		
Farnam Jahanian	Carnegie Mellon University	$1.29
George Hanbury II	Nova Southeastern University	$1.29
Marc Tessier-Lavigne	Stanford University	$1.28
Joseph Aoun	Northeastern University	$1.27
Joseph Nyre	Seton Hall University	$1.27
Paul. Leblanc	Southern New Hampshire University	$1.26
Barbara Snyder	Case Western Reserve University	$1.25
John. Jenkins	University of Notre Dame	$1.24

(*Continued*)

L. Rafael Reif	Massachusetts Institute of Technology	$1.23
Martha Pollack	Cornell University	$1.23
Nido Qubein	High Point University	$1.22
David Greene	Colby College	$1.22
$1+ Million Club		
John Degioia	Georgetown University	$1.18
Gary Brahm	University of Massachusetts Global	$1.17
Thomas Leblanc	George Washington University	$1.16
John Simon	Lehigh University	$1.15
Anthony Monaco	Tufts University	$1.13
Kwang-Wu Kim	Columbia College Chicago	$1.12
Robert Fisher	Belmont University	$1.12
Laurie Leshin	Worcester Polytechnic Institute	$1.12
Sherine Gabriel	Rush University	$1.11
Larry Arnn	Hillsdale College	$1.10
Ronald Vaughn	University of Tampa	$1.10
Wayne Frederick	Howard University	$1.10
Linda Livingstone	Baylor University	$1.10
Lawrence Bacow	Harvard University	$1.09
Christina Hull Paxson	Brown University	$1.08
Andrew Martin	Washington University in St. Louis	$1.07
Kimberly Cline	Long Island University-C.W. Post	$1.06

Laverne Harmon	Wilmington University (Del.)	$1.05
Christopher Eisgruber	Princeton University	$1.04
A. Gabriel Esteban	DePaul University	$1.03
Marvin Krislov	Pace University	$1.02

* There are several caveats: (1) the 2020 salaries listed in Table 4.2 are lower for some presidents since they reflect Covid-based salary cuts; (2) this excludes perks such as housing, retirement, and expense accounts. For instance, Harvard's Lawrence Bacow received $1.04 million in salary in 2019, plus almost $178,000 in other compensation. Yale's Peter Salovey earned $1.8 million plus almost $268,000 in additional compensation. (See ProPublica, Nonprofit Explorer, https://projects.propublica.org/nonprofits.)

Source: "How Much Are Private-College Presidents Paid? Base pay, bonuses, and benefits for 307 chief executives at private colleges with expenditures of $100 million or more in 2020," The Chronicle of Higher Education, July 18, 2023, www.chronicle.com/article/president-pay-private-colleges

Although the wages of public college presidents generally fall short of those of private nonprofit universities, their wages and benefits approximate those in the corporate sector. Table 4.3 examines the salaries and benefits of the top twenty-five highest-paid college presidents of public universities.

Some college presidents are rewarded financially even when their administration has failed. When Max Nikias resigned as president of the University of Southern California after a sex abuse and drug scandal in 2018, he left with a $7.7 million compensation package plus the $2.4 million he earned in 2017.[12] The late Ken Starr, former president and chancellor of Baylor University, was forced to step down in 2016 when his administration failed to address the sexual assaults perpetrated by football team members. Starr took home $4.5 million in severance pay plus almost $381,000 in salary.[13]

The corporate-level salaries of college presidents are not unique to the United States. The average package for a vice-chancellor in the Russell Group of twenty-four UK universities was £413,000 (roughly US $489,000) in 2021–2. Alice Gast, the former President of London's Imperial College, exited the university in 2022, having earned £714,000. Louise Richardson, the former vice-chancellor of Oxford University, earned £542,000 in 2022, while Baroness Shafik of the

Table 4.3 Highest Paid College Presidents at Public Universities, 2021

President	Institution	Total Pay	Bonuses	Benefits
Randolph Woodson	N. Carolina State University	$2.29 mill.	$1.7 mill.	$6,389
Mark Kennedy	Univ. of Colorado System	$1.95 mill.	0	$63,283
Michael Good	University of Utah	$1.65 mill.	0	$15,308
Renu Khator	University of Houston	$1.51 mill.	$300,000	$7,498
Jay Hartzell	University of Texas at Austin	$1.27 mill.	0	$91,079
Jeffrey Gold	Univ. of Nebraska-Omaha	$1.20 mill.	0	$18,221
James Clements	Clemson University	$1.20 mill.	$100,000	$135,271
W. Kent Fuchs	University of Florida	$1.16 mill.	0	$21,778
Eric Barron	Pennsylvania State University	$1.15 mill.	0	$15,837
Samuel Stanley Jr.	Michigan State University	$1.15 mill.	0	$16,606
Michael Crow	Arizona State University	$1.14 mill.	0	$5,381
Tedd Mitchell	Texas Tech Univ. System	$1.13 mill.	$200,00	$3,792
Ted Carter	U. of Nebraska System Office	$1.07 mill.	$140,190	$785
Neeli Bendapudi	University of Louisville	$1.03 mill.	$1,000	$19,885

President	Institution	Total Pay	Bonuses	Benefits
Jay Perman	Univ. System of Maryland	$1.03 mill.	$1,000	$39,089
Ana Mari Cauce	University of Washington	$1.01 mill.	0	0
Brooks Keel	Augusta University	$999,906	0	$93,418
Mitchell Daniels	Perdue University	$998,486	$300,000	$45,825
John Thrasher	Florida State University	$990,752	$361,250	$35,593
Mark Schlissel	Univ. of Michigan-Ann Arbor	$954,448	0	$49,715
Michael Schill	University of Oregon	$952,450	$200,000	$18,050
James Milliken	University of Texas System	$950,036	0	$20,377
F. King Alexander	Oregon State University	$942,658	0	0
Susan Cole	Montclair State University	$937,488	$123,200	$12,018
Mark Rosenberg	Florida International Univ.	$919,813	$360,000	$2,640

Source: Angelo Young, "Highest Paid College Presidents at America's Public Universities," *24/7 Wall St.*, August 30, 2022, https://247wallst.com/special-report/2022/08/30/highest-paid-college-presidents-at-americas-public-universities/6/

London School of Economics had a salary package of £539,000.[14] By comparison, the average 2020 salary for university staff in the UK was £40,761 for a lecturer, £51,590 for a senior lecturer, £64,356 for an associate professor, and £90,891 for a full professor.[15]

Australian universities also have high administrative salaries. The vice-chancellors of ten Australian universities (Melbourne, Australian Catholic, Flinders, Macquarie, Monash, Queensland University of

Technology, The University of Queensland, The University of Sydney, University of New South Wales, and University of Technology Sydney) earned upward of AUD $1 million a year in 2021. The highest-paid Australian vice-chancellor at the University of New South Wales earned AUD 1.15 million.[16]

Bringing Industry and the Academy Closer: Nontraditional College Presidents

Another manifestation of corporatization is hiring college presidents without academic experience or relevant educational credentials. While most provosts had academic credentials and previous faculty appointments, nontraditional college presidents come straight from business, law, or government. In 2016, the American Council on Education (ACE) found that 15 percent of college presidents came from outside academia.[17] A 2018 Virginia Commonwealth University study found that 40.5 percent of college presidents in public land-grant institutions had never had a tenure-track position in higher education.[18]

Proponents of nontraditional college presidents argue that they promote innovation, control university budgets, drive fundraising efforts, and manage complex organizations. These presidents are often part of important financial networks that can benefit the university with fundraising and endowments. On the other hand, lacking academic credibility, nontraditional presidents are viewed with suspicion or contempt by faculty who believe that the mission of higher education is to produce knowledge, not profits. Many faculty members are also critical of nontraditional college presidents who use corporate-style strategies to cut costs, such as replacing tenured faculty with low-paid adjuncts and are antagonistic toward unions. Some faculty argue that nontraditional administrators are unfamiliar with the academic culture and that a college campus is a complex environment best understood by those within its ranks.[19]

College presidential appointments are sometimes given as a perk or gift, such as John Thrasher, a former Florida speaker of the house, who was appointed president of Florida State University from 2014 to 2021. Other nontraditional college presidents include Margaret

Spelling, former president of the North Carolina System and former Secretary of Education under George W. Bush; Janet Napolitano, former president of the University of California System and former Secretary of Homeland Security; William McRaven, a four-star admiral, and the former chancellor of the University of Texas system; and Mitch Daniels, former governor of Indiana and former president of the Purdue university system.[20]

In 2022, the University of Florida hired former Nebraska Republican Senator Ben Sasse as its new president, despite the Faculty Senate's no-confidence vote of sixty-seven to fifteen. While the search committee claimed to have reached out to 700 possible candidates, Sasse was the single finalist. His candidacy sparked controversy due to his track record of being vehemently anti-abortion, anti-LGBTQ rights (he was opposed to gay marriage), and against student loan forgiveness.[21] Sasse also had little experience managing a large university since his academic experience was as president of Midland Lutheran College, a small college of less than 3,500 students compared to the 61,000 students at the University of Florida. Sasse's base salary began at $1 million a year.[22]

Nontraditional presidential appointments often end badly. Margaret Spelling left her position in North Carolina midway through a five-year contract, citing the "tough" nature of the job and personal reasons. Businessman Timothy Wolfe resigned as president of the University of Missouri due to campus tensions and deteriorating relationships with students and faculty. He was accused of acting autocratically when he failed to consult with faculty and disregarded student concerns. Wolfe lasted in the position from 2012 to 2015.[23] The California State Auditor reported in 2017 that Janet Napolitano engaged in misleading budget practices. According to one report, Napolitano approved a plan that pressured the ten University of California (UC) campuses to change their survey responses about her administration from negative to positive. Disciplinary action was taken against Napolitano.[24] She stepped down from UC in 2019.

One of the more extreme cases of political nepotism involved Manny Aragon, who served in the New Mexico Senate from 1975 to 2004. Aragon became the president of New Mexico Highlands University (NMHU) in 2004 despite having no experience in higher education administration. The Board of Regents fired Aragon in 2006 but provided him with a $200,000 settlement.[25] In 2009, Aragon pleaded guilty to three counts of conspiracy and mail fraud and was sentenced to sixty-seven months in prison. He was ordered to pay up to $1.19 million in restitution for his role in a scheme that skimmed $4.3 million from construction contracts.[26]

High Administrative Salaries across the Board

Top administrative staff in most universities are well paid. Table 4.4 lists the 2019 salaries of key administrative positions at Northwestern University, a private nonprofit university typical of many high-prestige institutions.

Table 4.4 Key 2020 Administrative Salaries for Northwestern University*

Position	Salary (millions are rounded off)	Other Compensation
*Head Football Coach	$5.3 million	$69,087
*Head Basketball Coach	$2.86 million	$66,364
*VP & Investment Officer	$2.31 million	$889,821
*VP Athletics	$2.29 million	$307,289
*President	$1.64 million	$627,782
*Managing Director, Investment	$989,266	$275,007
*Managing Director, Investment	$960,884	$334,119
*VP for Development	$947,077	$31,524
*VP Budget and Planning	$941,990	$18,358
*VP General Counsel	$896,054	$55,013
*Executive VP	$796,668	$124,998
*Provost	$598,149	$21,184

Position	Salary (millions are rounded off)	Other Compensation
*VP Medical Affairs	$570,802	$25,614
*VP Student Affairs	$537,089	$21,677
*VP for Facilities Management	$518,669	$1,995
*VP & Chief Information Off.	$478,828	$29,530
*VP Research	$474,110	$102,352
*Senior VP and Treasurer	$459,414	$38,412
*VP Admin & Planning	$447,018	$46,941
*VP Human Resources	$421,512	$30,265
*VP Global Marketing	$420,098	$21,825
*VP Operations	$395,672	$49,213
*VP for International Relations	$213,632	$21,657

* Due to the fiscal impact of Covid, these 2020 salaries are lower than in 2019.

Source: "Northwestern University, Return of Organization Exempt from Income Tax (2020), Form 990," Department of the Treasury, Internal Revenue Service, *ProPublica*, https://projects.propublica.org/nonprofits/display_990/362167817/IRS%2F362167817_202108_990_2022080220263735

Highly corporatized universities have several key features in common, including a board of directors (sometimes called Trustees, Regents, Governors, etc.). In most states like Michigan, Colorado, Nebraska, Nevada, Florida, and Texas, appointments to public university governing boards are made by governors, sometimes with the state legislature's approval. Boards of private universities are selected either by an alumni vote or by the board members.

Until recently, little attention was paid to board appointments in public universities. However, these appointments have taken on a new significance as part of the strategy to advance an ideological and political agenda in highly conservative states. For example, two-thirds of board members overseeing thirty-six Texas public universities are donors of conservative Governor Greg Abbott. These high-money donors are concentrated on larger boards, such as the University of Texas System and Texas A&M University System, and wield significant influence over these institutions.[27]

Public universities are impacted by conservative state governments trying to curtail what they view as a leftist college environment. One of the more draconian measures to control course content was the 2021 Florida House Bill 233, requiring the Florida Board of Governors to measure the intellectual freedom and diversity of viewpoints among students and faculty. The bill also allowed students to record class lectures for personal use, as evidence for a university grievance, or as evidence in a court proceeding.[28] Compliance with this act could constitute part of the criteria for dismissing tenured and tenure-seeking faculty whose teaching or personal politics do not fit that mold. It would also allow students to claim that an instructor was trying to indoctrinate them. These Draconian measures around thought control are more reminiscent of totalitarian regimes than Western democracies.

The commodification of higher education has led to the creation of a professional managerial class of university presidents, chief financial officers, human resource managers, development staff, and others with little or no academic background. Without a firm understanding or commitment to academic values, some university presidents are willing to sacrifice traditional values like academic freedom to appease legislators. Working with corporate-style college presidents, university governing boards often are rubber stamps for the agenda of governors who appointed them.

The commodified higher education system and its top-down hierarchy contradict a university culture rooted in academic freedom, shared governance, and job security. As such, traditional academic culture is an anomaly in the corporate world of at-will employees, gig economy workers, and employees covered under porous and virtually meaningless labor contracts.

In *The Fall of the Faculty*, Benjamin Ginsberg reminisces how American universities were traditionally led by faculty members who saw intellectual discovery and teaching as the institution's core mission. He warns that "deanlets" and "deanlings" (administrators lacking a serious academic background and experience) are dictating the direction of higher education; as a result, students are being denied an education enriched by intellectual rigor.[29]

A Compliant Labor Force: The Attack on Tenure, Shared Governance, and Unionization

For corporate university managers, tenure is an obstacle to creating a compliant labor force and an anachronism in the modern US economy. The attack on tenure by conservative pundits and government officials is based on several beliefs lodged in a political and corporatist agenda, including that it protects "dead wood" who are neither active researchers nor good teachers. A second criticism is that tenure protects instructors who brazenly bring their liberal views into the classroom to convert naive students. These arguments miss the fact that faculty members must exercise caution even with tenure to secure research funding. They must also placate administrators lest they find themselves with unmanageable course loads or are required to teach courses not in their field.[30] Moreover, most universities hold tenured professors accountable through a post-tenure review process.

Tenure thwarts the political agenda of conservative governors and state legislatures who want to curtail classroom discussions on race and gender. The goal is to replace critical thinking with career and job-ready skills and knowledge.[31] Multiple states, including Texas, Florida, North Dakota, South Carolina, Iowa, and Georgia, have entertained proposals to limit or terminate tenure.[32] The attack on tenure also complements the corporate need for a flexible labor force unimpeded by ironclad contracts or unions. The shift to an increasingly casual labor force has occurred mainly below the radar over the last fifty years. By 2020, 61.5 percent of faculty members had non-tenure track appointments.[33]

Shared governance is another obstacle to creating a disciplined corporate workforce. A 2021 AAUP study on shared governance found that the overall involvement of faculty in institutional decision-making declined from 1971 to 2021, especially in areas such as the allocation of faculty positions and budgetary input. In contrast, some local decision-making areas, such as curriculum decisions or the selection of department chairs, have seen an increase in faculty input.[34]

A significant driver for universities is the budgetary process, which is frequently off-limits to faculty bodies. The lack of influence in budgetary matters has important consequences since university administrations set the agenda and wield power through budgetary control. Given the current emphasis on austerity, partly attributable to lingering Covid-19 financial problems, tight budgets are used to justify program cuts, eliminate entire departments or colleges, and curb new tenure-track faculty positions. In paying lip service to shared governance, decisions around new buildings, athletic complexes, or new programs are often referred to faculty governance bodies only after a decision has been made. Faculty efforts to gain greater involvement in the budgetary process are often met with resistance from administrators.[35]

Administrators can neutralize the impact of shared governance through surveillance, including attending departmental and Faculty Senate meetings. Apart from the chilling effect of their presence at meetings, administrators can dominate meetings with lengthy reports, leaving little time for discussion and feedback. Administrators may also prohibit faculty members from directly contacting members of the board of trustees. Contact with the press around college issues may be discouraged, with faculty fearing repercussions if they are labeled disloyal to the university. In other cases, activist faculty are co-opted by lucrative administrative positions.

For corporate managers, unionization is an obstacle to maintaining a compliant and flexible labor force. Despite the downward trend in unionization (overall union membership fell from 20 percent of workers in 1983 to 10 percent in 2022), 118 newly recognized or certified faculty bargaining units covered 36,264 members from 2013 to 2019. Broken down, there were sixty-five new bargaining units at private non-profit institutions, fifty at public institutions, and three at private for-profit institutions.[36] The number of faculty bargaining units at non-profit colleges grew by 81 percent from 2012 to 2020.[37] Despite this rise, only 25 percent of college faculty and 12 percent of graduate assistants are unionized.[38]

The struggle for faculty unionization faces significant obstacles. For example, the University of Pittsburg spent nearly $3 million on Ballard Spahr, a union-avoidance company, to fight the ultimately successful unionization of its faculty. Temple and Pennsylvania State University employed the same firm. Columbia University hired Proskauer Rose, a law firm known for union busting. Even after a successful unionization vote, some universities challenge the results, refuse to acknowledge the bargaining unit, and even refuse to sit at the negotiating table.[39] Some administrators and boards of trustees argue that unions are antithetical to academic governance since they relieve management of the obligations associated with shared governance.[40] Moreover, governance issues are often murky, as in the reappointment, tenure, and promotion process, where faculty bodies make recommendations to deans and other university committees. A potential conflict occurs when a union member votes against the reappointment of another union member.

While some universities graciously accept a faculty vote to unionize, others fight it. In 2017, 71 percent of Hawai'i Pacific University's (HPU) faculty voted to unionize due to low salaries, job insecurity (HPU has no tenure), heavy teaching and service loads, little transparency around university decisions, and weak shared governance. The American Association of University Professors (AAUP) was to be the bargaining agent. HPU President John Gotanda refused to recognize the vote and framed unionization as threatening shared governance. He warned that all hiring, performance reviews, and promotions would be left to the administration under collective bargaining.[41] (Those decisions were already in the hands of the administration.) Gotanda further claimed that any faculty member who sat on a hiring, promotion, or retention committee was a manager, and therefore, only twenty out of 150 faculty were eligible for union membership. His anti-union strategy was based on the 1980 Supreme Court ruling (*National Labor Relations Board* v. *Yeshiva University*) that faculty at private colleges have "managerial status" since they make academic and personnel decisions. In response, the AAUP chapter filed an Unfair Labor Practice complaint with the National Labor Relations Board (NLRB), charging that the administration had violated the National Labor Relations Act by not recognizing the union. The NLRB dismissed the complaint, which squashed the union effort.

The Academic Gig Economy: Fostering the Casual Labor Force

The vacuum left by the gradual reduction of tenured and tenure-track faculty is filled by part-time adjuncts, contract workers, and graduate assistants. Part-time adjuncts are "as-needed" workers without benefits, perks, or job security. Since they are paid per course, they receive no compensation if the class fails to attract the requisite number of students. In some cases, adjuncts are informed of their teaching assignment only a few days before the course begins. The exploitation of adjuncts is even starker. In 2022, the average remuneration for a three-credit-hour course ranged from $2,839 in two-year-only institutions to $4,969 in doctoral institutions.[42] The average reimbursement was about $3,500, or $233 weekly for fifteen weeks. This amount supposedly compensates adjunct faculty for developing and delivering lectures, mastering the course management software, creating course syllabi, grading papers and assignments, keeping office hours, and travel time. An adjunct earning $3,500 a course and teaching four courses a semester for the entire academic year would earn $28,000 a year. By comparison, a full-time senior faculty member earning $75,000 a year and teaching three courses a semester will cost the university $25,000 for that same course. After paying high tuition, students expect and deserve a full-time faculty member rather than an adjunct instructor, regardless of their competence. Moreover, using lower-paid adjuncts should reduce the course cost for students.

Universities use a gig economy model similar to Uber, Lyft, and GrubHub, where a casual or ad hoc labor force is on an as-needed basis. Some adjuncts use the job to supplement their wages; others teach part-time, hoping to secure a regular faculty appointment someday. Others try to eke out a subsistence living by teaching multiple courses at different institutions. This last group constitutes an academic precariat, or a class of disenfranchised workers without a predictable source of income or job security.[43]

Colleges and universities increasingly rely on people ineligible for tenure to teach classes, including contract workers, visiting faculty, graduate assistants, and post-doc students. Some universities offer non-renewable teaching contracts to ensure contract workers cannot claim tenure rights due to time on the job. For instance, non-tenure track or contract faculty at Miami University of Ohio can only get annual reappointments for up to five years.[44]

Graduate assistants, whose numbers increased 44 percent from 2002 to 2021, form another tier of "cheap academic labor." These students typically function as quasi-faculty by teaching or working as lab assistants, sometimes doing both. In some schools, graduate assistants have unionized due to low wages, rules limiting what they can teach, limited healthcare benefits, lack of job security, and poor working conditions.[45] By 2023, graduate assistants at the University of Southern California, Northwestern University, Columbia, Yale University, Temple, and Johns Hopkins were unionized or starting to unionize.[46]

Universities differed in their approach to student unionization. In response to a 2023 strike by graduate assistants, Temple University played hardball by withdrawing tuition assistance (valued at $20,000 a year), required that students pay their total tuition balance by a specific date or face a financial hold on their account and a $100 late fee, and stripped students of their health insurance. The six-week strike was settled in March 2023, resulting in a 30 to 40 percent increase in the minimum pay for graduate students.[47]

The Cost of Commodification: Big Profits, Low Risk, and a Captive Market

Taking advantage of the lucrative higher education market and the financial desperation of some colleges, for-profit corporations provide a range of services, such as branding and logo consulting, enrollment and marketing, and assessments of institutional performance. However, the most significant corporate involvement in higher education is developing and managing online courses and degrees.

Online Program Managers (OPM)

Faced with enrollment challenges, high debt levels, and local and national competition from colleges and universities, schools desperate to increase enrollment have offered online courses leading to certificates and degrees. Although online programs are not burdened by maintaining a physical space and do not need a cap on class sizes based on available classroom space, they incur significant costs, including new course development, online assessments, support and technical services, and marketing. The Florida Board of Governors estimated that an online class costs $41.48 *more* per credit hour than an in-person class.[48] Online education advocates argue that many of the above expenses are startup costs that will be recouped through larger class sizes and recycling the course content and the instructional platform.

While some universities design and deliver their own online courses and degrees, others turn to Online Program Managers (OPM) like 2U, Pearson, Wiley, Academic Partnerships, and Keypath Education. These corporations provide turnkey services, including market research, course design, course delivery platforms, technology, enrollment, student and advising services, and internship and training placements.[49]

Estimated to be a $7.5 billion industry by 2025, OPMs serve many nonprofit and public institutions, including some of the most prestigious universities in the United States and abroad. For example, the client base of 2U (the largest OPM) includes Case Western, Washington University, Harvard, Yale, Northwestern, New York University, Pepperdine, Rice, Stanford, University of North Carolina at Chapel Hill, University of Pennsylvania, Vanderbilt, University of Southern California, and multiple University of California campuses. Its international reach extends to the London School of Economics, University of Birmingham, Oxford, Cambridge, University of London, University of Toronto, and the Australian universities of Sydney, Monash, Adelaide, and Western Australia.[50]

While OPMs can help grow enrollment for ailing institutions, the rub is that a college or university must agree to revenue-sharing that can range from 20 to 60 percent of tuition income. In turn, this high level of revenue sharing squashes any incentive for an institution to lower tuition.[51] These OPM partnerships can include long contracts from six to ten years, have strict exiting terms, include automatic contract renewals, and may prohibit schools from contracting with other companies for similar services after termination. There is also the question of how OPMs use student data. Faculty members and departments give up some autonomy as OPMs take over program management, including advisement and course assessments. One faculty member said my university should be named "Pearson U" since the company controls it.[52]

The course, degree program, or certificate template can be transferred to other schools once an OPM develops and implements it. Since OPMs receive a percentage of tuition per student head, they are incentivized to sign up as many schools as possible, including competing schools. For instance, 2U "partner schools" that offer a Masters of Social Work (MSW) degree include Baylor, Case Western, Fordham, Howard, Simmons, Syracuse University, University of Denver, and the University of Southern California. Since the online programs above are private nonprofit universities (without an in-state tuition option), they are competing for the same students. Because 2U's tuition cut is based on enrolled students, any competition between MSW programs will likely only have a limited effect on the company's bottom line. As the growing number of online degree programs saturates the market, it is hurting the long-term enrollment prospects of each participating university since only a finite number of students are interested in a given field. Lower-prestige schools experiencing the sharpest enrollment declines are further hurt by students who find better deals in more prestigious online degree programs.

The question nevertheless remains whether OPM-managed degrees contain quality standards similar to those of their in-person counterparts. For example, the University of Southern California (USC) partnered with 2U for an online MSW degree that saw enrollment soar from 300 to over 3,000 students. Disgruntled graduates of the USC online MSW program filed a class-action lawsuit in 2023, claiming that the program misrepresented itself as being on par with the in-person classroom version, citing that large parts of the degree were outsourced to 2U. The lawsuit accuses USC of misrepresenting facts, false advertising, and illegal recruitment practices. In particular, the graduates of the online MSW maintain that the instructors, content, curriculum, advising, and internship placements managed by 2U were inferior to the in-person program. Moreover, the lawsuit also alleges that 2U's employees used predatory enrollment tactics (similar to some for-profit institutions) targeted at students of color and veterans. For instance, 2U recruiters used usc.edu emails while communicating with prospective students despite not working for the university. Not coincidentally, the online and in-person MSW program charged students $100,000 in tuition and fees.[53] Ironically, USC claims to have lost money on its MSW program since so much of the tuition went to 2U.[54]

Subcontracting academic programs to for-profit corporations further blurs the line between public colleges and the commercial marketplace. Moreover, there is little evidence that OPMs manage educational programs more efficiently, and even if they do, that efficiency does not translate into lower tuition. OPM-managed degree programs expose students to the same risks as for-profit degree mills but with fewer protections since they are for-profit corporations hiding behind the legitimacy of public institutions purportedly concerned with student welfare.

As OPMs begin to take over more degree programs, there is a risk that public and private colleges and universities will become brokers rather than higher education providers. From the university's standpoint, offloading the delivery of courses would relieve them from dealing with unions and obstreperous faculty. It would also free up faculty time for more funded research. Conservative legislators would find it easier to influence for-profit corporations around course content than dealing with some college administrators hamstrung by Faculty Senates. Unrestrained by issues of shared governance, OPMs could realize further savings by using AI to develop lectures, course content, and syllabi and even employ virtual instructors.

The Textbook Market

In 2021, first-year undergraduate students spent between $1,000 and $1,250 a year on books and related materials. Since that estimate includes technology products and services, the actual textbook cost is likely closer to between $300 and $600 a year. A 2019 study of eighty-three college campuses by the Public Interest Research Group (PIRG) found that 63 percent of students skipped buying a textbook altogether; 90 percent worried that not buying a textbook would hurt their grade; 25 percent worked extra hours to pay for textbooks; 19 percent chose classes based on the cost of course materials; and 11 percent skipped meals to pay for course supplies.[55]

Textbooks are a significant cost for most college students. College textbook publishing is a $3.1 billion industry that includes large publishing houses like Pearson, McGraw-Hill, Cengage, Routledge Taylor and Francis Group, Wiley, and Springer, among others. Control of the textbook industry by a few players and a captive student market has allowed prices to balloon by 1,041 percent from 1977 to 2015, outpacing inflation by 238 percent. From 2002 to 2012, textbook prices also outpaced the growth in the consumer price index by almost 193 percent. Despite its high cost (hardcover books sell anywhere from $80 to $400 with the average at $105), industry revenue fell from $4.81 billion in 2013 to $3.1 billion in 2020.[56] The loss of revenue seems odd since publishers have outsourced the book's production to less expensive venues in India and Singapore. They have also reduced the production quality of books by substituting softcovers for hardcovers, using photocopying instead of setting print, and using thinner paper that is not durable enough to pass on to classmates. Despite this cost-cutting, lower production costs have not translated into lower textbook prices.

One reason for the drop in textbook revenue is the used booksellers. Students flock to resellers to retrieve a portion of the original cost of their textbooks. The subsequent resale brings no additional income to the publisher nor royalties to the author. Publishers try to address this problem by revising textbooks every three to four years, each increasing in price. Since instructors typically assign the newest edition, students pay for the latest version regardless of how much or how little the textbook has been updated.[57]

Three corporations control 80 percent of the college textbook market. These companies are adapting to lower revenues using innovative means to maintain their revenue while, at the same time, appearing to lower costs for students. For example, textbook publishers promote less expensive, time-limited digital media to reduce student costs and eliminate book resellers. However, this is a shell game where the real costs are hidden. In particular, using digital textbooks has not resulted in significant savings for students since the change from print copies has curtailed cost-saving strategies that students traditionally use, such as textbook sharing, library reserve books, used books, or passing down free copies when a student graduates. Using a captive market, publishers use tactics like bundling books with access codes and promoting custom edition textbooks that cannot be resold. A 2020 U.S. PIRG study found that students were experiencing high textbook prices at roughly the same rate as before the widespread use of digital materials.[58]

Some instructors use digital platforms to assist in grading, administering examinations, and submitting assignments. This platform can include practice exams and interactive videos explaining course concepts. Accessing this content often requires purchasing an additional digital code, and 80 percent of students surveyed in 2013 reported that they were required to buy an access code for at least one course. Failure to purchase the code and foregoing the use of the digital platform can negatively impact a student's grade (17 percent of students in the PIRG study failed to buy codes to complete their assignments).[59] The required use of course access codes double taxes students—they pay for the course and then have to pay again to get a good grade. The use of digital media lends itself to publishers potentially harvesting and selling student data.

In some college bookstores, textbook rentals are the only option available. These rentals expose students to a potentially predatory return policy, where if there is any damage to the book either by a spill, highlighting, or writing in the book, the student is responsible for paying the total price of a new book, which is often marked up.[60] Keeping the textbook in good order can be challenging given the shoddy production quality of some books (i.e., thin paper stock), especially when the book is carted around from class to class.

Many instructors are unaware of the cost of textbooks since sales representatives often fail to disclose prices.[61] Although concerned about high textbook prices, some instructors are unaware of open education resources (OER), such as free textbooks like OpenStax's *Introduction to Sociology*. On a positive note, the percentage of college faculty using OER resources rose from 5 percent in 2015–16 to 22 percent in 2021–2.[62]

In 2018, President Joe Biden signed the Open Textbook Pilot Act. This federal grant program supports projects at colleges and universities that create or expand the use of open textbooks in high-enrollment degree-granting courses. Since 2018, $47 million has been appropriated to the program, resulting in student savings of $250 million.[63] Other estimates suggest that OERs have saved students, parents, schools, and governments in the United States and Canada at least $1 billion.[64] The widespread use of OER materials can further impact higher education by including learning modules, videos, quizzes, and other supplemental materials alongside textbooks.

Despite the innovations in the textbook industry, the future of traditional textbooks is murky at best. Apart from OER materials crowding out the for-profit textbook sector, an even more ominous development is the prospect of using AI to write textbooks. For instance, an instructor could input the required course content in AI and produce a free textbook tailored to the individual course. The specter of this loss of revenue may be one reason that textbook publishers are barreling headlong into OPMs.

Conclusion

The conventional strengths of capitalism include innovation, consumer choice, and greater efficiency in producing goods and services. Spurred on by competition, these characteristics are expected to lead to high-quality goods and services, along with lower consumer prices. Unfortunately, this scenario has failed to materialize in higher education as commodification and corporatization have not led to higher quality education or lower student costs. The opposite has occurred—the more intense the corporatization, the higher the cost of college. Part of that cost dynamic is attributable to many highly paid administrative staff, including some college presidents whose salaries rival or exceed CEOs in medium-sized corporations.

Similarly, some mid-level managers have salaries higher than wages in the mid-range corporate sector. In addition to high administrative salaries, corporations and consultants are making profits paid for by students through their tuition and fees. Added to this brew are highly paid nontraditional college presidents who come directly from the business or government world and have little understanding of academic culture and the value of scholarship.

The corollary damage of corporatization is the harm done to the morale of university employees who are expected to transition from independent scholars to well-behaved and compliant corporate employees, something anathema to the fabric of academic culture. This behavioral expectation underlies the attacks on shared governance, tenure, and unionization. In effect, the corporatization of higher education has led universities to adopt some of the most abhorrent corporate practices that exploit adjuncts, contract workers, and graduate students.

Potentially useful innovations, like online education and digital course materials, have been usurped by OPMs and textbook publishers (often the same) who use them to increase their profits rather than provide actual student savings. Overworked instructors are enticed into using online platforms requiring digital codes to save time in grading examinations and homework. In turn, students pay for the course and, then again, for the codes and the privilege of adding to the profits of educational corporations. Textbook publishers may go the way of Blockbuster Video, given OERs and the potential for AI to create unique textbooks and other course materials.

The increasingly blurred line between public colleges and for-profit educational corporations may be a harbinger of longer-term trends similar to what occurred in healthcare and other public services. Namely, while the government funds certain public services, delivering those services is devolved to the lower-cost private sector. This change would accomplish three things for the university. First, the government can tighten the spigot when revenues are scarce. The results of any budget cuts or redundancies then become the private sector's responsibility. Second, the government is absolved from covering expensive health and retirement plans, a significant cost incurred by tenure-track or tenured faculty. Third, the government is unencumbered by faculty unions, civil service rules, and mores around shared governance. This would also make it easier to discipline or terminate employees. Devolving the delivery of educational content to potentially less expensive OPMs will further widen the gap between the elite nonprofit tertiary sector and its cheaper public facsimile. In particular, private sector corporations would be more willing to pander to student demands around reducing required liberal arts courses in favor of more courses in their STEM majors.

The predictable result is that public institutions will become more like vocational schools, leaving higher education to the families that can afford it.

As OPMs oversee more degree programs, their influence grows within the university. At the same time, the power of the faculty is reduced as their teaching role becomes less clear. Outsourcing teaching responsibilities is a gift to college administrators pressured to cut costs and conservative legislatures who see the shift to OPMs as a way to rid college campuses of liberal troublemakers. Unburdened by traditional academic values, private corporations would be more amenable to legislative pressure that limits academic freedom. Moving to a skills-based vocational-style curriculum allows OPMs to hire adjuncts with narrow workplace skills rather than liberal arts instructors with less workplace-specific knowledge. As OPMs take over more academic programs using low-cost adjuncts, tenured or tenure-track teaching faculty risk becoming superfluous and redundant. This vocational scenario impacts Ph.D. graduates whose academic choices would be narrowed to prestigious and highly competitive nonprofit colleges and universities.

In this scenario, the university would be divided with most courses taught under the aegis of OPMs, while grant-based research faculty would be assigned to designated research centers. The knotty issue is the cost of tuition, which, at present, is no cheaper than using OPMs to deliver online content. However, as the OPM market grows, educational administrators can reduce their operating costs based on higher enrollments and the recoupment of startup costs. While this scenario is bleak for some academics, it is becoming more plausible as the pressure to reduce costs is growing from students, their families, legislatures, and taxpayers.

Administrators have adroitly deflected the criticism for the high costs of college onto greedy faculty rather than themselves. The commodification and corporatization of higher education serve administrators who feel justified in earning exorbitant salaries and corporations that benefit from the captive student market and the desperation of colleges struggling with enrollment issues. As the next chapter demonstrates, the high cost of tuition can also be traced to the commodification and corporatization of college sports that are draining the coffers of many institutions.

5

The College Sports Industrial Complex

Almost nowhere in higher education are the effects of commodification more evident than in the hyper-commercialized world of college sports. Moreover, there is no equivalent in any of the world's universities to the iconic role that college sports play in American society. Fans' enthusiasm for a university team is one of the few bridges that unite disparate social, economic, and demographic groups. Despite its popularity, college sports are a significant resource drain on most universities, reflected in higher tuition.

The Hypocrisy of the National Collegiate Athletic Association (NCAA)

College sports had a humble beginning in 1852 when Harvard and Yale held a rowing competition. In the ensuing years, intercollegiate sports grew in popularity with the addition of football, basketball, baseball, and track and field. In 1906, the Intercollegiate Athletic Association of the United States (IAAUS) was formed to protect athletes from the brutality of football that left eighteen students dead and 159 seriously injured in 1904. The IAAUS became the NCAA in 1910, and after the Second World War, it adopted rules to ensure that college sports remained amateur. Longtime NCAA executive director Walter Byers (1951–87) was credited with creating a system to investigate violations and enforce penalties.[1] As college sports became increasingly popular, larger schools spent more on their sports programs, which disadvantaged less well-off smaller colleges. In response, the NCAA established separate divisions in 1973 and strengthened academic requirements for prospective student-athletes.[2]

Despite the NCAA's commitment to protect amateur sports, the big money behind college sports came to light in the corruption scandal surrounding the 2017–18 NCAA Division I men's basketball division. The investigation, led by the FBI and the Southern District Court of New York, involved bribery, money laundering, and wire fraud. It implicated Adidas, coaches, players, agents, and several well-known college basketball teams such as Arizona State University, Auburn University, University of Miami, Oklahoma State University, University of Alabama, University of Maryland, University of South Carolina, North Carolina State University, and University of Southern California (USC).[3] The investigation into college basketball was a wake-up call for the NCAA, resulting in sweeping reform proposals.[4]

By 2023, the NCAA had oversight of more than 500,000 student-athletes participating in two dozen sports across more than 1,000 universities. It had revenues of $1.4 billion, mainly from television and marketing rights and ticket sales for championships. According to the NCAA, 60 percent of its revenue goes to Division I schools and conferences.[5] Despite their well-publicized concern for student-athletes, the organization seems more concerned with the welfare of coaches and universities than students. Of the $15.8 billion in NCAA revenues in 2019 for Division I athletics, only $2.9 billion, or 18.2 percent, went to athletic scholarships, and only 1 percent went toward medical treatment and insurance for students. In contrast, 35 percent went to administrators and compensation to coaches, and 18 percent to facilities.[6]

The values driving college sports are evident when examining the priorities in the NCAA Power Five conference (Atlantic Coast Conference, Big Ten Conference, Big 12 Conference, Pac-12 Conference, and Southeastern Conference), encompassing sixty-five of the most successful schools in college sports. In 2020,

Power Five schools spent $936 million on student aid compared to $1.2 billion on coaching salaries. These schools had roughly 45,000 student-athletes and 4,400 coaches.[7] The coach-to-student ratio of 10:1 would be the envy of almost any public university where the student-faculty ratio is from 14:1 to 18:1.[8]

The NCAA's nonprofit status and its opposition to paying student-athletes seem hypocritical given former president Mark Emmert's 2020 salary of $2.9 million, on top of the almost $1.7 million paid to Executive Vice President Donald Remy, the $1.37 million paid to Executive Vice President Stanley Wilcox, and the $857,000 paid to Chief Medical Officer Brian Hainline.[9] Perhaps the NCAA's opposition to paying college athletes is less about their well-being and more about kowtowing to universities and coaches whose sports programs line the NCAA's pockets.

The opposition to player salaries may also be related to coaches' fear that payments to student-athletes could come from their substantial paychecks. This might not be such an unreasonable proposal. For example, the former University of Alabama's head football coach Nick Saban's annual salary of $11.7 million could have been divided among his ninety-nine players, giving each $100,000 a year, leaving Saban with a still generous $1.8 million a year.

NCAA's public opposition to paying student-athletes is based on their mission to keep college sports "amateur." Acknowledging the winds of change and knowing they will eventually lose the battle around student compensation, NCAA President Charlie Baker offered a proposal in 2023 whereby Division I schools would set aside educational trust funds of at least $30,000 per year for at least half of their athletes.[10] Given the conservative nature of the NCAA, it is uncertain whether that proposal will fly. Moreover, the horse may have already left the barn since, in 2024, Dartmouth's men's basketball team overwhelmingly voted to be represented by a union.[11] In all likelihood, other university teams will follow Dartmouth's lead.

While paying student-athletes seems fair, many universities are concerned that their already bloated athletic budgets would rise even higher. Paying student-athletes also leads to other questions, such as whether all college athletes will be paid, including those in money-losing sports like golf, tennis, hockey, swimming, baseball, rowing, and lacrosse. Paying athletes only for revenue-generating sports like football and basketball would lead to a two-tier system rife with resentment and conflict. If salaries were paid across the board, sports like golf, hockey, and tennis might have to be terminated to save money. Moreover, more minor and less-resourced schools would be disadvantaged in attracting top student-athletes, making the playing field in college athletics even more uneven.

Many struggling smaller colleges and universities use sports programs to maintain or grow enrollment. In particular, they provide scholarships for various sports, most of which lose money. For example, Hawai'i Pacific University (HPU) has about 4,000 students and fourteen sports teams, including golf, soccer, tennis, acrobatics and tumbling, and beach volleyball. In addition, it has almost fifty sports-related coaches and other staff.[12] Short of dramatically increasing tuition, providing athletes with a wage on top of (or instead of) a scholarship would not be financially viable for small institutions.

The College Sports Industrial Complex

For many large universities, college athletics is a lucrative business disguised as a branch of an academic institution—the vast sums of money involved in college sports support that critique. In 2021, the U.S. Department of Education valued America's college sports industry at $16.6 billion, including broadcast rights, merchandise sales, product promotion, and ticket sales. This was almost four times higher than the $4.3 billion in 2003 and nearly double the $8.4 billion generated in 2009.[13] Apart from a brief downturn due to the Covid pandemic, revenue growth in college sports is a linear trajectory that would be the envy of most corporations. Chart 5.1 illustrates the phenomenal revenue growth of the college sports industry.

Of the $16.6 billion generated in 2021 by 2,078 colleges with sports programs, $323 million went for recruiting, $3.9 billion for

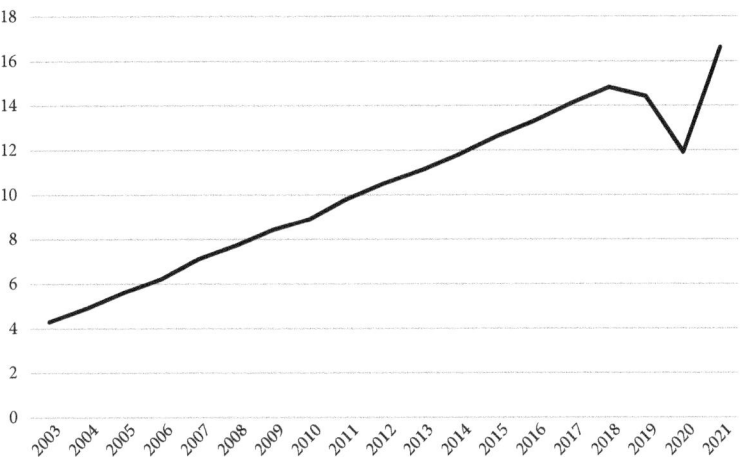

Figure 5.1 *Revenues (in Billions) for College Sports Based on 2,027 Institutions*

Source: U.S. Department of Education, Office of Postsecondary Education, "Equity in Athletics Data Analysis (EADA)," Equity in Athletics Data Analysis, 2023, accessed April 2023, https://ope.ed.gov/athletics/Trend/public/#/answer/6/601/trend/-1/-1/-1/-1

operating expenses, and $4.6 billion for athlete-based student aid. These sports programs supported 27,243 head coaches with a median salary of $507,650 and 56,599 assistant coaches with median earnings of $248,463.[14] By comparison, there were 57,680 English language and literature teachers in higher education in 2022, earning a median wage of $74,280.[15] Thirty-six thousand engineering faculty earned $103,550.[16]

The sheer scope of college athletics is illustrated by the University of Georgia's athletic foundation, whose 2021 revenues totaled $203 million. Of that amount, salaries accounted for $75.6 million, with other expenses totaling another $88 million, leaving a profit of almost $23 million.[17] The 2023 University of Georgia's football roster of ninety-nine players has been parlayed into hiring eleven coaches and forty-one support staff.[18] Some support staff titles include:

Culinary Service
Football Nutrition
Equipment Operations
Head Performance Chef
Football Creative Services & Videos
Football Creative Design
Football Administration
Football Technology
Football Management
Football Operations
Football Equipment & Apparel
Offensive Analyst
Player Connections
Player Development
Player Support and Operations
Quality Control—Offense
Quality Control—Special Teams
Recruiting Operations and Relations
Recruiting Administration
Strength and Conditioning Coaches
Special Teams Analyst
Special Teams Coordinator[19]

This level of staffing and support would be the envy of most academic units in America, where departmental support staff often consists of one or two overworked secretaries or program assistants, as well as IT support staff.

Television broadcast rights are a significant source of revenue for college sports. The Big Ten football conference comprises sixteen universities: Indiana, Michigan, Maryland, Michigan State, Ohio State, Pennsylvania State, Rutgers, Illinois, Iowa, Minnesota, Nebraska, Northwestern, Purdue, Wisconsin, UCLA, and the University of Southern California. In 2022, the conference signed a seven-year agreement with Fox, CBS, and NBC worth at least $7 billion, allowing the sixteen-member conference to share more than $1 billion annually.[20] By comparison, the previous media deals with Fox and ESPN earned only $440 million annually.[21]

The Big Ten is not the only television deal in college sports. ESPN's deal with the American Athletic Conference averages $83.3 million a year, the Atlantic Coast Conference's ESPN deal is worth about $240 million annually, Mountain West's six-year agreement with Fox and CBS Sports is worth $270 million, Pac-12 had a (twelve-year) $3 billion contract with Fox and ESPN, and Southeastern conference's contract with ESPN is worth $300 million a year. The annual College Football Playoff costs ESPN $470 million a year.[22] All told, televised game contracts are worth more than $10 billion annually for NCAA sports teams.

Dangling big broadcast dollars under the noses of under-resourced universities incentivizes them to ramp up their sports programs, often at the expense of their academic operations. The lure of big money is dragging marginally resourced schools into direct competition with prestigious and well-resourced institutions. The difference is that highly ranked schools are typically well-funded and can mount sports programs without compromising their academic mission. Since lower-ranked schools are typically underfunded, they cannibalize their academic programs to fund their sports teams.

Several private companies make money on college sports. Learfield, a large sports marketing company, employs 2,200 employees in 100 national offices and provides sponsorship, ticketing, licensing, and other services.[23] Companies like Nike and Adidas advertise by outfitting student-athletes. When 100 million people tune into NCAA's March Madness, every Nike or Adidas on a jersey or a shoe is a direct advertisement. Not surprisingly, Nike, Adidas, and Under Armour have exclusive rights to outfit almost all football and basketball programs.[24] College sports are lucrative for everyone except student-athletes.

Neither the NCAA nor college sports programs adequately protect college athletes. Nor do they have the best interest of college athletes at heart. Instead, their concern is to support the financial interests of broadcasters, apparel companies, and athletic departments. If the NCAA wants to restore its shattered credibility, it should start by decommodifying college sports and putting the players first, including finding ways to reimburse them for their labor. Even conservative Supreme Court Justice Brett Kavanaugh wrote, "Nowhere else in America can businesses get away with agreeing not to pay their workers a fair market rate on the theory that their product is defined by not paying their workers a fair market rate. The N.C.A.A. is not above the law."[25]

College Sports Betting

In the 2018 *Murphy v. NCAA* case, the US Supreme Court struck down the Professional and Amateur Sports Protection Act that barred states from legalizing gambling for professional and college sports. By 2023, thirty-seven states had legalized sports betting, leading to the proliferation of gambling companies or sports books. College athletics followed in the wake of that decision. The American Gaming Association (AGA) predicted that 68 million Americans would wager $15.5 billion on NCAA sports in 2023.[26] Roughly $8 billion is bet in an average college football season alone, with 25 percent of the adult population betting on championship matches.[27]

The power of athletic departments, the dire financial straits of universities, and the Supreme Court ruling ushered in university-sponsored online campus betting.[28] By 2021, at least eight universities had partnered with online sports betting companies. Michigan State University partnered with Caesars Sports Book for a deal worth $8.4 million over five years, which included displaying Caesars' prominent ads on game day.[29] Louisiana State University signed a similar deal in 2021 with Caesars and sent a promotional signup code to its Geaux-Mail email list, including people under age twenty-one.[30] In 2020, the University of Colorado Boulder signed a $1.6 million deal with PointsBet that gave the school $30 each time a student bet using the company's app.[31] While betting companies claim to target only students twenty-one or older, their advertising is so porous that younger students invariably get the message.[32]

The love affair between universities and sports books began to fizzle by 2023. The AGA updated its Responsible Marketing Code for Sports Wagering in 2023 to prohibit college partnerships that promote, market, or advertise sports wagering activity other than to alumni networks or other responsible parties. Many betting companies are not part of the AGA; even for its members, the code is a collection of guidelines rather than enforceable rules.

Despite the potential revenue, the University of Colorado bowed to community pressure and ended its partnership with PointsBet early, as did the University of Maryland (not surprising since a state law prohibiting these partnerships was sent to the governor). Michigan State University ended its partnership with Caesars, which included removing signage and promotional materials. Caesars also took down its signage at LSU.[33] New York State proposed rules prohibiting advertising on college campuses aimed at students under age twenty-one, and both Ohio and Massachusetts banned sports betting marketing on college campuses. Maryland and Connecticut moved to ban sports books from signing deals with public universities.[34]

Although universities are distancing themselves from betting companies, it does not eliminate the impact of sports betting on student-athletes' well-being. Apart from a tiny cluster of top athletes, most student-athletes receive little or no remuneration. At the same time, they are surrounded by coaches who earn millions while they struggle to balance practice sessions with their studies. The resentment around this imbalance and the need for money make student-athletes vulnerable to the influence of gamblers. Sometimes, they only have to provide insider information about injuries or other information that can affect the outcome of a game. Other times, they have to miss a throw, fumble a pass, or miss a pitch.

Gambling impacts college sports even though the NCAA rules state that student-athletes and other members of athletics departments are forbidden to bet on any NCAA-sponsored sport or share information used for sports wagering. To formalize that rule, the NCAA requires student-athletes to sign a yearly statement acknowledging that they understand the rules on sports betting. Students are also expected to report any violation of those rules to their director of athletics.[35] Despite this, the NCAA has no blanket punishment for breaking the gambling rule.

In spite of NCAA rules, there is a strong temptation among some students and coaches to bet on college sports. In 2023, the University of Iowa announced that twenty-six athletes across five sports (baseball, football, wrestling, men's basketball, and men's track and field) were suspected of violating the NCAA rule on sports betting. More than 100 people were linked to the investigation. The Iowa investigation came shortly after the University of Alabama fired baseball coach Brad Bohannon in 2023 following a report involving two suspiciously large bets placed before Alabama's game with LSU.[36]

Most college athletes love the game. Yet, because of sports betting, they have the pressure of a national or state-wide audience and the pressure of bets placed on them or their team's performance. Sports betting puts much pressure on students, especially those aspiring to a sports career. This added pressure not only takes away from the love of the game but also exposes athletes to online abuse and threats from bettors who lost money.[37]

Sports betting embodies the commodification of amateur sports and the failure of the university and the NCAA to protect student-athletes. It exposes students to gambling addictions, and like alcohol and drug abuse on campus, gambling is a problem that colleges and universities are ill-prepared to handle. College gambling also has untoward consequences for financially vulnerable athletes who are sensitive to online scorn, mockery, and abuse.

The Status Race and the Edifice Complex

The arms race in college sports led some universities to pursue prestige through sports rather than academics. For example, despite Clemson University's drop in QS' World University Rankings from 601 in 2012 to 801–1,000 in 2023 (the lowest score is 1,200),[38] Clemson still paid head football coach Dabo Swinney $10.5 million in 2022. Swinney's salary is even more remarkable since Clemson has less than 29,000 students. By comparison, the University of Michigan has almost 51,225 students, and its head football coach, Jim Harbaugh, earned $7.34 million in 2022. Moreover, the University of Michigan's 2023 budget was $10.9 billion compared to Clemson's $1.4 billion. Both are public universities. The obsessive desire of many universities for sports dominance makes them fearful of their coaches being poached, which gives coaches considerable bargaining power and may explain the meteoric rise in their salaries.

Universities spend millions on athletic facilities to impress and recruit student-athletes, placate or entice coaches, and chase the elusive national championship. Power Five schools nearly doubled their spending on facilities between 2004 and 2014. Clemson claims to have spent $350 million over eight years on their athletic facilities. Their recent $55 million athletic complex resembles a theme park with a miniature golf course, sand volleyball courts, laser tag, bowling lanes, and a movie theater. University of South Carolina's athletic facilities include a TV and video game area, a movie theater, a video arcade room, and a sound studio for athletes to record music.[39] The University of Florida invested nearly $300 million into its sports facility over six years. Auburn University's $100 million Performance Center includes a players' lounge, meeting rooms, a barbershop, recording studios, and a flight simulator. Renovations to the University of Tennessee's Neyland Stadium are expected to cost $180 million. The University of Texas-Austin spent $10,000 on lockers with digital names and likenesses. Not to be outdone, the University of Washington spent $1 million on locker room upgrades, including one mile of purple LEDs. Ohio State University's upgrades include state-of-the-art locker rooms, a massive players lounge, a kitchen and nutrition area, a barber shop, a basketball court, a golf simulator, an arcade, a cryotherapy chamber, sleep pods, and an illuminated waterfall in a locker room. Despite deep budget cuts, Louisiana State University has a new $28 million futuristic locker room with customizable player pods. Texas A&M spent a whopping $485 million on their football complex. The University of Georgia spent $80 million on facility upgrades, including $30 million on an indoor athletic facility. Building indoor practice facilities is the newest trend embraced by schools like the University of Texas-Austin, Texas Tech, University of Florida, University of North Carolina-Chapel Hill, and the University of Notre Dame.[40] Coddling players in tony sports facilities is presumably necessary to extract their maximum performance. It would be helpful if the same presumption were applied to academic programs.

While most universities claim that most of the money earmarked for athletic renovations comes from private donations, whether those donations cover 100 percent of the project costs is unclear. (As a perk, large donors are repaid with adoration and VIP treatment at games.) Lavish spending on sports facilities obscures the difficulties faced by academic units in many universities suffering from deep budget cuts, a deteriorating physical infrastructure, the elimination of liberal arts degrees, and the replacement of tenure-track faculty with adjuncts. The question is whether sports-focused donors could be convinced to also invest in academic activities. The commodification of college sports ensures that contractors and architects are well-fed, university officials get bragging rights, and coaches get five-star facilities. Not coincidentally, student-athletes who make it all possible get the least long-term benefit.

Exploiting the Poorest Players

Student-athletes from low-income backgrounds are exploited in multiple ways. One is through the limited financial compensation they receive. In compliance with NCAA rules, compensation for college athletes is generally limited to scholarships and a modest living stipend of $6,000 a year. A 2020 National Bureau of Economic Research (NBER) study found that despite athletes' television and social media exposure, less than 7 percent of men's football and basketball revenue was transferred to them. In contrast, US professional football and men's basketball players receive roughly 50 percent of the revenues they generate.[41] This led to a 2023 lawsuit alleging that the NCAA and the Power Five schools are violating antitrust laws based on NCAA rules that prevent conferences from sharing broadcasting revenue with players and denying them a part of the lucrative market in college sports video games.[42]

Men's football and basketball teams are the only two college sports that generate significant revenues through ticket sales, broadcast rights, promotions, and other means. These two sports subsidize the losses incurred by predominantly white money-losing sports such as men's golf, tennis, baseball, women's basketball, soccer, tennis, rowing, and lacrosse.[43]

Researchers in one NBER study found significant differences between players in revenue-producing sports and other student-athletes. For instance, Black players account for nearly half of the football and basketball players in the Power Five schools studied, but they only represent 11 percent of the players in money-losing sports. Athletes participating in revenue-producing sports came from high schools with median family incomes of $58,400. In contrast, players in revenue-losing sports came from high schools with median family incomes of $80,000.[44] In short, college football and basketball revenues constitute a transfer of resources from heavily Black college sports to white-dominated ones. Not surprisingly, this mimics the transfer of wealth in American society.

Sexual Abuse in College Sports: See No Evil, Hear No Evil, Speak No Evil

The lure of winning can cause a university to ignore moral, ethical, and legal concerns. One egregious example is former Michigan State University (MSU) sports doctor Larry Nassar, who sexually abused more than 330 female gymnasts under the guise of medical treatment. Nassar was sentenced to multiple life sentences in 2018, leading to the resignation of MSU's president and sports director.[45] Nassar had worked at MSU for almost twenty years, and as the allegations mounted, the university reassigned him and finally fired him. When the case became public in 2016, MSU officials claimed they had no prior knowledge of his behavior despite a decades-old police report alleging sexual assaults. Several reports, lawsuits, and victim testimonials alleged that the university had known about Nassar for years but did nothing.[46] As late as 2023, the Board of Trustees declined the request by Michigan's attorney general to release nearly 6,000 documents relating to the investigation of Nassar.[47] In 2018, MSU paid $500 million to settle lawsuits involving more than 300 victims.[48]

College football brings in big money for Pennsylvania State University (Penn), and in 2021–2, its football division earned millions.[49] Jerry Sandusky worked as an assistant coach under head coach Joe Paterno from 1969 until his retirement in 1999. In 2012, Sandusky was found guilty of sexually abusing at least ten young boys over at least fifteen years. He was sentenced to thirty to sixty years in prison.[50] Former FBI Director Louis Freeh led an inquiry into Penn's response to the case. His findings lambasted former university leaders for their total disregard for these child victims and for covering up the actions of a longtime sexual offender. By early 2018, Penn had paid over $100 million in settlements and millions in legal fees. The Department of Education fined the university $2.4 million for failing to report assaults, and the NCAA announced a $60 million fine ruling that Penn State's share of Rose Bowl revenues would be donated to child abuse charities.[51] A casualty of the Sandusky scandal was legendary head football coach Joe Paterno, who was fired in 2011 for failing to report Sandusky's misconduct. Paterno died just seventy-four days after being dismissed from Penn State.

Dr. Richard Strauss was hired by Ohio State University in 1978 as a faculty member in the College of Medicine. He quickly volunteered to be a team physician and would later become the associate director of the sports medicine program. Strauss was suspended in 1997 after allegations surfaced about his conduct. He retired in 1998 and committed suicide in 2005.[52] A 2019 investigative report by Ohio State found that Strauss had sexually abused at least 177 students during his twenty years as an athletics and student health doctor. Investigators also found that Ohio State officials knew about Strauss' misconduct as early as 1979 but did nothing. Others, including former assistant wrestling coach and US Congressperson Jim Jordan, have been accused of concealing abuse allegations. By 2023, Ohio State had paid more than $60 million to 296 survivors.[53]

From 2012 to 2016, Christian-affiliated Baylor University was awash in a scandal involving rape and sexual misconduct by its football team. After dragging their feet, Baylor regents eventually acknowledged that seventeen women had reported sexual or domestic assaults involving nineteen players, including four alleged gang rapes.[54] One 2017 lawsuit alleged that fifty-two rapes were committed by thirty-one Baylor players from 2011 to 2014.[55]

In April 2012, a Baylor football player raped a student at an off-campus party. She reported the assault to the police. Another Baylor student alleged that she was gang raped by ten to fifteen football players at the same party. In response, Baylor suspended the athlete for twelve days for an "unspecified violation" of team rules. He was later arrested and sentenced to twenty years in prison. In 2013, a Baylor women's soccer player accused another football player of raping her. She notified the police, and two months later, the school ruled that the allegations could not be proven by a "preponderance of evidence." The rapist was subsequently investigated by local police, which resulted in a six-month jail sentence and ten years of probation.[56]

In 2015, Baylor University hired the Pepper Hamilton law firm to investigate Title IX and other compliance issues. Pepper Hamilton was engaged due to Baylor's history of discouraging student complaints, failing to address a hostile environment, and retaliating when students filed a sexual abuse complaint. Pepper Hamilton's findings described Baylor's football players as "above the rules" with "no culture of accountability for misconduct."[57] The report also found specific instances where the Athletics Department leadership had failed to respond to a pattern of sexual violence by a football player.[58]

The scandal led to the firing of head football coach Art Briles, who received a $15.1 million severance package; the resignation of Baylor president Ken Starr, who received a $4.5 million severance package; the resignation of athletic director Ian McCaw, whose severance package was $761,059, and the firing of two others connected with the football program.[59] Despite his culpability in the Baylor scandal, McCaw became the Athletics Director at Liberty University, a fundamentalist Christian university. In 2018, Briles testified that senior Baylor administrators knew about the sexual assaults but failed, as he did, to act. Despite being a Baptist university, the events at Baylor demonstrated how success in college sports had trumped its Christian values.

Sports programs in many universities exist as a subculture alongside mainstream academic culture. The underbelly of competitive sports at Northwestern University illustrates how this subculture operated in one school. In 2022, an anonymous complaint about hazing in Northwestern's football program was made. Lawsuits later alleged that hazing had occurred in rituals involving sexual and physical abuse, including "running," where a group forcibly held down a player and rubbed their genitals against him. A former football player reported seeing a player held underwater and sexually abused. At other times, players were coerced into playing football naked and sexually harassed in a "car wash" ritual where they had to walk through a row of naked teammates in the shower. The lawsuit also described the "Gatorade shake challenge," where players were pressured to drink protein shakes until they vomit. In the "Trading Block," coaches and players traded insults in a large-group setting and sometimes exposed personal details, such as infidelity or questions about an athlete's sexuality.[60] There were also reports of Black and Hispanic athletes facing racial taunts.[61]

In another lawsuit, a former Northwestern cheerleader alleged that coaches forced her team to socialize with donors in a sexualized manner and denied them meals to encourage weight loss. Black players and cheerleaders were also told to cut their hair to make them look "more American." Many minority athletes and cheerleaders had to comply since, without their scholarships, they could not afford to attend Northwestern. Finally forced to act, a 2023 independent investigation by Northwestern found evidence of hazing, leading to the firing of two coaches, including famed head football coach Pat Fitzgerald. Although the investigation found no credible evidence that Fitzgerald knew about the hazing, Northwestern's president, Michael Schill, maintained that he was ultimately responsible for the team's culture as head coach.[62]

What's the Real Graduation Rate for Student-Athletes?

NCAA's commitment to amateur college sports includes believing that student-athletes should not be paid. Despite endless hours of training, practice, and sacrifice, less than 2 percent of Division I college football and basketball players ever play a game in a national football or basketball league.[63] Many of the 98 percent who fail to make the cut in professional sports end up without the backup of a college degree.

The NCAA proudly touts the increase in the graduation success rates (GSR) for Division I athletes from 74 percent in 2002 to 90 percent in 2022. For Black athletes, the overall GSR rose from 56 to 81 percent; for Hispanic/Latino athletes, it rose from 64 to 88 percent. Broken down, the GSR for Black football players rose from 53 to 81 percent, and for Black men's basketball athletes, from 46 to 81 percent.[64] Despite these claims, Andrew Zimbalist argues that the NCAA's GSR rates exaggerate academic success by combining graduation results from all NCAA sports. Zimbalist maintains that the data underestimates the lower GSR of athletes who participate in sports that generate the highest revenues. For example, 52 percent of all Division I men's basketball players and 38 percent of all Division I football players on full scholarships failed to graduate on time.[65] Zimbalist's skepticism is reinforced by the Drake Group's finding that the NCAA's measures of comparing athletes and non-athletes are not equivalent.[66]

In many ways, student-athletes in revenue-producing sports like football and basketball are primed for less academic success. Jordan Acker, a University of Michigan Board of Regents member, observes that many student-athletes rarely enter a classroom. They attend their classes online and take proctored exams in hotel ballrooms.[67]

The influence of athletic departments on academic units virtually assures a compromised educational experience for student-athletes. In particular, athletic departments have an outsized influence on academic affairs and can easily manipulate student success rates. For example, it is common for instructors to feel pressure to pass athletes, even if they perform poorly or rarely attend class. Some faculty members are afraid to fail athletes for fear of retribution by powerful athletic departments. It is the rare instructor who dares to fail an athlete, especially a star. Even then, a dean or provost can overturn a failing grade. This is one reason why the NCAA's GSR numbers are essentially meaningless.

Almost everyone tacitly acknowledges that athletes are recruited to play sports, not to excel academically. These athletes often recognize they are just a cog in a system where everyone benefits more than them: coaches need wins to justify their inflated salaries, fans want entertainment, television networks want ratings, and administrators want winning teams to gain prestige for their university.[68]

The NILS (Name, Image, and Likeness) Wild West

In 2021, the US Supreme Court ruled in the *NCAA v. Alston* that the NCAA could not bar member schools from offering student-athletes certain education-related benefits. Students can now receive "cost of attendance" stipends up to about $6,000 and other benefits and awards. The Court also ruled against the NCAA by allowing student-athletes to receive payouts based on their NILs (name, image, and likeness) value. Following the ruling, the NCAA reversed its position on NILs and allowed athletes to be remunerated and to hire professionals to manage their NILs activities. Sports writer Justin Byers estimates that NILs could be worth as much as $1.5 billion for college athletes, with a few top athletes earning $6.5 million annually.[69]

The NILs payday has already arrived for some athletes. University of Alabama quarterback Bryce Young had a NILs valuation of $3 million and was reportedly offered more than $1 million in endorsement offers. Olivia Dunne, a junior gymnast at Louisiana State University, claims more than 10 million social media followers and has made seven figures in endorsements. Gonzaga University basketball star Drew Timme cited NIL deals as the reason why he returned to college instead of becoming a professional. He believed his NILs deals could be worth twice as much as a basketball contract.[70]

The commodification of college sports has helped many private companies to reap some of the spoils. Since a social media presence and a personal "brand" are essential to financial success, companies like INFLCR help athletes develop and track their social media presence, estimate their NILs monetization, find endorsements, and manage their business affairs.[71] Opendorse promotes itself as the largest NIL technology company that focuses on building, protecting, and monetizing an athlete's brand. The company represents over 100,000 athletes, 3,000 sports marketers, 2,000 sports organizations, and 1,000 sports agents. Endorsed by some head coaches, the company claims to have made more than 100,000 deals for athletes.[72]

Wealthy sports fans and boosters are capitalizing on NILs and student-athletes by organizing public appearances, autograph signings, and brand deals. While these third-party businesses started as for-profit enterprises, they are increasingly turning into nonprofits. Donors pay a few dollars a month (sometimes considerably more) to get access to athletes via online events or more intimate private events, with most of the proceeds going to players.[73] While NCAA rules prohibit colleges from offering monetary incentives as a recruitment tool, non-university-sponsored activities were exempt and could entice star athletes with promises of support and endorsements. To rein in these collectives (some with multi-million funding), the NCAA issued new guidance that bars boosters from talking with recruits.[74] In 2024, a federal judge temporarily blocked the NCAA from enforcing NILs restrictions.[75] This ruling further weakened the NCAA's hold on college sports and pried it open to even more corporatization.

Some legislators are trying to standardize NIL policies to rein in and stabilize college sports.[76] In particular, high NILS reimbursements threaten the stability of college sports by injecting market compensation into an otherwise tightly regulated "amateur" sports system. States that try to regulate NILs compensation will risk disrupting their recruitment efforts, as top high school athletes will gravitate to states without NILs regulations. Since star athletes bring in fans and TV viewership, colleges risk losing part of their sports-based revenue if their recruitment efforts fail.

One result of the commodification of college sports is the almost 7,000 college football and basketball players who want to transfer schools for a better financial deal using the NCAA's transfer portal. This website portal allows student-athletes to announce their interest in switching colleges. Coaches from other institutions can reach out to these students in minutes. One associated transfer portal assigns a score to student-athletes based on their transfer value, including their NILs value. Students get stars based on a "recruiting industry comparison."[77] Reducing college athletes to their market value is similar to the dehumanization discussed in 1972 when Gary Shaw's *Meat on the Hoof* showed how student-athletes at the University of Texas were little more than objects in the 1960s.[78]

The Winners (and Mostly) Losers

Of the 2,078 schools with sports programs, the sixty-five Power Five schools (3 percent of all sports programs) generate 54 percent of all college sports revenue.[79] The NCAA Division 1 (D-I) schools are considered the best for student-athletes, given their large sports budgets and generous athletic scholarships. The 363 D-I schools account for 97 percent of the NCAA's revenues and profit, even after paying for coach and assistant coach salaries, sports scholarships, training consultants, equipment, travel, training facilities, and other expenses. In contrast, most schools are losers left with dwindling sports budgets, fading cheers, and the cost of post-game clean-ups.

The Winners

The profitability (or lack thereof) of NCAA sports programs is difficult to measure given the large number of variables, such as school subsidies, donor gifts, product endorsements, and revenues returned to the university by sports teams. Determining profitability is also tricky since college sports budgets are sometimes nested in both athletic foundations and general university budgets. Despite this challenge, Scott Hirko calculated the total revenues minus expenses generated by college sports programs. Table 5.1 is Hirko's list of football programs that generated a profit of $1 million or more in 2020.

Table 5.1 Division I Football Where Revenue Exceeded Expenses 2020 (in millions)

School	Profit
University of Georgia	$36.0
University of Florida	$31.7
University of Texas at Austin	$22.1
Ohio State University	$15.2
University of Alabama	$11.5
Auburn University	$11.2
Texas A&M University	$7.5
Pennsylvania State University	$7.1
Kansas State University	$6.6
University of Washington	$4.2
University of Michigan	$3.7
University of Nebraska-Lincoln	$3.0
Purdue University	$2.1
Texas Tech University	$2.0
Mississippi State University	$1.7
Oklahoma State University	$1.0

Source: Scott Hirko, "I found 18 profitable & 211 money-losing NCAA Division-I public athletic programs in 2020," *LinkedIn,* September 3, 2022, www.linkedin.com/pulse/i-found-18-profitable-211-money-losing-ncaa-public-scott-hirko-ph-d-

See Syracuse University, Newhouse School of Public Communication, Knight Commission on Intercollegiate Athletics, College Athletics Database, 2023, accessed April 2023, https://knightnewhousedata.org/

The biggest winners in college sports are well-paid coaches, assistant coaches, and the legions of support staff needed to run multi-million-dollar sports programs. In 2020, more than 100 Division I head coaches earned over $1 million a year, with the top twenty-five football coaches earning an average of $5.2 million. The top twenty-five basketball coaches earned $3.2 million. College football and basketball coaches are the highest-paid public employees in forty-one out of fifty US states.[80]

While the average NCAA football coach in Division I earned $1.75 million in 2022 compared to $6.69 million for the average National Football League (NFL) coach, this obscures the extreme cases. For example, New England Patriots Bill Belichick was the highest-paid NFL coach at $12.5 million in 2023. The University of Alabama's Nick Saban was close behind, earning $11.7 million. Seattle Seahawks' Pete Carroll earned $11 million and was the second highest-paid NFL coach. Carroll's salary was less than the $11.25 million paid to the University of Georgia's Kirby Smart. Las Vegas Raiders coach Jon Gruden made $10 million in 2023, less than Clemson University's Dabo Sweeney's salary of $10.5 million and USC's Lincoln Riley, who earned $10 million.[81]

NCAA Division I basketball coaches earn less than football coaches. The top highest-paid National Basketball Association (NBA) coaches in 2023 earned from $6.5 million to $11.5 million. Most NBA coach salaries hovered around $8 million a year. By contrast, the University of Kentucky's John Calipari earned $8.5 million, Bill Self of the University of Kansas earned $6 million, Tom Izzo of Michigan State was paid $5.7 million, and Rick Barnes of the University of Tennessee and Auburn University's Bruce Pearl each earned $5.5 million.[82] In addition to these lavish salaries, coaches receive bonuses, endorsements, country club memberships, and expense accounts. Sometimes, they can even receive a negotiated percentage of ticket receipts.[83]

The size of coaching salaries is related more to the growth of the college industrial sports complex than to the size of the university or winning games. For example, after adjusting for inflation, the average wage for head football coaches in public universities rose by 750 percent from 1984 to 2020.[84] The sheer scope of this income growth is illustrated by examining the salary of Bear Bryant, the University of Alabama's legendary football coach. In 1982, Bryant earned $1.1 million after adjusting for inflation. His successor, Nick Saban, earned ten times that much in 2023.[85] They both won a similar number of national championships. In contrast to Saban, the Bear exhibited humility when he stipulated that he would earn $1 less than the university president.[86] That humility is long gone since many football coaches earn several times (sometimes ten times) more than their college presidents. The outsized role of college sports on some campuses is evident when comparing college football coaches' salaries with their university presidents (see Table 5.2).

Table 5.2 Salaries of Highest-Paid College Coaches Compared to Presidents of Their Universities (2022)

University	Coach	Salary (Millions)	President/ Chancellor	Salary
Univ. of Alabama	Nick Saban	$11.7	Stuart Bell	$804,407
Univ. of Georgia	Kirby Smart	$11.2	Jere Morehead	$917,729
Clemson Univ.	Dabo Swinney	$10.5	Jim Clements*	987,530
Univ. of S. Calif.	Lincoln Riley	$10+ (est.)	Carol Folt	$3.9 million
Louisiana State	Brian Kelly	$9.5	William Tate	$725,000
Michigan State	Mel Tucker	$9.5	Samuel Stanley*	$960,000
Ohio State	Ryan Day	$9.5	Kristina Johnson*	$927,000
Stanford Univ.	David Shaw	$8.9	Marc Tessier-Lavigne*	$1.4 million
Univ. of Miami	Mario Cristobal	$8.0	Julio Frenk	$1.7 million
Texas A&M	Jimbo Fisher	$7.5	Katherine Banks	$925,000 (2021)
Univ. of Mississippi	Lane Kiffin	$7.2	Glenn Boyce	$850,000

University	Coach	Salary (Millions)	President/ Chancellor	Salary
Univ. of Michigan	Jim Harbaugh	$7.0	Santa Ono	$975,000
Penn. State	James Franklin	$7.0	Eric Barron	$876,612
Northwestern	Pat Fitzgerald	$5.7	Morton Schapiro	$1.65 million
UCLA	Chip Kelly	$5.6	Gene Block	$639,953
Univ. of Texas	Steve Sarkisian	$5.45	Jay Hartzell	$1.25 million

*Former President

Sources: Julia Elbaba, "Looking at the top college football head coach salaries in 2022," NBC Sports, September 8, 2022, www.nbcsports.com/chicago/college-football-head-coach-salaries-kirby-smart-2022-new-contract. Chronicle of Higher Education, "How Much Are Private-College Presidents Paid?" Chronicle of Higher Education, August 17, 2022, https://www.chronicle.com/article/president-pay-private-colleges

The Losers

The winners in college sports are offset by the losers, including students and taxpayers who pay part of the bill for sports programs. Calculating revenue gains or losses in athletic departments is tricky since several kinds of revenues are often combined. Sports teams generate direct revenues through ticket sales, broadcast contracts, product endorsements, etc. Revenues can also include university subsidies and donations to sports teams, which can sometimes be hugely significant. For instance, Nike founder Phil Knight donated $100 million in 2007 to create the University of Oregon's Athletics Legacy Fund, which helped pay for the university's athletic programs. Some of these funds were earmarked for salary increases to keep coaches or to buy out their contracts. Knight also underwrote the bulk of money for the $270 million Hayward Athletic Field. In addition, Knight donated $100 million for the Matthew Knight Arena, $60 million for stadium renovations, $42 million for an academic center for student-athletes, and $10 million for a sports complex.[87] Author William Deresiewicz sarcastically refers to the University of Oregon as the University of Nike.[88]

As noted earlier, Scott Hirko found that only eighteen out of 229 NCAA Division I athletic programs were profitable in 2020,[89] an assessment that generally fits with the NCAA's 2019 data (2019 data is pre-Covid, reflecting a more normative year in college sports). That year, the median revenue *loss* among colleges was roughly $18.8 million for the highest-level football division. Only twenty-five institutions generated revenues that exceeded expenses, with a median net revenue gain of $7.9 million. Overall, the results ranged from a loss of $65 million to a surplus of almost $44 million. The median generated revenue loss for the lower football divisions was roughly $14.3 million, ranging from $2.2 million to over $42.1 million.[90] It is evident that losers in the college sports game far outnumber winners.

Students Carry the Heaviest Burden

An NBC News report found that some college students pay thousands of dollars (often hidden in tuition and fees) to support NCAA sports teams. More than 80 percent of the 230 Division I public universities billed students to subsidize their sports teams, with some of those fees being extremely high[91] (see Table 5.3).

Some universities twist NCAA rules at the expense of students. For instance, NCAA regulations require that colleges have an attendance at home games of 15,000 to qualify for NCAA Division I. Unable to meet that number, Miami University of Ohio billed students $1,044 in athletic fees in 2022 and used part of that money to buy 10,000 of its football tickets for each home game. The tickets were not resold.[92]

The subsidies for college sports are often hidden within university budgets and then surreptitiously bundled into tuition. As such, these fees become part of a student's overall tuition costs and are therefore incorporated into student loans. This lack of transparency is not surprising since many students who work one or two jobs to pay for college and have no interest in sports would be infuriated to know how much of their tuition and fees are going into athletics.

Table 5.3 Student Fees Used to Subsidize Athletics

Institution	Student Fee	Percent Dedicated to Athletic Budget
Virginia Military Institute	$3,340	43%
Citadel Military College of South Carolina	$2,713	39%
James Madison University	$2,340	75%
Longwood University	$2,012	66%
College of William and Mary	$1,900	50%
Old Dominion University	$1,678	63%
Norfolk State University	$1,538	47%
College of Charleston	$1,278	62%
Winthrop University	$1,225	46%
Radford University	$1,180	81%
Morgan State University	$1,177	71%
University of Maryland-Baltimore	$1,112	68%
Miami University-Oxford	$1,012	48%

Source: Merritt Enright, Andrew Lehren, & Jaime Longoria, "Hidden figures: College students may be paying thousands in athletic fees and not know it," *NBC News*, March 8, 2020, www.nbcnews.com/news/education/hidden-figures-college-students-may-be-paying-thousands-athletic-fees-n1145171

Reforming College Sports

Any attempt to fundamentally reform college sports would face immense challenges, given how deeply ingrained sports are in American culture. Moreover, radically restructuring or terminating multi-billion college sports programs would profoundly affect the salaries of coaches, the budgets of the minority of universities with profitable sports programs, broadcast networks, sports agents, corporate sponsors, and professional teams that recruit college athletes. Billions of dollars are behind the "student-athlete industrial complex" with its extensive network of influential and well-funded beneficiaries.

In 2017, Gerald Gurney et al. argued that the NCAA should be replaced since it cannot achieve real reform while placing commercial success above its duty to protect college athletes. The authors argued that while college sports belong in higher education, their administration and governance are the real challenge.[93] Gurney's argument misses the point that NCAA college sports are a runaway train that jumped its tracks. As the NCAA's control over college sports has weakened, the vacuum has been filled by entrepreneurs who want to further commodify and monetize college sports, making it indistinguishable from professional sports.

Difficult choices confront colleges facing massive financial losses in their sports programs. They can continue funneling scarce resources into the money pit of NCAA intercollegiate sports programs or end those programs and redirect the savings into scholarships, lower tuition, modernizing their infrastructure, and expanding their academic offerings.

Alternatives to the Intercollegiate Sports Programs

As this chapter demonstrates, NCAA-sanctioned sports have been a financial albatross around the necks of most colleges and universities for over fifty years. University funding for college sports has added to the cost of college attendance, student loans, and tax burdens.

College sports funding should be dislodged from university auspices, thereby removing all financial responsibility from the institution, students, and taxpayers. This radical move would accomplish several things. Offloading the financial responsibility for sports would free up funds for more remedial programs for struggling students. It would allow colleges and universities to refocus their resources and energies on strengthening their academic offerings. Tuition savings would reduce the amount students have to borrow. As universities stopped paying outrageous coaching salaries, those salaries would come down to earth and more closely reflect an organization's resources. Coaches could no longer blackmail university presidents by threatening to take a job at a competing school. While radical, this "uncoupling" is necessary to break the out-of-control spiral of the commercialization of college sports, which results in blurred lines between amateur and professional sports. The NCAA would be disbanded since its raison d'être would no longer exist. While intercollegiate sports programs severed from university coffers will face the challenge of sinking or swimming, this "uncoupling" would also bring US colleges closer to less expensive but equally high-quality European and Australian universities.

College students' participation in sports can occur outside university auspices through sports clubs, associations, or sports clinics funded by professional teams as part of their recruitment activities. Many college sports programs could be spun into nonprofit (or for-profit) organizations like university alumni associations, which are part of a university but do not receive university funding. Alumni associations generate revenues for the university through various forms of fundraising. If their commitment to college sports is sincere, fans, donors, professional sports leagues, broadcasters, and others will step up to meet the challenge.

There is no one-size-fits-all solution to the termination of college sports funding. Universities with revenue-producing football and basketball teams could still contribute to the university through donations to sports-based alumni associations. In addition, these teams could provide revenue to universities through leasing stadiums and training facilities. With the demise of the NCAA, college sports associations would be free to pay athletes salaries commensurate with their value to the team. Self-financing sports teams could continue to compete against each other but without cost to the university or students. If a sports team is not financially viable as a separate entity, it could join forces with similar clubs to form athletic associations or consortiums.

The revenue stream for privatized college sports organizations could include broadcast contracts, ticket sales, corporate sponsorships, donations from major leagues, and individual and fan donations and endowments. More aggressive professional teams might be willing to sponsor these clubs to scoop up the best players. In addition, the

NFL and NBA could use these organizations to set up minor leagues or farm teams. Instead of universities and students paying for developing player skills, those costs would fall back on professional teams who would pay their fair share for developing talented players.

European sports are structurally different from US sports because they are associated with "sporting clubs." The club system is a network of sporting organizations, ranging from small local recreational clubs to multibillion-dollar franchises similar to professional US sports teams. Another alternative model for college sports is the European University Sports Association (EUSA), a nonprofit and non-governmental (NGO) organization that links national university sports federations, universities, teams, individual competitors, volunteers, and other partners in European countries.

A valid argument for funding college sports involves its sociocultural implications. In particular, many low-income Blacks, Hispanics, and whites view sports scholarships as the only way they can attend college. Some see college sports as a door into professional sports. While a college degree can be a way out of poverty, admitting students based solely on their athletic abilities sets them up for failure if they cannot meet academic expectations. It is also unfair to low-income students who lack athletic abilities but have the motivation, drive, and wherewithal to complete a college degree but lack the resources. Even though students admitted solely on their athletic prowess may graduate, it is too often based on a truncated college experience that leaves them without the knowledge and skills expected of a college graduate. Alternatively, the money saved by eliminating NCAA sports programs could be redirected to mentoring low-income high school students, adding more scholarships for low-income students, or funding a pre-college year designed to aid students from low-performing high schools.

Conclusion

College sports initially aimed to balance intellectual pursuits with physical activity. Health was a primary concern. While college students in the 1800s were a driving force in intercollegiate sports, by the mid-1900s, it was taken over by the "adults," presumably under the guise of "in loco parentis." Under the NCAA's influence, college sports became semiprofessional, and only those students able to play at a high level were welcome on sports teams. College sports became exclusionary, with most students being shut out from participating.

Intercollegiate sports have changed dramatically from the 1920s when legendary coach Knute Rockne led Notre Dame's "Fighting Irish" to 105 victories. Today's NCAA Division I teams are semiprofessional (more "professional" than "semi") and amateur in name only. Division I sports teams in many universities are corporatized multibillion-dollar industrial complexes with sports agents, marketers, and coaches whose salaries run in the millions. Some college sports stadiums like the University of Michigan, Louisiana State University, Pennsylvania State University, Ohio State University, and Texas A&M seat upward of 100,000 spectators. Rome's Colosseum seated only 87,000 people.

Humbled by losing court cases and outmaneuvered by commercial interests, the NCAA is abandoning almost all pretenses of keeping amateur sports amateur. Complementing the NCAA's failure, universities have failed to counter the commercialization of college sports and have become little more than warehouses for business interests.

The commodification of higher education has permeated college sports and led to significant financial rewards for star athletes and coaches. As big and small businesses dangle lucrative opportunities in front of student-athletes, the potential financial windfall has led some high school graduates to attend college solely to play sports and earn money from NILs deals. The goal of earning a college degree is secondary to earning points in a game.

There are clear winners and losers in college sports, with most schools being losers. Fearing donors and alums will abandon them without a winning team, colleges funnel massive amounts of money into athletic departments. The myth around the importance of a winning sports team exists despite a 2019 study that found that while a winning football team correlates to increased college applications, it does not impact donations or state appropriations.[94] Myths die hard, especially when backed by millions of dollars.

For most universities, eliminating the financial drain of college sports will make education more affordable for more students. As athletic fees and other hidden sports-related fees disappear, the costs of attendance will be lowered for students who are taxed for college sports even though they never attend a game.

Professional basketball and football teams have a predatory relationship with colleges and universities since they use them as a free minor league. In contrast, Major League Baseball uses a farm system of minor league teams to develop young players, some of whom wind up on major league teams. On the other hand, the NBA and NFL invest almost nothing since star college athletes are already trained when a professional team recruits them. Colleges are a free farm system for the NFL and NBA, paid for by tuition, fees, and university subsidies.

Conservative columnist George Will argues that college football must shed its three most egregious pretenses: amateurism/amateur sports, student-athletes, and tradition. He argues against the absurdity of trying to graft a multibillion-dollar entertainment industry onto higher education. For Will, college football is simply an "unembarrassable" money machine.[95] Will is right since football factories like the Universities of Alabama and Georgia resemble Fortune 500 corporations more than the universities that house them. The NCAA and universities can't have it both ways. They can't pronounce their commitment to amateur sports while treating college sports like a business and student-athletes like unpaid professionals.

College students should not be forced to subsidize the salaries of millionaire coaches, professional sports teams (who use the university as a free recruiting venue), sports fans seeking entertainment, and college administrators searching for institutional prestige through sports achievements. Nor should taxpayers subsidize college sports programs that contribute little to the fundamental mission of education. In particular, the justification for using tax dollars to support higher education is to strengthen the economy and promote the common good. NCAA college sports programs meet neither of these goals. Moreover, the money earmarked for college sports could be better spent on hiring more quality faculty, providing more financial assistance for students, and providing campus childcare and healthcare.

One reason universities in Europe, Australia, New Zealand, and China can provide an education as good (and sometimes better) as American colleges at a lower cost is that they are not burdened with expensive sports programs that contribute little to education. Nor are their priorities as twisted as in the United States, where the highest-paid university employees are not college presidents, Nobel Laureates, National Medal of Science winners, or exemplary teachers but football and basketball coaches.

6

Inequality and the Corporatization of Higher Education

American higher education is at an inflection point, as evidenced by declining enrollment, administrative bloat, and public skepticism about the value of a college diploma. While 60 percent of students from the top quartile of family income graduate from college, only 12 percent from the bottom quartile receive a diploma. As the distance between the have-nots and have-yachts widens, Michael Crow and William Dabars have called for National Service Universities, institutions "facilitating access for all academically qualified American students and advancing research and workforce development to promote innovation and global competitiveness."[1] The impediments to that vision are substantial: a product of an array of institutions evolving under different auspices, the elevation of students as consumers, excessive salaries paid to university presidents, coaches, and star faculty, and the exploitation of athletes through intercollegiate sports. The nation's colleges and universities, once engines of upward mobility, are now complicit in exacerbating economic inequality, in contradiction to the American ethos.

An Emerging Market

Higher education in America evolved from European precedents. Private colleges like Harvard trained ministers to lead churches in the new colonies. Steeped in Greek and Latin, their religious curricula were later broadened by adopting the English Oxbridge model of the liberal arts. Subsequently, a focus on science was imported from Germany, leading to the establishment of Johns Hopkins University. The dominance of private Eastern colleges, subsidized by wealthy benefactors who established endowments to their alma maters, would be disrupted through the 1862 Morrill Act, which set aside lands to create public agricultural institutions. These "land grant" schools sprouted far beyond the East Coast, offering training in engineering, agronomy, and teacher education, skills needed for an expanding economy. During the twentieth century, this combination of private colleges and public universities gained wide respect for advancing the public good by virtue of the experts they produced, professionals who navigated the First World War, the Great Depression, and the Second World War.

After the Second World War, the Cold War prompted the injection of federal funding into universities for research to address Soviet space and nuclear achievements, advancing nuclear physics, aeronautic engineering, and biological sciences. At the same time, the GI Bill provided grants to veterans to attend college. A burgeoning population of Baby Boomers caused states to deploy community colleges to provide vocational education while serving as conduits to four-year institutions. Following the Civil Rights movement, Pell Grants supported individual low-income students, contributing to the emergence of for-profit schools. At the inception of the twenty-first century, these disparate institutions were ideally suited for a massive experiment in market solutions in higher education, a competition that grew fiercer as declining enrollments pitted institutions against one another for fewer students.

Complementing the rise of higher education, professional associations established during the Progressive Era contended that civil service positions should be reserved for university graduates to address the dislocations attendant with industrialization, immigration, and urbanization. As experts demonstrated their prowess by planning livable alternatives to slums, constructing the interstate highway system, inventing vaccines to defeat communicable diseases, and engineering labor-saving commercial products,[2] expertise became associated with progress despite retrograde errors, such as eugenics. The New Deal of the 1930s and Great Society of the 1960s would require legions of lawyers, administrators, doctors, nurses, accountants, statisticians, teachers, and social workers to oversee programs and provide benefits. The elaboration of silo programs of the welfare state may have added credence to the accusation that a "fourth branch" of government had emerged, but it certainly larded public agencies with well-credentialed experts.

The collusion between university-trained experts and the welfare state amplified a liberal, or "progressive," disposition in public affairs, a belief that expertise would benefit the public when harnessed by the state. That major social programs were entitlements, on autopilot, and not subject to annual appropriations anguished conservatives who perceived a specter of not only uncontrollable benefit expenditures but also increasing numbers of experts to manage them. This would implicate university professional schools, including Harvard's Kennedy School, but also liberal think tanks, such as the Urban Institute, as well as advocacy organizations, including the Children's Defense Fund and the Center on Budget and Policy Priorities, in a seemingly infinite expansion of government social programs. The right's umbrage to liberal designs in public policy was registered by Lewis Powell's 1971 memo to the U.S. Chamber of Commerce alleging that radical university students, abetted by Ralph Nader, represented a direct threat to American capitalism.[3] While Powell's suggestions of a speakers bureau and pamphlets distributed at airports were quaint, his colleagues had a grander vision. Under the banner of a "marketplace of ideas,"[4] they funded an alternative network to the nation's universities: conservative think tanks. Within a decade, the previously staid American Enterprise Institute was refurbished to lead the right's charge against unrestrained liberalism. It was soon joined by new think tanks: the Heritage Foundation, the Manhattan Institute, and the Cato Institute, among others. While these organizations would evolve distinct signatures—AEI being more centrist, Heritage going full Trump MAGA, and Cato consistently libertarian—their work during the latter decades of the twentieth century disrupted the hegemony enjoyed by liberal academics accustomed to shuffling in and out of the Brookings Institution and the Urban Institute.

The shift in public philosophy, away from faith in the state and favoring markets, would be underscored by the election of Ronald Reagan in 1980, who inveighed against the government, cut taxes, and opposed economic regulation while staffing his administration with personnel from conservative think tanks. The Reagan administration's assault on the welfare state would capitalize on market-compatible precedents established by more liberal predecessors. For example, the GI Bill, updated after military adventures in Vietnam, Iraq, and Afghanistan, allowed veterans to select the college they wished to attend. The Higher Education Act of 1965 offered students grants and loans, which expanded via Pell Grants in the 1970s, establishing individual students as sovereign consumers with a choice of which college to attend, a solution congruent with Milton Friedman's thinking of the period. Ditto 529 plans, deployed in 1995, providing tax breaks to parents who saved for their children's college education. Even as the federal government focused on college students as consumers of higher education, states continued to subsidize colleges and universities directly.

A Flawed Meritocracy

Awash in prestige and cash following the Second World War, American higher education became the envy of the world, accruing Nobel Prizes, securing patents for innovative technology, and attracting students from around the globe. Exclusive institutions became *de rigueur* destinations for the affluent. Elite universities vetted applicants, provided a stellar education, and arranged internships, their graduates eventually rotating through executive offices in government, consulting firms, and think tanks, forming a new and distinct social class: the meritocracy. Coined by Michael Young in 1958, "meritocracy" appeared in his satire *The Rise of the Meritocracy*. A Labour Party and Fabian leader preoccupied with increasing distance between politicians and citizens, Young was skeptical about a society predicated on scientific efficacy criteria, anticipating social cleavage exacerbated by education accessed by IQ tests. "No longer is it just the brilliant individual who shines forth; the world beholds for the first time the spectacle of a brilliant class, the five percent of the nation who know what five percent means," Young quipped. "Every member is a tried specialist. In his own sphere."[5] To that end, Young offered an equation: "Intelligence and effort together make up merit (I+E=M)."[6]

The American meritocracy selected and nurtured students at exclusive colleges and universities, claiming their success rested on merit, but critics identified a skewed process,[7] including tutors, test coaches, and prep schools, reinforced by restrictive zoning and inequalities in funding public education, which gave affluent applicants to elite colleges a decided advantage.[8] "The elite invest heavily in their progeny and in political control," observed Branko Milanovic, "Investment in their children's education enables the children to maintain high labor income and the high status that is traditionally associated with knowledge and education."[9] As the Varsity Blues scandal demonstrated, affluent parents would pursue even illegal means to get their children admitted to elite schools. Paying an intermediary to divert tens of thousands of dollars to exclusive schools based on phony sports portfolios, several parents would be convicted of fraud, jailed, and their children's admissions retracted.[10]

Recent studies of elite schools show the meritocratic selection process at work. Researchers from Harvard's Opportunity Insights found that, among Ivy League schools, exclusive private colleges, and select public flagship universities, "applicants from families in the top 1 percent (incomes above $611,000) are 55 percent more likely to be admitted to Ivy-Plus colleges [Ivy League schools plus Duke, MIT, Stanford, and. Chicago] than applicants from middle-class families," those reporting between $83,000 to $116,000 per year. Moreover, "the marginal student" entering an Ivy-plus school "is about 60 percent more likely to reach the top 1 percent of the income distribution at age thirty-three, nearly twice as likely to attend a highly ranked graduate school, and three times as likely to work at a prestigious firm" compared to the classmate attending a public flagship school. Thus, the authors concluded, "highly selective private colleges serve as gateways to the upper echelons of society in the United States. Because these colleges currently admit students from high-income families at substantially higher rates than students from lower-income families with comparable academic credentials, they perpetuate privilege across generations."[11]

This conclusion was echoed by researchers from the *New York Times*, who found a similar advantage for students from wealthy families: "At Georgetown, someone from the top 1 percent was 2.7 times as likely to attend as a typical student with [a high test] score, while a student from the bottom 20 percent was about half as likely to attend." More broadly, Ivies showed a disinterest in admitting less affluent applicants but a clear preference for legacies coming from the wealthiest 1 percent of households.[12] The issue here is not merit, per se, but that less affluent students simply don't align with the business model of elite universities, the endowments of which are sustained by infusions that only the rich can provide. As Paul Tough observed, "Enrollment managers know there is no great shortage of deserving low-income students applying to good colleges; they know this because they regularly reject them—not because they don't want to admit those students, but because they can't afford to."[13]

Except for MIT, which does not prefer legacies, this favoritism for the affluent is subscribed to by private schools and even most public flagships, except for Florida, Berkeley, Ohio State, and UCLA. Indeed, it is not until less-exclusive schools are included in the mix that, controlling for identical test scores, less affluent students are admitted. Such less-exclusive schools are essential to equipping youth with the skills to become accountants, military officers, schoolteachers, business owners, nurses, and the like, who populate the middle class.[14] Despite the gratifying futures promised by academies of lesser stature, the mad scramble for admission to elite schools validates the realization among meritocrats that having a career of affluence and consequence depends on being admitted to an exclusive school.[15] By comprising the meritocracy, graduates of elite schools choreograph the policies that define the options for the middle class. Members of the middle class are productive but unlikely to ascend to leaders of the polity, business, the arts, and nonprofit organizations—or, for that matter, cabinet members, university presidents, and star faculty who script higher education.

In this way, the nation's leadership class reflects the economic stratification of the population, at least among those pursuing higher education, in effect creating a "diploma democracy."[16] The Ivies have risen to the top, followed by exclusive private colleges and a handful of public flagships, but most college students are admitted to less prestigious schools. "Higher education in America is highly unequal and disturbingly stratified. Youth from poor families of all races, but especially those from black and Latino families, are less likely to go to college than their wealthy peers," observed Abraham Jack:

> Although half of all undergraduates in the United States are the first in their family to go to college—with most of those coming from poor backgrounds—first-generation college students are disproportionately relegated to community colleges, for-profit colleges, and less selective four-year colleges. Those institutions share some troubling traits: resources are few, student aid is scarce, and retention is low.[17]

This is not to say that students can't and don't migrate among them. Certainly, ambitious graduates of public schools strive to attend Ivies for professional and post-graduate degrees, and some of those attending Ivies transfer to less challenging public institutions, but the route to meritocratic affluence and influence is conspicuously upward.

Regardless, a meritocracy produced by elite education is hardly foolproof. Aside from debacles at scale, such as military incursions in Vietnam and Iraq and the Great Recession, meritocrats have been complicit in mismanaging entire industries, including public polling, which consistently erred about national elections in 2016 and 2020.[18] Since the War on Poverty, a cottage industry of researchers has been dedicated to understanding Americans struggling with inadequate resources, proposing, then debating contradictory measures of poverty.[19] The Covid-19 pandemic generated a firestorm of criticism when public health officials from the Centers for Disease Control and Prevention proposed efforts to contain infections, which some state officials disputed. These incidents question the public value of "peer-run institutions," as Tom Nichols admitted: "Mechanisms like peer review, board certification, professional associations, and other organizations and professions help to protect quality and to assure society—that is, the expert clients—that they're safe in accepting expert claims of competence."[20] Except when they don't.

Setbacks notwithstanding, the meritocracy in higher education has adopted a corporate mindset, replete with paying presidents and

CEOs million-dollar salaries, competing cost centers, and favoring revenue producers, such as patents and sports. David Graeber lamented the consequence as "managerialist ideologies [are] put into practice in complex organizations. As managerialism embeds itself, you get entire cadres of academic staff whose job it is to just keep the managerialist plates spinning—strategies, performance targets, audits, reviews, appraisals, renewed strategies, etc., etc.— which happen in almost wholly and entirely disconnected fashion from the real lifeblood of universities: teaching and education."[21] Managerialism in higher education would result in administrative bloat, the cost of which was passed on to students and their families, who were unaware of increased tuition and hidden fees obscured by conveniently opaque academic budgets. "Between 1976 and 2018, full-time administrators and other professionals employed by those institutions increased by 164% and 452%, respectively," noted. Paul Weinstein. "Meanwhile, the number of full-time faculty employed at colleges and universities in the U.S. increased by only 92%, marginally outpacing student enrollment which grew by 78%." A top-heavy academy will soon be confronted with an expected 15 percent decline in enrollment between 2025 and 2029.[22] For academic meritocrats, the disconnect between plummeting enrollment and institutional budgets will likely be addressed by jacking up tuition, making their conceit affordable because they would not be adversely affected since *their* children would be enrolling in exclusive schools, tuition, and fees for their education already secured.

 Policies that provided federal grants to students presumed that college presidents and trustees would be held accountable by the consumers of the education their institutions provided, as opposed to relying on government regulators. Furthering the absence of accountability, American colleges and universities and their accreditors have been private organizations independent of direct governmental control. In recent decades, trustees and presidents authorized increases in tuition and fees to cover sunk costs, such as buildings and tenured faculty, hoping students and their families would realize the long-term earnings benefits of college credentials despite any short-term financial pain. As inequality increased, affluent families had little difficulty enrolling their children in college. At the same time, working-class households struggled with static wages, finding a child's college degree difficult to justify, especially given the decline in the value of Pell Grants, which were not indexed for inflation. Much of the realization by blue-collar families that college was an iffy proposition resulted from impressionistic evidence, the collective experiences of youth who found higher education difficult to navigate, many having dropped out. It would not be until the Obama administration that "scorecards" would allow nonprofit organizations to provide information on college costs and projected earnings by institution and field of study, but this even provoked stiff resistance from college leaders.

Populist Blowback

A flawed meritocracy that gave short shrift to the masses, who were de facto consumers of policies and programs established and managed by their betters, contributed to a populism that was understandably skeptical of elites and occasionally virulently so. Such polarization can be attributed to different worldviews: a meritocracy that is objective and adept with data-infusing policies and programs versus a less credentialed sensibility that is subjective and pedestrian and informed by daily experience. Accordingly, the British essayist David Goodhart differentiated "somewheres," people anchored to locality and embedded in local social networks, from "anywheres," cosmopolitans whose education and aspirations made them comfortable on the global stage. After Brexit, Goodhart published *The Road to Somewhere* to reconcile the two factions. "The tension between a declining market position for many employees and the political promise of some kind of respect, security and share in prosperity accounts for at least some of the Somewhere public disaffection of recent times. And the declining status of non-graduate employment," Goodhart observed, "has been exacerbated by other economic trends: falling income after the financial crash, the decline in home ownership especially in big cities, in-work poverty, and that reduction in the number of middle status jobs."[23] That tableau has been replicated in America.

By the 2020s, a working class that had migrated to the Republican Party was thoroughly disenchanted with college as a path to upward mobility. Consider: in 2015, 28 percent of respondents to a Gallup poll had a "great deal" of confidence in higher education compared to 9 percent who had "very little." By 2023, that had reversed with 17 registering "great deal" but 22 percent "very little."[24] A 2017 poll found that of Republican respondents, 33 percent had "a great deal/quite a lot" of confidence in higher education, compared to 67 percent who had "some/very little,"[25] an ominous development since Republican-dominated legislatures controlled the purse strings for state universities.

An open society guarantees that collective frustration and passion will erupt periodically in ways that meritocrats could not have imagined. Indeed, close on the heels of the passage of "Obamacare," the Tea Party mobilized in 2010, a populist movement initially critical of liberal and conservative elites alike. Soon, a liberal "occupy" movement was spawned, also unanticipated; suddenly, America was in the grips of ground-up organizations that defied traditional political parties. The throes of polarization would prove more consequential for Republicans once Donald Trump seized control of the GOP, improbably vaulting himself into the White House. His corrupt and deceitful administration exasperated liberal Democrats who tried unsuccessfully to impeach him, the second effort in response to the January 6 insurrection in the Capitol. Months later, Trump was confronted with four unprecedented trials as a former president; unbowed, he suggested to his base that they were being indicted with him.

In retrospect, flustered meritocrats might have taken notice of Trump's appeal to his base while campaigning, "I love the poorly educated!" Having organized the data and crafted corrective policies, the meritocracy was faced with populists who *opposed* the very programs liberals insisted were in *their* best interests. Grown deaf to a working class that was once the backbone of its party, Democrats had embraced the meritocracy, professionals who, having graduated from exclusive colleges and universities, had come to control essential social institutions. Endorsing immigration, universal basic income, and Black Lives Matter, liberal meritocrats chose issues that exacerbated the anxieties and fears of white men who had, only a generation earlier, taken pride in supporting their middle-class families, purchasing homes in suburbia, and sending their kids off to college. In response to their defection, few liberals took seriously the tectonic shift in blue-collar support for the Democratic party, an exception being Joan Williams, who warned, "Changing working-class attitudes will require a mind shift for progressives whose instinct has been to highlight the benefits of government help for the poor."[26] Clueless about the angst felt by blue-collar workers whose job loss and employment demotion pushed them downward toward the welfare poor, meritocrats, who lacked any direct exposure with either experience, pontificated about their superior morality.

Rather than being an invitation to step on the ladder of upward mobility, college for lower-income students has been disastrous. Despite the best intentions, fragile family finances subverted even the most modest aspirations, such as obtaining an associate degree and transferring to a public university. Erratic income from secondary labor market employment, based on hourly wages without benefits, unpredictable schedules, and few options for promotion, collided with expense shocks, such as a needed car repair, a babysitter no longer available, or a utility shut-off to derail attendance, a missed class morphing to a semester's withdrawal to concluding that college is not worth the hassle. Those persevering may have taken out loans to weather a financial storm, but student debt could not be discharged through bankruptcy, saddling a college dropout with weighty obligations far into the future.[27] Such scenarios could have been the subject of economic modeling by researchers at elite schools, who would have suggested ways to increase retention and graduation for low-income students, but the academy has shown little interest, assuming that such students were expendable. For most lower-income students, a two-year community college degree offered the ticket to a vocation paying decent wages, but such prospects were a galaxy away from exclusive colleges. Consider: in 2018, Michael Bloomberg gave Johns Hopkins University $1.8 *billion*, while gifts to all of the nation's community colleges totaled $174 *million*.[28] Understandably, lower-income voters would become skeptical about college, contributing to the collapse of support for higher education among Republicans.

In fact, most of the working-class and working poor valued education, hoping their children would be able to leave behind the shopfloor and fast food for a salaried job with benefits. Yet, once again, meritocrats, who controlled higher education among other institutional remits, offered token support. Certainly, exclusive colleges provided scholarships, and government grants mitigated tuition increases, but the former were so few as to be symbolic, and the latter declined in relation to inflation, leaving students and families resorting to loans. Although elite schools had ample staff and knowledge to conduct the necessary research to smooth the path of upward mobility for working-class students, academic administrators preferred a business model that favored the "rents" they had assiduously constructed through accreditation, administrative bloat, and tenure along with endowments battened by legacy admissions. Unacknowledged altogether, another economic term loomed in the background: "opportunity costs" of college for low-income students—the increased income foregone in favor of current earnings.

In retrospect, the failure to generate data on opportunity costs is an indictment of the nation's leading schools, virtually all with departments of economics and research centers. While the nation would be awash in data from Obama's scorecards and data from the Pell Institute, aside from Abraham Jack's interviews, none bothered to generate rigorous data on how lower-income youth actually perceived college. For a worker earning a minimum wage and receiving a Pell Grant, it would be a struggle to be self-supporting while covering tuition and fees at a public institution, whether a community college or a four-year institution. As wages increased due to a tight labor market, even a $20/hour job would be problematic simply because attending school full-time would require reduced working hours. Certainly, a two-earner household could compensate, but figuring children into family finances effectively defeated increased earned income. Low-income households might have accessed welfare benefits and tax refunds, but these require separate applications with different due dates, causing students to forfeit income supports due to "administrative burden." As Jack summarized, "Money remains a requirement for full citizenship in college, despite institutional declarations to the contrary."[29] Although college leaders have been reluctant to address the predicament of less affluent students, it does show up in graduation rates, which were extended from a previous norm of four years to six years; even then, this failed to account for significant numbers of dropouts.[30]

Instead, colleges dived into identity politics, timid administrators eager to assuage the anxieties of students. A catalyst of the degradation of higher education was Ernest Boyer's 1990 *Scholarship Reconsidered,* which advocated scrapping a core curriculum in favor of a smorgasbord of electives, effectively conceding academic rigor to the preferences of student consumers.[31] Two education scholars would observe the consequences; surveying 2,300 students with the Collegiate Learning Assessment, they found "no statistically significant gains in critical thinking, complex reasoning, and writing skills for at least 45 percent of the students in our study. An astounding proportion of students are progressing through higher education today without measurable gains in general skills assessed by the CLA."[32] Despite critics concerned about the quality of instruction, such as Mark Bauerlein,[33] and the future of the academy, such as Kevin Carey,[34] leaders of American higher education dithered.[35]

An overwhelmingly liberal faculty endorsed Affirmative Action and objected to the intimidation of minority and female students by white males.[36] Soon, "speech codes" articulated a regime of "political correctness," which morphed into academic tribalism with the establishment of programs in university departments dedicated to studies of African Americans, Latinos, and women; later, LGBTQ+ would be added. Speaking "truth to power," student activists blocked speakers on campus, sometimes intimidating classmates and resorting to violence.[37] To placate students, academies established Diversity, Equity, and Inclusion policies to increase the presence of minorities on campus, some policies degenerating into de facto progressive loyalty oaths necessary for faculty employment and promotion. Two events would disrupt ordinarily tranquil campuses: the murder of George Floyd in 2020 animated Black students; the 2024 war between Hamas and Israel generated conflict between Jewish students and advocates of Palestine. These disparate agendas were conflated into "woke" by conservatives alarmed about what they perceived to be the politicization of the academy by the left. Although the right had little influence at private universities, it had considerable leverage with public universities through Republican state legislatures. By the 2020s, "red states" promulgated dozens of laws to reverse academic policies that offended conservatives, the Governor of Florida, Ron DeSantis, becoming the paragon of the movement, his signature legislation, the "Stop WOKE Act," which opposed DEI programs in state universities, coupled with inserting conservatives as trustees of New College of Florida.

Dénouement

No surprise to anyone acquainted with self-interest in politics and policy, institutions of higher education have been complicit in the divisions now raging in America. By elevating the exclusively educated over those of lesser means, a new polemic has emerged: meritocracy v. populism. By replacing the public service model with a corporate mindset, leaders of colleges and universities have commodified learning, turning it from an opportunity for all Americans to gain admission to great art, philosophy, literature, and history to a vocational pursuit that is increasingly elusive for the middle class; for the working class and welfare poor, higher education generates deep skepticism. The result has been increasing rigidity by social class, with meritocrats trained at exclusive schools establishing the priorities, policies, and programs in which those toiling at lesser institutions then labor. Not even an afterthought, the opportunity costs of the working class and the working poor make higher education a chimera. Is it any wonder that those left behind are attracted to authoritarian nationalism?

Like capitalist enterprises in general, universities implementing market strategies to cope with declining enrollment attributable to Covid-19, a declining birthrate, constricted immigration, and a tight labor market have been struggling to adapt. The signs of a reckoning are unmistakable: establishing nonprofit entities to partner with commercial colleges, contracting with for-profit enrollment firms that charge up to 50 percent of tuition generated, marketing degrees to uninformed students who are unlikely to repay loans from meager post-graduation earnings, replacing instruction by professors with cadres of adjuncts and graduate assistants, relying on revenues from major sporting events that detract from higher learning, cashiering humanities to amplify more lucrative majors, and paying unjustifiable salaries to presidents as well as star faculty who view themselves as free agents in a competitive market.

As independent institutions not subject to direct governmental regulation, colleges and universities are free to thrive or whither. Accordingly, during the twentieth century, the nation's schools became the envy of the world, but that luster is badly tarnished as a corporate mindset infects the academy. Indeed, "disruptive innovation" is necessary to reorganize America's fonts of higher learning and make them international beacons of science, humanities, and the arts once again.[38]

Conclusion: A Framework for Reforming Higher Education

University students in the 1960s experienced college life very differently than students in 2024. Campuses in the late 1960s were rife with political activity, and many students chose interesting classes rather than those directly related to a career. Interdisciplinary baccalaureate degrees were created for students with varied interests that didn't fit into an established discipline. Faculty and student interactions were often informal, and it wasn't unusual for faculty members to have lunch with students, even going for a beer at a student bar. It was also not unusual for small seminars to be held in an instructor's home. These days, instructors fear possible allegations, and many only meet students with their doors open and avoid discussing anything that could be construed as personal. In many places, the interactions between students and faculty are primarily instrumental and business-like.

The college experience has become increasingly as faculty pressured to generate research dollars rush from classes to their labs or offices. Poorly paid adjuncts have little incentive to stay after class. The impersonality of the college experience is further amplified as working students shuffle from classes to their jobs. As a result, colleges are no longer places where one wants to be but are now places that must be endured to get a good job.

Higher education today is far removed from its traditional teaching, research, and service roles. As such, the former balance between these roles has been lost in commodified and corporatized universities. Righting the balance and returning higher education to a more humane, inclusive, and cost-efficient system is more complicated than applying one or two simple solutions. The following recommendations are meant only as a starting point to address problems that have been festering for decades.

Reestablishing a Moral Center: Protecting Families and College Employees

Much of what was assumed to be at the moral core of the university has been eroded by commodification and corporatization. Instead of being bastions of knowledge and moral integrity, universities are increasingly mimicking the corporate world, especially in exploiting consumers and vulnerable parts of the labor force.

Exploitation in the Academic Workplace

The commodification and corporatization of higher education have eroded the formerly core value of workplace security. Most universities are influenced, if not run, by "bean counters" who champion cost-cutting wherever possible, especially in labor costs. (A notable exception is protecting administrative positions.) In contrast to the academic value of job security through tenure, the solutions posed by corporate-minded administrators involve reliance on low-paid adjuncts and contract workers who have no job security. This creates a gig economy similar to Lyft, Uber, and GrubHub that relies on on-call workers who lack retirement plans, health insurance, paid holidays, and sick leave. This cost-cutting measure has led to the creation of precariat academics who have little or no hope for a permanent position. Instead of continuing to propagate this exploitation, universities should use casual faculty only for special-purpose classes where they bring a unique and specialized knowledge or skill set. Adjunct and contract workers should not be used to replace full-time faculty members.

The Use of Retail Market Strategies

Some colleges have adopted retail market strategies to hide the actual costs, including confusing tuition, fees, and living expenses estimates. This approach leaves students and families perplexed about the real cost of college, including full versus discounted tuition. A 2023 Government Accountability Office report found that 91 percent of colleges understate degree costs, 65 percent omit critical details about aid packages, and 31 percent list loans as grants. Instead of leaving it up to parents and students to figure it out, colleges should be required to provide a clear written explanation of the terms and conditions of their aid, including any loans, grants, and scholarships. Loans and loan terms should be clearly and fully laid out.

Unlike tuition and cost estimates left to colleges' discretion, the federal Housing and Urban Development (HUD) agency requires a detailed mortgage closing statement, including loan terms, projected monthly payments, fees, and other closing costs. Using the HUD precedent, all colleges should be required to use a binding standardized form that explicitly states the total costs of attending the institution.

Protecting against Zombie Colleges

While some universities, especially the Ivies, are generally doing well financially, others are near death or are like zombies who are already dead but don't know it. These zombie colleges include some small nonprofit and for-profit universities struggling with low enrollment and high costs. From 2020 to 2023, at least forty-four colleges closed, merged, or announced plans to that effect.

Seventy percent of students impacted by a college closure experience it as abrupt.[1] For instance, for-profit Argosy University-Hawai'i closed in 2019, leaving 800 students in the lurch.[2] Seven hundred students were left scrambling when West Virginia's Alderson Broaddus University, a private nonprofit Baptist university, suddenly closed in 2023. Having graduated from a college or university that no longer exists devalues the legitimacy of a degree and hurts graduates seeking references from past instructors. It can also make it challenging to obtain an official transcript.

Transparency is essential when determining whether a particular college or university is a worthwhile investment. The Securities and Exchange Commission (SEC) requires all publicly traded companies to post their financial statements in annual reports; otherwise, few investors would invest in a corporation without having crucial financial information. Yet, students and families are expected to invest their tuition dollars in a college without having essential knowledge about their investment. While the tax records of for-profit and nonprofit institutions are available, they are not easy to access or easily understandable for ordinary people.

To protect students and parents, all nonprofit, for-profit, and public institutions should be required to provide a simplified financial statement that lists assets, loans, financial obligations, and endowments. This statement should also include any plans for growth, mergers, and planned cuts to programs, courses, and degrees. A financial statement can help families assess the risks and benefits when comparing colleges. While some comparative data can be accessed through the Department of Education's College Scorecard (https://collegescorecard.ed.gov/), it does not address the long-term viability of an institution.

Predatory For-profit Colleges

Categorizing for-profit educational institutions is confusing since it covers everything from cosmetology schools to four-year colleges. In this context, for-profit colleges refer to four-year institutions that offer at least a baccalaureate degree.

For-profit colleges potentially threaten low-income students since they often falsely promise nonexistent jobs and lucrative careers after graduation. Some of this deception is partly attributable to admissions counselors who are paid per recruited student. What recruiters and for-profit colleges hide is their high dropout rate, averaging as high as 34 percent in the first year. While some for-profits claim graduation rates of 62 percent,[3] those high rates are suspect. In particular, instructors may be pressured to give students passing grades despite a lack of effort or regular attendance.

Even if students graduate, they don't necessarily receive an education that prepares them for success or a sufficient income to repay their student loans. The more unlucky graduates are often left unemployed with high debt and low salaries since their degrees are undervalued and not competitive in the job market. While the Biden administration's Gainful Employment rule denies federal funding to higher education programs where student debts are too high or earnings are too low, for-profits can easily evade this penalty by becoming nonprofit or selling their operations to a nonprofit corporation.[4]

For-profit colleges have few valuable purposes not met by public two- and four-year institutions. For instance, the primary role of for-profits is as "second chance" institutions that provide hassle-free enrollment and convenient online degrees. Those roles, however, are now being usurped by aggressive public universities that have online degree programs and charge lower tuition. Another function of for-profits is to minimize unnecessary course requirements by allowing credit for life experience. Open-enrollment public institutions are now replicating those functions. Public colleges' institutional legitimacy is an important asset, something for-profit colleges lack.

One problem facing public universities is the lag time in tooling up for online education, a historical strength of for-profits. Buying up struggling for-profit colleges at bargain prices has shortened this lag time. For example, the University of Idaho bought the struggling University of Phoenix, once the largest for-profit university in America. The University of Arizona purchased Ashford University, while Purdue University purchased Kaplan University and rebranded it Purdue University Global. Although for-profits are becoming obsolete, they are still important to American higher education.

Reinforcing the Core Values of Higher Education

While commodification and corporatization erode the moral center of higher education, they also erode the core values that traditionally undergirded the academy.

Freedom of Expression

A fundamental academic value is the freedom to think about and openly discuss various issues without fear of intimidation or retribution. Nevertheless, there are limits to that freedom. For instance, the disastrous House of Representatives testimony on antisemitism by the presidents of Harvard, University of Pennsylvania, and MIT demonstrated that freedom of expression and free speech have limits when singling out and attacking a group's ethnicity and religion.

In 2014, the University of Chicago published the Chicago Statement, a set of principles to protect freedom of expression and free speech on college campuses. By 2022, eighty-four US colleges and universities had adopted all or part of the statement. Some of the statement's fundamental principles include the belief that universities should not protect students from ideas and opinions they disagree with. The statement maintained that free speech is essential to campus culture and can have multiple forms of expression. On the other hand, the statement points out that freedom of expression does not include blocking commencement speakers because a group of students disagrees with them.

One element of "woke" culture is the provision of "safe spaces" for students, which too often translates into spaces where their ideas, opinions, and values are unchallenged. Colleges need to be safe from intimidation, coercion, threats, taunts, and hate speech, but not from ideas. Returning to the basics of higher education would include guaranteeing the free expression of ideas and speech on campus without fearing harassment or intimidation from students or faculty members.

Strengthening the Core Curriculum

American colleges are obliged to educate and prepare students for living in a liberal democracy. A knowledge of history, literature, government, science, sociology, anthropology, social psychology, and economics, among other subjects, is vital in developing the critical thinking skills needed to repudiate the misinformation and conspiracies rampant in social media. Critical thinking skills are also necessary to combat the global rise in authoritarian populism that threatens the fragile experiment in democracy.

A fundamental market principle is to give consumers what they want, or at least what the company thinks they want (or wants them to want). This view is also embedded in a commodified system of higher education. It is reflected in the diminishing importance of the core curriculum, which many students view as an obstacle to their major.

The nonprofit American Council of Trustees and Alumni (ACTA) collects data on the state of core curriculums nationwide. Their 2022 report titled "What Will They Learn?" found that as core curriculums weaken across the United States, many colleges fail to graduate students with the broad knowledge and critical thinking skills necessary for responsible citizenship. Specifically, the 2022 ACTA study found that fewer than one-fifth of colleges and universities require students to study government or history, and less than one-third require a literature course.[5] Of the 1,130 US colleges and universities ACTA ranked in 2022, only twenty-two received an "A" grade, while 68 percent received a "C" or worse.[6]

Some universities include a broad range of course options in their core curriculum, and students can choose from various courses in different columns or themes. As a result, graduates could lack a core knowledge of science, math, economics, political science, world and US history, philosophy, literature, and social sciences that is expected of a university-educated graduate. Strengthening the core curriculum, which defines the knowledge expected of an educated person, would require a full two years of introductory courses in core areas, including a required semester-long course in world civilizations that focuses on the history, art, music, poetry, law, medicine, social science, and physical science.

Teaching First

Students attend college to learn and be taught. In contrast, the main perks in academia (salary, promotion, and a lighter teaching load) come from success in research rather than teaching. Many large research-based universities employ a hierarchal model in allocating faculty resources and perks. For instance, a grant-funded researcher is usually at the top of the hierarchy and will likely be tenured and promoted. Well-published scholars who bring prestige but no research dollars are valued below grant-based researchers. The last rung of the hierarchy is reserved for faculty who predominantly teach. Faculty in research-intensive universities that primarily teach have diminished chances for tenure and promotion, even while they carry the brunt of the department's teaching load. Teaching faculty are often seen as disposable since, unlike researchers, adjuncts can readily replace them. Returning to basics would place good teaching on par with research and scholarship for tenure, promotion, and merit. In effect, teaching faculty would be accorded the same status as research and scholarship faculty since undergraduates benefit more from good teaching than research or scholarship.

Institutional Reform

Corporate business values increasingly drive significant decisions about how a university operates, for whom, and for what purpose. These values determine the winners, the losers, and the beneficiaries.

Putting Colleges Back into the Hands of People Who Understand Them

Chapter 4 notes that the proliferation of administrative positions has outstripped the growth in faculty positions, as most universities now have more administrators than faculty members. The large number of highly paid administrators is draining university resources and adding to the cost of higher education. One way to address the administrative bloat in public colleges is for an independent organization or governmental entity to evaluate a university's workflow to determine if there are administrative positions that can be merged or eliminated. This administrative audit could also establish guidelines for the reasonable remuneration of various administrative positions, including dean, provosts, and chancellor/presidents.

College administrators are appointed through different routes. Some administrators come from teaching, others are recent graduates who go straight into administration positions, and others come from business. While colleges were once managed on a more or less collegial basis with strong Faculty Senates having a voice in determining a university's direction, most colleges now use a top-down model that replaces the power of the faculty with the power of professional administrators. In turn, many of these administrators make decisions without fully understanding the mission and culture of the university. Those decisions are too often based on short-term planning and cost-cutting that ignore the longer-term implications of the decision.

Instead of occupying open-ended administrative positions, college presidents, provosts, and deans could serve on a rotating time-limited basis, similar to some European universities where senior faculty members assume administrative appointments for a limited period. Appointing existing senior faculty members to administrative positions would ensure continuity and an institutional memory. Moreover, an administrator's decisions would be tempered, given the knowledge that they would eventually return to the faculty. Besides, there is no easily definable knowledge or skill set unique to the role of a college president that senior faculty members involved in university committees could not master. College presidents without an academic background are sometimes hired directly from government or business based on the assumption that they know how to manage. Unfortunately, this often doesn't always work out for the institution or the candidate.

Ensconced in their offices, administrators risk losing touch with students, faculty, and the larger university community. To stay in touch with the university community, students, and faculty, college presidents, provosts, deans, and department chairs should be required to teach at least one course a year.

Accomplished researchers and well-known scholars are often exempt from teaching responsibilities, or their teaching is restricted to small doctoral seminars. Undergraduate students are, therefore, denied exposure to active researchers and productive scholars. This unfairness (undergraduates pay the salaries of researchers and scholars) could be remedied by requiring active researchers and scholars to teach at least one introductory undergraduate course in their field. Undergraduate students should not be taught solely by adjuncts and graduate assistants.

Institutional Overreach

Many colleges and universities are forced to "punch above their weight class" due to competition from neighboring institutions, tight budgets, declining enrollment, and the need for grant-funded research to compensate for budget shortfalls. Some colleges have tried to become research institutions by adding low-quality graduate programs based on low admissions standards to survive. While lowering admissions standards can draw students rejected from other graduate programs, it can also lead to unemployed and debt-burdened students who graduate from colleges with poor reputations. To combat a "race to the bottom," state licensing and national accrediting bodies should stiffen the requirements for accrediting graduate programs. One way to ensure that accrediting bodies reject low-quality degree programs is to require them to include representatives from state education departments or independent organizations. This oversight is critical since accrediting bodies derive revenue from accrediting programs and, therefore, have limited incentive to be overly rigorous.

Raising Taxes on University Endowments

As Chapter 3 demonstrates, endowments in nonprofit universities run in the billions of dollars and, in some cases, close to $50 billion. By comparison, Missouri's state budget was $51 billion in 2023. The 2017 Tax Cuts and Jobs Act and the Bipartisan Budget Act of 2018 levied a 1.4 percent excise tax on the endowment income of universities with at least 500 tuition-paying students and net assets of at least $500,000 per student. Despite the intent, the 1.4 percent tax raised only minimal revenue. Doubling the tax on endowments could help level the playing field by funneling additional tax revenues into Pell Grants or student loan forgiveness.

Improving Relationships with Trustees.

Boards of Regents or Trustees often do not include (or purposely exclude) stakeholders like students, staff, or faculty members. Board members are consequently kept in the dark since they are only fed information from the administration. To control the flow of information, administrators sometimes erect impenetrable firewalls between faculty and the board, and in some cases, faculty are expressly prohibited from communicating with board members. Having faculty, staff, and students elected to these oversight boards would enhance the flow of ideas and help cement a more unified academic community.

Making College More Affordable

The good news is that college costs are declining in relation to inflation. According to the College Board, before adjusting for inflation, the average 2023–4 tuition and fees for a full-time in-state student in public universities was $11,260, or 2.5 percent higher than in 2022–3. Out-of-state students in public universities paid $29,150, or 3 percent higher than in 2022–3, and students in private nonprofit schools paid $41,540, or 4 percent higher than in 2022–3, before adjusting for inflation.[7]

The bad news is that much of that stabilization is related to a decline in quality. For instance, it is unlikely that significant savings came from reducing administrative bloat, ending the use of consultants, cutting managerial wages, or cutting major NCAA sports programs. Instead, most of the savings came from cuts in teaching, namely, fewer course offerings, fewer sections with larger class sizes, fewer degree offerings, and the increased use of adjuncts, graduate students, and contract workers to replace faculty members who retired or moved to another university.

A metric helps plot the real rise and fall of college costs. One way to view the costs of attending college is in relation to the average wage. In 1989, college tuition at a four-year public university was

$1,780, and the average yearly wage was $20,099. College tuition was equal to roughly 9 percent of the average wage. Tuition at a four-year public college in 2023 jumped to $11,280 while the average wage rose to $59,428. Hence, college tuition in 2023 equaled 19 percent of the average wage, or double that of 1989. It is little wonder some working-class students consider college beyond their financial reach.

One way to cut costs is to calibrate public college tuition to the average wage in a state. Using 1989 as a metric, public college tuition would correlate to 9 to 10 percent of the average yearly wage. This would lower tuition costs and calibrate the rise in college costs to wage growth. The amount of state funding would be based on meeting that metric.

Increase Pell Grants

Finding the money to pay for college is daunting for many students. As Chapter 1 points out, the value of Pell Grants (which makes college possible for low-income students) has plummeted. In 2023, Pell covered less than 30 percent of the costs at a public university and less than 20 percent at private nonprofit institutions. To make higher education more accessible to low-income students, Pell Grants should be doubled to cover 60 percent of the costs of a public university and 40 percent of the costs at nonprofits. Pell Grants should also be updated yearly (like Social Security) based on rising college costs to slow the downward slide.[8] On the other hand, the value of Pell Grants has fallen so far that even these increases will not bring it back to 1983 funding levels.

Social Welfare Supports

Many students are unaware of financial assistance besides Pell grants, such as SNAP (food stamp), housing assistance, EITC (Earned Income Tax Credit for working students), and other social welfare programs. One innovative approach is Up$tart, a software program that integrates applications for Pell grants, federal student loans, and social benefits for low-income students. Accessing these services can increase student income by an average of $8,144 per year and contribute to a 5 percent increase in student retention.[9]

Alternative Ways to Afford College.

An alternative way for students to pay for higher education is through a community service option started before college. This could include AmeriCorps VISTA, FEMA Corps, or Peace Corps. The Segal AmeriCorps Education Award is awarded after completing an AmeriCorps term of service and enrolling in the National Service Trust. This award is used to repay student loans and to cover educational expenses at eligible institutions. The amount is based on the length of the completed service.

A significant problem in the Segal AmeriCorps Education Award is that the maximum award is only equivalent to the maximum value of a Pell Grant in the year the award was approved. Since the maximum Pell Grant ($6,895) covered only 30 percent of college costs in 2023, volunteers must find the additional 70 percent. In addition, this option makes little sense from a financial standpoint since the median yearly salary of a sixteen to nineteen-year-old was $31,668 in 2022,[10] or almost five times more than a Pell Grant. If a student saved just 22 percent of their income, it would be higher than the maximum Pell Grant. Alternatively, a reform could provide volunteers with free tuition in a public institution plus the full value of the Pell Grant. Since the average US college tuition was $11,744 in 2023, this would increase the value of the total award to $18,639 a year, making public service more attractive to a broader group of students.

Cutting Textbook Costs

The high cost of textbooks, sometimes hundreds of dollars, is a significant cost burden for students. The $11 million the Biden administration targeted for the Open Textbooks Pilot program in 2022 was a step in the right direction. However, more funding is still needed to make a broader range of free college textbooks available. Not coincidentally, free textbooks could be created by training instructors to use AI.

Standardize the Transfer of College Credits

Another expense for students involves the transfer of credits when moving between colleges and universities. One in three students transfer to a new school at least once, and about 62 percent attend another public university. On average, students who transfer schools lose 20 to 43 percent of their transfer credits, equal to one or more semesters. Often, this loss occurs when moving from a community college to a four-year institution.[11] The decision about which credits to accept and for how many hours can be inconsistent and may relate more to garnering additional tuition dollars than legitimate academic concerns. To counter this, states should require that all courses completed in an accredited public institution be accepted as transfer credits in the discipline in which they were taken.

Provide Lower-Cost Student Housing

In addition to tuition, a significant cost of attending college involves housing. The National Center for Education Statistics (NCES) estimates that in 2021, the yearly room and board in a four-year public institution cost $11,963, and $13,488 in a private university.[12] Aside from on-campus housing, there are no other options except in the private housing market. The rising costs of private market rentals can cause students to jam as many people and beds into an apartment as possible, leading to conflicts and unhealthy living conditions.

By contrast, off-campus student housing in Norway is run by a student organization that manages 8,900 housing units for singles, couples, and families. The units are small for single students, with a single bed, a bathroom, and a shared kitchen on each floor. There are supermarkets nearby, and students are responsible for their food. This housing arrangement is notably less expensive in cities with high rental rates, such as Oslo. While austere by American standards, this type of student housing may be preferable to a severely overcrowded apartment or couch-surfing. In the US context, colleges wanting to curtail student housing costs could collaborate to develop less expensive joint housing solutions.

A Student's Bill of Rights

Since a college education has become a commodity, student consumers should have the right to refuse to pay for things that do not directly improve the quality of their education. This could include college sports programs, stadiums, state-of-the-art gyms, educational consultants, and other questionable expenses paid for by tuition and fees.

As consumers, students should also be represented on all college committees and the Board of Trustees. As part of a Student Bill of Rights, they should be provided with full-time instructors who are mentors and available for consultation around coursework. Graduate teaching assistants should be paid a fair wage plus benefits and not be exploited by teaching multiple courses with large student enrollments. In addition, students should not be pawns for politicians' political aspirations. Colleges and universities should be independent and devoid of party politics and political meddling by ambitious politicians. Lastly, students should not be caught off guard by having courses and degree programs cut without their input.

Low-Income Students

As the book notes, low-income students face the greatest risk in attending college. In particular, the deck is stacked against them due to inadequate academic preparation resulting from underfunded and underperforming public schools, a shortage of high school guidance counselors, the limited ability of their families to provide financial help, and colleges' reliance on SAT and ACT scores. Unlike middle- and upper-class students, low-income students often lack enhancement opportunities like one-on-one tutoring, SAT and ACT exam preparation, and enrichment-focused after-school activities. The result is that the graduation rate for low-income students, especially students of color, is below that of white students. Moreover, when low-income students drop out, they remain responsible for repaying their student loans. This explains why students from families with the lowest income have a long-term default rate of 41 percent compared to the overall federal student loan default rate of 2.3 percent.[13] In short, comprehensive reforms are needed to mitigate the financial risks for low-income students and lessen the punishment for their potential failure.

Cutting Institutional Costs

High institutional costs are embedded in the tuition and fee structure and help to make college unaffordable for many working-class families.

Cutting Administrative Costs

One way to curb institutional costs is to reduce both administrative salaries and the number of administrators. In many places, the salaries of college presidents eclipse that of CEOs in mid-size corporations. As Chapter 4 illustrates, many university presidents earn millions, and some earn multiple millions. One way to curb exorbitant administrative salaries is to calibrate them to full professors' salaries plus a modest administrative stipend. For example, a college president's salary could be based on their previous salary plus a 40 to 50 percent stipend. Alternatively, their salary could be based on multiples of a median professor's salary in that institution, including in-kind benefits, such as a campus residence and use of a car. A similar metric could be developed to determine the salary for provosts and deans.

Eliminating Unnecessary Consultants.

It is enigmatic why universities with business schools, law schools, education departments, public administration, and other departments use expensive outside consultants. Consultants often know little about a university's culture since their charge is to recommend ways to cut costs, often by eliminating courses and degree programs (rarely administrative positions). To cut costs, in-house resources should be utilized before employing consultants, and faculty should help vet that decision. In addition, consultants like McKinsey should not be allowed to hide behind "confidential, proprietary information" that conceals their recommendations, proposals, and fees.

End the Use of Online Program Managers (OPM)

The popularity of online education is growing, and schools without a robust online component risk losing tuition dollars. Scrambling to meet student demand, colleges are increasingly relying on for-profit OPMs to deliver their online courses and degrees. Some of this reliance is due to laziness since OPMs offer a quick, turnkey solution compared to the work of developing an online degree or course. This decision comes at a high cost since OPMs can take from 45 to 60 percent of tuition dollars, a loss supposedly compensated by increased enrollment. On the other hand, some schools have realized that the tuition going to OPMs results in a net revenue loss, and aggressive OPMs who sign up for competing programs reduce the overall number of applicants.

Instead of relying on OPMs, colleges should use their IT and education resources to develop their online programs. While high development costs are a stumbling block, those costs will be recouped in the long term by reclaiming 100 percent of online tuition. Schools lacking the technical capacity to develop online programs could become part of a consortium to share knowledge and resources. Despite their success, OPMs will eventually become obsolete as universities recognize that losing over 45 percent of their tuition is unsustainable.

Shutting or Consolidating Low-Enrollment Colleges

Surges in college enrollment in the 1960s and beyond led to building new colleges and enlarging older ones. The current sharp enrollment decline (projected to drop even further) has resulted in low-enrollment colleges that are increasing overall college costs.

Choosing the location of a public college is often the result of pork barrel legislation. For instance, New York State has 20 million people and forty four-year public colleges and universities. Many New York state colleges, like Morrisville, SUNY Potsdam, and SUNY Purchase, have less than 4,000 students, with some having less than 2,000. New York also has thirty community colleges; a third have less than 2,000 students. New York is not alone in its large number of public colleges. North Carolina has 10 million people, sixteen four-year public universities, and fifty-eight community colleges. Of those sixteen colleges, three have enrollments of under 3,000 students. While no established guideline exists for the minimal size of a public college, institutions with small enrollments are costly and nonviable in the long term.

Despite the costs, significant community benefits are realized from a local college. For instance, even though New York's SUNY Plattsburgh has less than 10,000 students, the yearly tax revenues generated by the university totals more than $56 million, injecting more than $172 million into the region. Students contribute nearly $55 million to the area by spending on off-campus housing, food, transportation, etc. Plus, the college helps locals to stay in rural New York State. If the public college system is to remain financially viable, tough choices will have to be made around closing or merging low-enrollment colleges. Policy choices will involve the issue of quantity versus quality: Is having a larger number of universities with inadequate funding more desirable than fewer but better-funded universities?

Reducing Duplicate Degree Programs and Courses

Colleges and universities near each other that offer the same degrees drive up the cost of education. For instance, there are thirty-five Masters of Social Work (MSW) programs in New York State, with thirteen in the New York City metropolitan area alone. Five of those programs are in public institutions. North Carolina has twelve MSW programs and twenty-three Bachelor of Social Work (BSW) programs. Ohio has twenty-seven BSW and eleven MSW programs. There are 800 accredited MSW and BSW programs in the United States compared to 120 in the UK. The saturation of social work degree programs is similar to other professions. For instance, California has eighteen law schools, the District of Columbia has six, Florida and Illinois have ten, New York has sixteen, Texas has nine, and Virginia has eight. The Council on Education for Public Health accredits 252 schools and programs: sixty-seven schools of public health, 158 public health programs, and twenty-seven standalone baccalaureate programs. By comparison, ninety-eight UK universities offer degrees in public health.

Since only a finite number of students are interested in a given field, saturating that field by offering the same degree in multiple locations thins out the applicant pool, reduces enrollment, and increases the per-student cost. A saturated degree market also weakens existing programs by pressuring them to lower admissions standards to maintain enrollment.

The higher education market does not respond to competition like the private marketplace. While marketplace competition often leads to better quality goods at lower prices, competition in tertiary education does the opposite: it can lead to lower quality and higher prices as institutions make up for lost revenues by increasing class sizes and employing adjunct faculty.

Degree programs in close proximity can be economically rationalized by reducing the duplication of courses through course sharing. Specifically, two or more institutions can collaborate to make their courses available to each other's students. Sharing can be cost-effective (the home institution charges students more than they pay the other institution) when colleges have extra space for online classes or want to add new programs but lack the resources. It can also help colleges replace low-quality courses with higher-quality ones from other institutions. Most schools use academic brokers like Acadeum, who get 25 percent of the tuition for course hosting and platform access. Instead of paying brokers, university-run consortiums could manage course-sharing projects themselves without losing tuition.

NCAA College Sports Programs

Chapter 5 notes that most universities lose money (sometimes in the millions) in their NCAA sports programs. Addressing this issue, however, poses a conundrum. For one, NCAA college sports like football and basketball are high-stakes games, with top college competitors spending millions on training facilities, coaching salaries, nutritionists, physical therapists, physicians, and other support personnel. Since vast sums of money are required to compete in the top echelons of NCAA sports, any sports-related budget cuts will likely make a university's team less competitive. The decline in competitiveness means less revenue since sports fans generally don't attend games for teams that rarely win. Here lies the conundrum. If colleges continue to fund NCAA sports at the current level, they lose money. If they cut funding for NCAA sports, they also lose money. As discussed in Chapter 5, the only viable action is to exit the merry-go-round and remove money-losing NCAA sports from university funding.

Final Thoughts

American exceptionalism is moored in the belief that solutions to social problems must be uniquely American and that nothing can be gained from the experiences of other countries. Rejecting this exceptionalism would permit the United States to learn how other countries educate their students at far lower costs and with equal, if not better, educational outcomes. For instance, the United States spent $35,346 to educate a tertiary student in 2019 compared to $29,687 in the UK, $26,046 in Sweden, $25,019 in Norway, $22,334 in Canada, $21,658 in Denmark, $21,329 in Austria, $20,625 in Australia, $19,608 in Germany, and $18,135 in France.[14] The lower per-student expenditures in OECD universities did not come on the backs of faculty. The average US faculty salary in 2022 was $79,640 compared to $77,000 in Germany, $105,000 in Australia, $77,000 in the UK, $73,000 in Canada, and $74,000 in France. Nor did the high costs of US tertiary education come from ambitious research and development. In 2019, per student expenditure on research and development in the United States was $4,093 compared to $17,527 in Switzerland, $13,961 in Sweden, $8,460 in Germany, $7,589 in the Netherlands, $6,644 in Australia, $5,803 in the UK, and $5,405 in France.[15] It is difficult to argue that the results justify the high costs of US education.

MIT, Harvard, Stanford, and University of California-Berkeley took the top four slots in the 2024 QS World University Rankings.[16] While an impressive showing, it belies the fact that only a tiny fraction of the 20+ million US undergraduates attend these universities. Most students attend less stellar state universities like the University of Nebraska, Appalachian State University, the University of South Dakota, St. Mary's University, and thousands of other colleges and universities. While America has some of the best universities in the world, it is mistaken to claim that America has the best universities. In fact, US universities are in the middle range of world universities based on world rankings.

Americans are falling behind other countries in college graduates. As Paul Tough points out, the number of British undergraduates rose 12 percent since 2016 compared to an 8 percent drop in America. Sixty-seven percent of Canadians between twenty-five and thirty-four graduated from a two- or four-year college, which is 15 percentage points higher than in America. OECD countries have increased the number of their college graduates by 20 percentage points since 2000, and eleven smaller countries now have a better-educated labor force than the United States.[17] In short, Americans are rejecting college in large numbers while students in the rest of the world are flocking to campuses. Recent polls demonstrate that this decline corresponds to Americans' increasingly hostile view of higher education.[18]

Several factors explain the skepticism and distrust of higher education, including the view of college graduates as elitists who abhor the values of the 60 percent of Americans without a college degree. Right-wing politicians and pundits also stoke the long-standing anti-intellectualism. Trump typified the anti-intellectualism in 2016 when he stated that, "We won with young. We won with old. We won with highly educated. We won with poorly educated. I love the poorly educated."

College education is being sold in the same way that home ownership was sold in the early 2000s. In both instances, the road to the American middle class involved either mortgage debt or student loans. The real cost of these two commodities was obscured by the debt instruments that made them appear affordable. Nowadays, consumers are seeing through the ruse. As another marketplace commodity, higher education must listen to the market. The latest polls show that the market has spoken, and the public is losing interest in the product. It will be dangerous for colleges and universities not to heed the message. To regain its appeal, higher education must become more financially feasible for a larger number of students and families. Tuition needs to be lowered instead of relying on student loans to make education look financially possible.

Making higher education more inclusive will require a return to the basics. This means ending wasteful spending on consultants, runaway administrative salaries, out-of-control bureaucratic growth, and expensive sports programs. It will also involve implementing austerity measures that move universities from resort venues to ones whose primary mission is education, not entertainment. Public universities must stop spending on gourmet food courts, tony student centers, four-star dormitory rooms, world-class gyms, and the edifices administrators build to memorialize themselves.

American universities have been criticized for not meeting a series of impossible expectations. While a college education can bring some people out of poverty and into the middle class, it was never meant to be an anti-poverty program. Consequently, it is unfair to saddle higher education with the direct responsibility to end poverty or promote social equality since other social policies have that responsibility. If higher education brings people out of poverty, it is only because it helps them to develop their human capital.

Colleges have the simple responsibility to affordably and roundly educate students without regard to race, gender, ethnicity, or religion. In 2007, the Committee of Ministers of the European Union defined higher education goals as preparation for sustainable employment, preparation for being an active citizen in a democratic society, personal development, and the development of a broad and advanced knowledge base through teaching, learning, and research.[19] Driven off course by commodification and corporatization, colleges and universities must rediscover their mission and reinvigorate higher education's fundamental principles and goals.

Notes

Preface

1. Jill Barshay, "Poll: Nearly half of parents don't want their kids to go straight to a four-year college," *The Hechinger Report,* April 7, 2021, https://hechingerreport.org/poll-nearly-half-of-parents-dont-want-their-kids-to-go-to-a-four-year-college/#:~:text=A%20Gallup%20survey%2C%20commissioned%20by,no%20obstacles%2C%20financial%20or%20otherwise.
2. Jessica Bryant, "69% of Students Say You Don't Need College to Be Successful," *Best Colleges,* September 14, 2022, www.bestcolleges.com/research/do-you-need-college-to-be-successful/

Chapter 1

1. Drew Desilver, "For most U.S. workers, real wages have barely budged in decades," *Pew Research Center,* August 7, 2018, www.pewresearch.org/short-reads/2018/08/07/for-most-us-workers-real-wages-have-barely-budged-for-decades/
2. Margaret Cahalan et al., "Indicators of Higher Education Equity in the United States: 2022 Historical Trend Report," *The Pell Institute for the Study of Opportunity in Higher Education,* 2022, https://pellinstitute.wpengine.com/wp-content/uploads/2022/10/publications-Indicators_of_Higher_Education_Equity_in_the_US_2022_Historical_Trend_Report.pdf
3. "Social Capital and Economic Mobility," *Opportunity Insights,* Harvard University, 2022, https://opportunityinsights.org/
4. Josh Moody, "A Guide to the Changing Number of U.S. Universities," *U.S. News & World Report,* April 27, 2021, www.usnews.com/education/best-colleges/articles/how-many-universities-are-in-the-us-and-why-that-number-is-changing

5   Cahalan et al., "Indicators of Higher Education Equity in the United States."
6   "America's elite universities are bloated, complacent and illiberal," *The Economist*, March 4, 2024.
7   "Columbia whistleblower on exposing college rankings: 'They are worthless,'" *The Guardian*, September 16, 2022, www.theguardian.com/us-news/2022/sep/16/columbia-whistleblower-us-news-rankings-michael-thaddeus
8   Amanda Ripley, "Why is college in America so expensive?" *The Atlantic*, September 11, 2018, www.theatlantic.com/education/archive/2018/09/why-is-college-so-expensive-in-america/569884/
9   Anthony Carnevale, Ban Cheah, & Emma Wenzinger, *The College Payoff: More Education Doesn't Always Mean More Earnings* (Washington, DC: Georgetown University, 2021), www.cew.georgetown.edu/collegepayoff2021/
10 Ibid.
11 Malcolm Harris, *Kids These Days: Human Capital and the Making of Millennials* (New York, NY: Little Brown, 2017).
12 Carmen DeNavas-Walt & Bernadette Proctor, "Income and Poverty in the United States: 2014, Current Population Reports," U.S. Department of Commerce (U.S. Census Bureau, September 2015): 60–252, www.census.gov/content/dam/Census/library/publications/2015/demo/p60-252.pdf
13 Ibid.
14 "Unemployment rate by educational attainment and age, monthly, not seasonally adjusted: 25 to 34 years," Federal Reserve Bank of St. Louis, April 2023, https://fred.stlouisfed.org/release/tables?eid=1197546&rid=50
15 Ibid.
16 Bureau of Labor Statistics, "Weekly earnings by educational attainment in second quarter 2018," *TED: The Economics Daily*, July 28, 2018, www.bls.gov/opub/ted/2018/weekly-earnings-by-educational-attainment-in-second-quarter-2018.htm
17 Bureau of Labor Statistics, "Highlights of women's earnings in 2020," *BLS Reports*, September 2021, www.bls.gov/opub/reports/womens-earnings/2020/home.htm
18 Women's Bureau, "Women's median weekly earnings by educational attainment, race, and Hispanic ethnicity (annual)," *US Department of Labor*, 2021, www.dol.gov/agencies/wb/data/earnings/Women-median-weekly-earnings-educational-attainment-race-Hispanic-ethnicity. Erin Bisesti & Marc A. García, "The Cost of Being a Woman,"

Research Brief #79 (Syracuse University, October18, 2022), https://surface.syr.edu/cgi/viewcontent.cgi?article=1194&context=lerner

19. DeNavas-Walt & Proctor, "Income and Poverty in the United States: 2014, Current Population Reports."
20. Deborah Weiss et al., "When Does Selective College Matter?" *Northwestern Now* (Northwestern Center on Law, Business and Economics, 2021), https://news.northwestern.edu/stories/2021/12/when-does-selective-college-matter/
21. Gillian White, "Does going to a selective college matter? For many majors, not so much," *The Atlantic*, August 17, 2015, www.theatlantic.com/business/archive/2015/08/does-college-matter/400898/
22. Raj Chetty et al., "Mobility Report Cards: The Role of Colleges in Intergenerational Mobility," *National Bureau of Economic Research Working Paper Series 23618*, July 2017, www.nber.org/papers/w23618
23. Pell Institute, "Indicators of higher education equity in the United States: 2016 historical trend report," *Pell Institute for the Study of Opportunity in the United States*, 2016, www.pellinstitute.org/downloads/publications-Indicators_of_Higher_Education_Equity_in_the_US_2016_Historical_Trend_Report.pdf
24. Joel McFarland et al., "The Condition of Education 2017," *U.S. Department of Education*, 2018 (NCES 2017–144), https://nces.ed.gov/pubsearch/pubsinfo.asp?pubid=2017144.; Pell Institute, "Indicators of higher education equity in the United States: 2016 historical trend report."
25. Eric Eide, Michael Hilmer, & Mark Showalter, "Is It Where You Go or What You Study? The Relative Influence of College Selectivity and College Major on Earnings," *Contemporary Economic Policy* 34, no. 1 (January 2016): 37–46.
26. Stacy Dale & Alan Krueger, "Estimating the return to college selectivity of the career using administrative earning data," *Journal of Human Resources* 49, no. 2 (Spring 2014): 323–58.
27. Frank Bruni, *Where You Go Is Not Who You'll Be* (New York: Grand Central Publishing, 2016).
28. Jonathan Wai, "Frank Bruni is wrong about Ivy League schools," *Quartz*, March 22, 2015, https://qz.com/367077/frank-bruni-is-wrong-about-ivy-league-schools
29. Anthony Carnevale, Ban Cheah, & Martin Van Der Werf, "A First Try at Roi: Ranking 4,500 Colleges," *Georgetown University Center on Education and the Workforce*, 2019, https://cew.georgetown.edu/cew-reports/collegeroi/

30 Danielle Douglas-Gabriel & Susan Svrluga, "More elite universities settle suit over alleged 'price-fixing' aid policies," *The Washington Post*, January 24, 2024, www.washingtonpost.com/education/2024/01/24/colleges-price-fixing-financial-aid-settlement/

31 Melanie Hanson, "Pell Grant Statistics," *Education Data Initiative*, June 5, 2023, https://educationdata.org/pell-grant-statistics#:~:text=Nationwide%2C%2034%25%20of%20undergraduate%20students,Pell%20Grant%20award%20is%20%244%2C491.

32 Council for the Opportunity in Education, "Indicators of Higher Education Equity in the United States: 2022," *Pell Institute*, 2023, https://www.pellinstitute.org/pell-institute-indicators-2022/

33 McFarland, Hussar, de Brey, Snyder, Wang, Wilkinson-Flicker, Gebrekristos, Zhang, Rathbun, Barmer, Bullock Mann, & Hinz, "The Condition of Education 2017."

34 Tyler Kingkade, "Pell Grants cover smallest portion of college costs in history as GOP calls for cuts," *The Huffington Post*, August 29, 2012, www.huffingtonpost.com/2012/08/27/pell-grants-college-costs_n_1835081.html

35 Melanie Hanson, "Average Cost of College & Tuition," *Education Data Initiative*, April 3, 2023, https://educationdata.org/average-cost-of-college#:~:text=The%20average%20cost%20of%20attendance,or%20%24218%2C004%20over%204%20years.

36 National Center for Education Statistics (NCES), "Trends in Ratio of Pell Grant to Total Price of Attendance and Federal Loan Receipt," *Data Point,* August 2019 (NCES 2019–489), https://nces.ed.gov/pubs2019/2019489rev.pdf

37 Meris Stansbury, "Is it time to rethink the term nontraditional student?" *Ecampus News*, September 30, 2016, www.ecampusnews.com/2016/09/30/nontraditional-student-nces/

38 Annette Lareau, *Unequal Childhoods* (Berkeley, CA: University of California Press, 2011).

39 American School Counselor Association, "School Counselor Roles & Ratios," 2023, www.schoolcounselor.org/About-School-Counseling/School-Counselor-Roles-Ratios#:~:text=Although%20ASCA%20recommends%20a%20250,Counselor%20Ratios%20(2021%2D2022)

40 Jill Barshay, "Proof points: New poll points to college and career benefits of Greek life despite criticism," *The Hechninger Report*, July 19, 2021, https://hechingerreport.org/proof-points-new-poll-points-to-college-and-career-benefits-of-greek-life-despite-criticism/

NOTES

41 Gallup, "Fraternity, and Sorority Membership Linked to Higher Well-Being for College Grad," May 27, 2014, https://news.gallup.com/opinion/gallup/173630/fraternity-sorority-membership-linked-higher-college-grads.aspx

42 Barshay, "Proof points: New poll points to college and career benefits of Greek life."

43 Tyler Epps, "Is Greek Life Worth It?" *Best Colleges*, May 5, 2023, www.bestcolleges.com/blog/is-greek-life-worth-it/

44 NCES, "The Condition of Education 2020, COE—College Student Employment," 2020, https://nces.ed.gov/programs/coe/indicator/ssa/college-student-employment

45 Anthony Carnevale, "Working while in college might hurt students more than it helps," *CNBC*, November 21, 2019, www.cnbc.com/2019/10/24/working-in-college-can-hurt-low-income-students-more-than-help.html

46 Walter Ecton, Carolyn Heinrich, & Celeste Carruthers, "College students who work more hours are less likely to graduate," *The Conversation*, January 11, 2023, https://theconversation.com/college-students-who-work-more-hours-are-less-likely-to-graduate-196183

47 Walter Ecton, Carolyn Heinrich, & Celeste Carruthers, "Earning to Learn: Working While Enrolled in Tennessee Colleges and Universities," *AERA Open*, January 7, 2023, https://journals.sagepub.com/doi/10.1177/23328584221140410

48 The Hope Center for College, Community, and Justice, "Basic Needs Insecurity during the Ongoing Pandemic," *The Lumina Foundation*, March 31, 2021, www.luminafoundation.org/wp-content/uploads/2021/04/real-college-2021.pdf

49 Ibid.

50 Devon Payne-Sturges et al., "Student Hunger on Campus: Food Insecurity among College Students and Implications for Academic Institutions," *American Journal of Health Promotions* 32, no. 2 (February 2018): 349–54.

51 Kristin Blagg, et al., "Assessing Food Insecurity on Campus," *Urban Institute*, August 2017, www.urban.org/sites/default/files/publication/92331/assessing_food_insecurity_on_campus_4.pdf

52 U.S. Government Accountability Office, "Food Insecurity: Better Information Could Help Eligible College Students Access Federal Food Assistance Benefits" (GAO-19-95), January 9, 2019, www.gao.gov/products/gao-19-95

53 Ibid.

54 Matt Taylor, "Here's fresh evidence student loans are a massive, generational scam," *Vice*, October 17, 2018, www.vice.com/en_us/article/pa9899/heres-fresh-evidence-student-loans-are-a-massive-generational-scam

55 U.S. Census Bureau, "Census Bureau Releases New Educational Attainment Data," CB22-TPS.02, February 24, 2022, www.census.gov/newsroom/press-releases/2022/educational-attainment.html. Courtney Brown, "Veering Off-Track: 'Some college, no degree' numbers spike to 39 million," *Lumina Foundation*, May 10, 2022, www.luminafoundation.org/news-and-views/veering-off-track-some-college-no-degree-numbers-spike-to-39-million/

56 Richard Fry & Anthony Cilluffo, "A Rising Share of Undergraduates are from Poor Families, Especially at Less Selective Colleges," *Pew Research Center*, May 22, 2019, www.pewresearch.org/social-trends/2019/05/22/a-rising-share-of-undergraduates-are-from-poor-families-especially-at-less-selective-colleges/

57 William Bowen, Matthew Chingos & Michael McPherson, *Crossing the finish line: Completing college at America's public universities* (Princeton: Princeton University Press, 2009).

58 Ibid.

59 National Center for Education Statistics (NCES), "Undergraduate Retention and Graduation Rates," Department of Education, Institute of Education Sciences, 2022, https://nces.ed.gov/programs/coe/indicator/ctr.

60 NCES, "Indicator 23: Postsecondary Graduation Rates," February 2019, https://nces.ed.gov/programs/raceindicators/indicator_red.asp

61 Alanna Bjorklund-Young, "Family income, and the college completion gap," *Johns Hopkins University School of Education*, March 10, 2016, http://edpolicy.education.jhu.edu/family-income-and-the-college-completion-gap/

62 Carnevale et al., "A First Try at Roi: Ranking 4,500 Colleges."

63 John Matarese, "Before you go gambling: The best and worst casino game odds," *Newsnet*, January 23, 2017, www.news5cleveland.com/money/consumer/don't-waste-your-money/before-you-go-gambling-the-best-and-worst-casino-game-odds

64 National Assessment of Educational Progress (NAEP), "School Composition and the Black-White Achievement Gap," *National Center for Education Statistics*, September 24, 2015, https://nces.ed.gov/nationsreportcard/pubs/studies/2015018.aspx

65 Lauren Camera, "Study Finds Students Underperform in Schools with Large Black Populations," *U.S. News & World Report*,

NOTES

September 24, 2015, www.usnews.com/news/articles/2015/09/24/study-finds-students-underperform-in-schools-with-large-black-populations

66 Sean Leaver, "What drives increases in University fees? Bennett hypothesis vs Baumol's cost disease," *The Misbehaving Economist*, December 27, 2015, https://themisbehavingeconomist.com/2015/12/27/what-drives-increases-in-university-fees-bennett-hypothesis-vs-baumols-cost-disease/

67 Imed Bouchrika, "15 Best Companies to Work for without a Degree," *Research.com*, October 4, 2022, https://research.com/careers/best-companies-to-work-for-without-a-degree

68 The Editorial Board, "See Workers as Workers, Not as a College Credential," *The New York Times*, January 28, 2023, www.nytimes.com/2023/01/28/opinion/jobs-college-degree-requirement.html?action=click&module=Well&pgtype=Homepage%C2%A7ion=Editorials.Rachel Cohen, "Stop requiring college degrees for jobs that don't need them," *Vox*, March 19, 2023, www.vox.com/policy/23628627/degree-inflation-college-bacheors-stars-labor-worker-paper-ceiling

69 Ben Wildavsky, "Let's Stop Pretending College Degrees Don't Matter," *The New York Times*, August 21, 2023, www.nytimes.com/2023/08/21/opinion/skills-based-hiring-college-degree-job-market-wage-premium.html?smid=nytcore-android-share

70 Annie Lowrey, "How ChatGPT Will Destabilize White-Collar Work," *The Atlantic*, January 20, 2023. www.theatlantic.com/ideas/archive/2023/01/chatgpt-ai-economy-automation-jobs/672767/

71 Joe McKendrick, "Most Jobs Soon to Be 'Influenced' by Artificial Intelligence, University of Pennsylvania Suggests," *Forbes*, March 26, 2023, www.forbes.com/sites/joemckendrick/2023/03/26/most-jobs-soon-to-be-influenced-by-artificial-intelligence-research-out-of-openai-and-university-of-pennsylvania-suggests/?sh=735884cc73c7

72 Aaron Mok & Jacob Zinkula, "ChatGPT may be coming for our jobs," *Business Insider*, June 4, 2023, www.businessinsider.com/chatgpt-jobs-at-risk-replacement-artificial-intelligence-ai-labor-trends-2023-02.Aaron Mok, "ChatGPT will most likely impact your job if you work in tech, went to college, and make up to $80,000 a year, research says," *Business Insider*, March 21, 2023, www.businessinsider.com/chatgpt-ai-impacts-white-collar-college-educated-high-salary-jobs-2023-3

73 Center for American Progress, "The Inflation Reduction Act Is Building a Clean Energy Economy and Good Paying Jobs," *Cap20*, April 27, 2023, www.americanprogress.org/article/the-inflation-reduction-act-is-building-a-clean-energy-economy-and-good-paying-jobs/

74 Associated Builders and Contractors (ABC), "Construction Workforce Shortage Tops Half a Million in 2023, Says ABC," *ABC News Release*, February 9, 2023, www.abc.org/News-Media/News-Releases/entryid/19777/construction-workforce-shortage-tops-half-a-million-in-2023-says-abc

75 Robert Reich, "Why college isn't (and shouldn't have to be) for everyone," *Huffington Post*, May 22, 2015, www.huffingtonpost.com/robert-reich/why-college-isnt-and-shouldnt-have-to-be-for-everyone_b_6920436.html

76 Jennifer Ma, Matea Pender, & Meredith Welch, "The Benefits of Higher Education for Individuals and Society" (College Board, 2019), https://research.collegeboard.org/trends/education-pays

Chapter 2

1 Christopher Newfield, *The Great Mistake* (Baltimore: Johns Hopkins University Press, 2016).

2 "Education at a Glance 2022, OECD Indicators," OECD, October 3, 2022, www.oecd.org/education/education-at-a-glance/

3 William Deresiewicz, "How to Overhaul Higher Education, A few modest proposals for fixing a broken system," *Persuasion*, July 31, 2023, www.persuasion.community/p/how-to-overhaul-higher-education

4 Richard Arum & Josipa Roksa, *Academically Adrift Limited Learning on College Campuses* (Chicago: University of Chicago Press, 2011).

5 "Margaret Thatcher: A life in quotes," *The Guardian*, April 18, 2013. Retrieved December 2022, www.theguardian.com/politics/2013/apr/08/margaret-thatcher-quotes

6 Peter Wilby, "Margaret Thatcher's education legacy is still with us — driven on by Gove," *The Guardian*, April 5, 2013, www.theguardian.com/education/2013/apr/15/margaret-thatcher-education-legacy-gove

7 Steven V. Roberts, "Ronald Reagan Is Giving 'Em Heck," *The New York Times*, April 25, 1970, www.nytimes.com/1970/10/25/archives/ronald-reagan-is-giving-em-heck-ronald-reagan-is-giving-em-heck.html

8 Thom Hartmann, "Student loan debt is an American malignancy born of Ronald Reagan," *The Panama News*, August 27, 2022, www.thepanamanews.com/2022/08/hartmann-ronald-reagan-and-student-loan-debt/

9 "Percentage of US students' expenses for tuition fees, room, and board covered by Pell grants from 2002/2003 to 2022/2023," *Statista*,

November 2, 2022, www.statista.com/statistics/222444/share-of-us-students-expenses-covered-by-pell-grant/. "Double Pell," National College Attainment Network, December 2022, www.ncan.org/page/Pell#:~:text=At%20its%20peak%20in%201975,it's%20worth%20less%20than%2030%25.

10. Lilia Vega, "The history of UC tuition since 1868," *The Daily Californian*, December 22, 2014, https://dailycal.org/2014/12/22/history-uc-tuition-since-1868
11. "Tuition & Cost of Attendance," University of California Office of Admission, 2023, https://admission.universityofcalifornia.edu/tuition-financial-aid/tuition-cost-of-attendance/
12. Emma Kerr & Sarah Wood, "A Look at College Tuition Growth Over 20 Years," *US News & World Report*, September 13, 2022, www.usnews.com/education/best-colleges/paying-for-college/articles/see-20-years-of-tuition-growth-at-national-universities#:~:text=Tuition%20and%20fees%20at%20private,the%20most%2C%20increasing%20175%25.
13. Nisha Kurani et al., "How has US spending on healthcare changed over time?" *Petersen-KFF Health System Tracker*, February 25, 2022, www.healthsystemtracker.org/chart-collection/u-s-spending-healthcare-changed-time/#Contribution%20to%20change%20in%20total%20national%20health%20expenditures,%20from%202019-2020,%20by%20spending%20category
14. Eric Levitz, "How the Diploma Divide Is Remaking American Politics," *Intelligencer*, October 19, 2022, https://nymag.com/intelligencer/2022/10/education-polarization-diploma-divide-democratic-party-working-class.html
15. Ibid.
16. Ruth Igielnik, Scott Keeter, & Hannah Hartig, "Behind Biden's 2020 Victory," *Pew Research Center*, June 30, 2022, www.pewresearch.org/politics/2021/06/30/behind-bidens-2020-victory/
17. Megan Brenan, "Americans' Confidence in Higher Education Down Sharply," Gallup, July 11, 2023, https://news.gallup.com/poll/508352/americans-confidence-higher-education-down-sharply.aspx
18. George Will, "How to build a university unafraid of true intellectual diversity," *The Washington Post*, December 16, 2022, www.washingtonpost.com/opinions/2022/12/16/university-of-austin-intellectual-diversity/
19. Andrew Atterbury, "How DeSantis and Florida Republicans are reshaping higher education," *Politico*, October 16, 2022, https://www.politico.com/news/2022/10/16/how-desantis-and-florida-republicans-are-reshaping-higher-education-00061980

20 Miami Herald Editorial Board, "DeSantis' aides offer a glimpse of what "woke" means to him. Resentment, mostly," *Miami Herald*, December 7, 2022, www.miamiherald.com/opinion/editorials/article269675311.html

21 Atterbury, "How DeSantis and Florida Republicans are reshaping higher education."

22 Steven Walker, "New College of Florida graduates turn backs, wear masks in protest of leadership, changes," *Sarasota Herald-Tribune*, May 20, 2023, www.heraldtribune.com/story/news/education/2023/05/19/new-college-of-florida-graduates-protest-desantis-appointees-at-commencement/70232553007/

23 Emma Camp, "New College of Florida Embraces Affirmative Action for Men," *Reason*, August 16, 2023, https://reason.com/2023/08/16/new-college-of-florida-embraces-affirmative-action-for-men

24 Dana Goldstein, "Florida Approves Classic Learning Test for Use in College Admissions," *The New York Times*, September 8, 2023, www.nytimes.com/2023/09/08/us/florida-classical-learning-test-approval.html

25 "Preliminary Report of the Special Committee on Academic Freedom and Florida," American Association of University Professors (AAUP), May 24, 2023, https://www.aaup.org/report/preliminary-report-special-committee-academic-freedom-florida

26 Iowa State University, "Frequently Asked Questions, Iowa House File 802 — Requirements Related to Racism and Sexism Trainings at Public Postsecondary Institutions," August 5, 2021, accessed January 2023, from www.provost.iastate.edu/policies/iowa-house-file-802—requirements-related-to-racism-and-sexism-trainings

27 Ibid.

28 Samantha Ketterer, "Gov. Greg Abbott signs anti-DEI, tenure bills," *Houston Chronicle*, June 19, 2023, www.houstonchronicle.com/news/houston-texas/education/article/dei-programs-banned-texas-higher-education-18152792.php

29 Tom Nichols, "Florida Has a Right to Destroy Its Universities," *The Atlantic*, January 30, 2023, www.theatlantic.com/newsletters/archive/2023/01/florida-desantis-universities/672898/

30 April Rubin, "University leaders hammered after congressional hearing on antisemitism," *Axios*, December 7, 2023, www.axios.com/2023/12/06/harvard-university-presidents-congress-hearing-antisemitism-campus.

31 Zach Montague & Tracey Tully, "Education Dept. Is Investigating Six More Colleges Over Campus Discrimination," *The New York Times*, December 13, 2023, www.nytimes.com/2023/12/13/us/politics/education-department-campus-discrimination.html

32 Elissa Nadworny, "Why the Supreme Court decision on affirmative action matters," *National Public Radio* (NPR), June 29, 2023, www.npr.org/2023/06/29/1176715957/why-the-supreme-court-decision-on-affirmative-action-matters

33 Tom Norton, "Fact Check: Did Clarence Thomas Go to Yale Under Affirmative Action Policy?" *Newsweek*, June 30, 2023, www.newsweek.com/fact-check-did-clarence-thomas-go-yale-under-affirmative-action-policy-1810180

34 Collin Binkley, "Activists Spurred by SCOTUS Affirmative Action Ruling Sue Harvard Over Legacy Admissions," *HuffPost*, July 3, 2023, www.huffpost.com/entry/affirmative-action-education-legacy-admissions-lawsuit_n_64a2d94be4b0dcb22c46b63e

35 Aatish Bhatia, Claire Miller, & Josh Katz, "Study of Elite College Admissions Data Suggests Being Very Rich Is Its Own Qualification," *The New York Times*, July 24, 2023, www.nytimes.com/interactive/2023/07/24/upshot/ivy-league-elite-college-admissions.html

36 Ibid.

37 Andrew Hacker & Claudia Dreifus, *Higher Education*? (New York: Times Books, 2010).

38 National Center for Education Statistics (NCES), "Undergraduate Degree Fields."

39 Michael Nietzel, "College enrollment losses continue, but at a slower rate, according to a new report," *Forbes*, October 20, 2022, www.forbes.com/sites/michaeltnietzel/2022/10/20/college-enrollment-decline-continues-but-at-a-slower-rate-according-to-new-report/?sh=17aff7ba3910

40 Lisa Corrigan, "The Evisceration of a Public University," *The Nation*, August 16, 2023, www.thenation.com/authors/lisa-m-corrigan/

41 Ibid.

42 Anemona Hartocollis, "Slashing Its Budget, West Virginia University Asks, What Is Essential?" *The New York Times*, August 18, 2023, www.nytimes.com/2023/08/18/us/west-virginia-university-budget-cuts-deficit.html

43 West Virginia University, WVU Procurement Contract and Payment Services, April 18, 2023, https://transformation.wvu.edu/files/d/c25b20f3-cf7a-43b0-a4aa-1fe7cca3ace7/rpk-contract.pdf

44 Jenna Chernega & Patrick Clipsham, "Cuts to arts programs at St. Mary's created a huge void in Winona," *Minnpost*, June 6, 2022, www.minnpost.com/community-voices/2022/06/cuts-to-arts-programs-at-st-marys-created-huge-void-in-winona/

NOTES

45. Bret Devereaux, "Colleges Should Be More Than Just Vocational Schools," *The New York Times*, April 2, 2023, www.nytimes.com/2023/04/02/opinion/humanities-liberal-arts-policy-higher-education.html
46. Nathan Heller, "The End of the English Major," *The New Yorker*, February 27, 2023, www.newyorker.com/magazine/2023/03/06/the-end-of-the-english-major
47. Devereaux, "Colleges Should Be More Than Just Vocational Schools."
48. Will Geiger, "Top Esports Scholarships for Gamers in January 2023," *Scholarships360*, January 4, 2023, https://scholarships360.org/scholarships/esports-scholarships-for-gamers/
49. Roger Lee, "Layoffs.fyi, 2023," https://layoffs.fyi/
50. Jack Turner, "Tech companies that have made layoffs in 2023," *tech.co*, January 18, 2023, accessed January 2023, from https://tech.co/news/tech-companies-layoffs
51. Corrigan, "The Evisceration of a Public University."
52. Laura Pappano, "The Master's as the New Bachelor's," *The New York Times*, July 22, 2011, www.nytimes.com/2011/07/24/education/edlife/edl-24masters-t.html
53. NCES, "Graduate Degree Fields," May 2023, https://nces.ed.gov/programs/coe/indicator/ctb/graduate-degree-fields
54. Pappano, "The Master's as the New Bachelor's."
55. Jennifer Ma & Matea Pender, "Trends in College Pricing and Student Aid 2021," *College Board*, October 2021, https://research.collegeboard.org/media/pdf/trends-college-pricing-student-aid-2021.pdf
56. Richard Fry & Anthony Cilluffo, "A Rising Share of Undergraduates Are from Poor Families, Especially at Less Selective Colleges," *Pew Research Center*, 2023, www.pewresearch.org/social-trends/2019/05/22/a-rising-share-of-undergraduates-are-from-poor-families-especially-at-less-selective-colleges/#:~:text=The%20overall%20number%20of%20undergraduates,uniformly%20across%20the%20postsecondary%20landscape. Meris Stansbury, "Is it time to rethink the term nontraditional student?" *Ecampus News*, September 30, 2016, www.ecampusnews.com/2016/09/30/nontraditional-student-nces/
57. NCES, "Digest of Education Statistics, Table 303.40, Total fall enrollment in degree-granting postsecondary institutions," 2022 Table of Figures, accessed July 2023, https://nces.ed.gov/programs/digest/d22/tables/dt22_303.40.asp
58. NCES, Digest of Education Statistics, Table 303.40 and Congressional Budget Office, "The Demographic Outlook: 2022 to 2052," July 2022, www.cbo.gov/publication/58347

NOTES **193**

59   Matthew O'Brien, "Happy Birthday, Alan Greenspan: The Housing Bubble Wasn't Your Fault," *The Atlantic*, March 7, 2012, www.theatlantic.com/business/archive/2012/03/happy-birthday-alan-greenspan-the-housing-bubble-wasnt-your-fault/254089/. Federal Reserve Bank of St. Louis, Median Sales Price of Houses Sold for the United States (MSPUS), 2023. Retrieved July 2023, from https://fred.stlouisfed.org/series/MSPUS

60   Howard Karger, *Shortchanged: Life & Debt in the Fringe Economy* (San Francisco: Berrett-Koehler, 2005).

61   Quoted in Johann Neem, "The Problem with the Push for More College Degrees," *The Conversation*, September 12, 2019, https://theconversation.com/the-problem-with-the-push-for-more-college-degrees-122525

62   Melanie Hanson, "College Enrollment & Student Demographic Statistics," *Education Data Initiative*, July 26, 2022, https://educationdata.org/college-enrollment-statistics

63   Alicia Hahn, "2023 Student Loan Debt Statistics: Average Student Loan Debt," *Forbes*, July 16, 2023, www.forbes.com/advisor/student-loans/average-student-loan-debt-statistics/

64   Federal Student Aid, "Federal Student Loan Programs," Department of Education, June 2022. Accessed July 2023, https://studentaid.gov/sites/default/files/federal-loan-programs.pdf

65   Ben Luthi, "Types of private student loans," *Bankrate*, June 9, 2023, www.bankrate.com/loans/student-loans/types-of-private-student-loans/

66   Annie Nova, "Despite the economic recovery, student debtors' 'monster in the closet' has only worsened," *CNBC Markets*, September 22, 2018, www.cnbc.com/2018/09/21/the-student-loan-bubble.html

67   Adam Looney, Constantine Yannelis, Carolyn Hoxby, & Karen Pence, "A crisis in student loans?" *Brookings Papers on Economic Activity* (Fall 2015): 1–68.

68   Nova, "Despite the economic recovery, student debtors'."

69   Ama Takyi-Laryea, Ilan Levine, & Phillip Oliff, "Government Hits Reset on Student Loan Defaults, But Many Could Experience Default Again," *Pew Charitable Trusts*, June 14, 2022. Retrieved July 2023, www.pewtrusts.org/en/research-and-analysis/articles/2022/06/14/government-hits-reset-on-student-loan-defaults-but-many-could-experience-default-again

70   Melanie Hanson, "Student Loan Default Rate," *EducationData.org*, January 8, 2022, https://educationdata.org/student-loan-default-rate#:~:text=An%20average%20of%207.1%25%20of,is%20in%20defaulted%20student%20loans.

71 Statista Research Department, "Percentage of recent college graduates in the United States working in low-wage jobs from June 2017 to June 2023," Statista 2024, www.statista.com/statistics/642040/share-of-recent-us-college-graduates-working-low-wage/

72 NEA, "Teacher Salary Benchmarks Report, 2024," *NEA*, April 2023, www.nea.org/resource-library/educator-pay-and-student-spending-how-does-your-state-rank/starting-teacher#:~:text=Only%205%20states%20and%20DC%20pay%20starting,Teacher%20Salary%20Benchmark%20Report%2C%202021%2D22%2C%20April%202023.

73 Federal Student Aid, Student Loan Delinquency and Default, U.S. Department of Education, 2023, accessed July 2023, https://studentaid.gov/manage-loans/default

74 Federal Student Aid, "Student Loan Forgiveness," U.S. Department of Education, 2022, accessed July 2023, https://studentaid.gov/manage-loans/forgiveness-cancellation

75 Federal Student Aid, "The Biden-Harris Administration's Student Debt Relief Plan Explained," U.S. Department of Education, 2023, accessed June 2023, https://studentaid.gov/debt-relief-announcement. Kelley Taylor, "Student Loan Forgiveness: What You Need to Know," *Kiplinger*, February 28, 2023, www.kiplinger.com/biden-forgives-student-loans-what-it-means.

76 Sam Fossum, "Biden administration announces $39 billion in student debt relief following administrative fixes," *CNN*, July 14, 2023, www.cnn.com/2023/07/14/politics/student-loan-relief-biden-administration

77 James McWilliams, "To Understand the High Cost of Colleges, Think of Them as Investment Banks," *Pacific Standard*, October 25, 2018, https://psmag.com/education/to-understand-the-high-cost-of-colleges-think-of-them-as-investment-banks

78 James Nguyen Spencer, "Higher Ed Is a Public Good. Let's Fund It Like One," *Chronicle of Higher Education*, December 8, 2022, www.chronicle.com/article/higher-ed-is-a-public-good-lets-fund-it-like-one. Karin Fischer, "The Return of College as a Common Good," *Chronicle of Higher Education*, October 3, 2022, www.chronicle.com/article/the-return-of-college-as-a-common-good

79 Rachel Gillett, "The 19 college degrees that lead to the most satisfying careers," *World Economic Forum*, November 13, 2015, www.weforum.org/agenda/2015/11/the-19-college-degrees-that-lead-to-the-most-satisfying-careers/

80 Anthony Carnevale, Stephen Rose & Ban Cheah, "The college payoff: Education, occupations, lifetime earnings," *The Georgetown University Center on Education and the Workforce*, 2014, https://cew.georgetown.edu/cew-reports/the-college-payoff/

81 Scott Jaschik, "Redefining 'Value' in Higher Education," *Inside Higher Education*, May 12, 2021, www.insidehighered.com/news/2021/05/12/gates-foundation-attempts-redefine-value-higher-education

82 Neem, "The Problem with the Push for More College Degrees."

83 "Simons Foundation Announces Historic $500 Million Gift to Stony Brook University Endowment," *Stony Brook University News*, June 1, 2023, https://news.stonybrook.edu/newsroom/press-release/general/simons-foundation-announces-historic-500-million-gift-to-stony-brook-university-endowment/

84 Brian Bushard, "Elon Musk Endorses Debunked 'Pizzagate' Conspiracy Theory—And Deletes Post," *Forbes*, No. 28, 2023, www.forbes.com/sites/brianbushard/2023/11/28/elon-musk-endorses-debunked-pizzagate-conspiracy-theory-again/?sh=3d00fb2c4f26

85 Perry Bacon, "Education Reform Is Dying," *Washington Post*, May 8, 2023, www.washingtonpost.com/opinions/2023/05/08/how-to-reform-education/

86 James Kunetka, "When America's scientists knew sin," *Politico*, August 6, 2015, www.politico.eu/article/when-americas-scientists-knew-sin-hiroshima-70-years-anniversary/. Ross Andersen, "Oppenheimer's Cry of Despair in The Atlantic," *The Atlantic*, July 25, 2023, www.theatlantic.com/technology/archive/2023/07/j-robert-oppenheimer-ideas-history/674814/

87 David Brooks, "Let's Smash the College Admissions Process," *The New York Times*, June 1, 2023, www.nytimes.com/2023/06/01/opinion/college-admissions-affirmative-action.html

Chapter 3

1 Sean Leaver, "What drives increases in university fees? Bennett hypothesis vs Baumol's cost disease," *The Misbehaving Economist*, December 27, 2015, https://themisbehavingeconomist.com/2015/12/27/what-drives-increases-in-university-fees-bennett-hypothesis-vs-baumols-cost-disease/

2 Jessica Dickler, "Inflation-adjusted college costs decline for the second-straight year," *CNBC*, October 24, 2022, www.cnbc.com/2022/10/24/college-tuition-falls-in-2022-23-after-adjusting-for-inflation.html

3 National Center for Education Statistics (NCES), "Table 330.10. Average undergraduate tuition, fees, room, and board rates charged

for full-time students in degree-granting postsecondary institutions, by level and control of institution: Selected years, 1963–64 through 2020–21," 2022, nces.ed.gov/programs/digest/d21/tables/dt21_330.10.asp. See also NCES, "Table 330.40. Average total cost of attendance for first-time, full-time undergraduate students in degree-granting postsecondary institutions, Selected years, 2010–11 through 2020–21," nces.ed.gov/programs/digest/d21/tables/dt21_330.40.asp

4 William Bennett, "Our Greedy Colleges," Opinion, *The New York Times*, February 18, 1987, www.nytimes.com/1987/02/18/opinion/our-greedy-colleges.html

5 Robert Martin & R. Carter Hill, "Baumol and Bowen Cost Effects in Research Universities," *COB Journal*, September 13, 2021, www.subr.edu/assets/subr/COBJournal/Baumol-and-Bowen-Effects-13sept21.pdf

6 William Baumol, *The Cost Disease: Why Computers Get Cheaper, and Health Care Doesn't* (New Haven: Yale University Press, 2012).

7 Nicole Goodkind, "Some colleges cost $95,000 per year, and they're only getting more expensive. Here's why," *CNN*, July 16, 2023, www.cnn.com/2023/07/16/investing/curious-consumer-college-cost

8 David Levy, "Stop coddling underworked professors," *The Week*, January 8, 2015, https://theweek.com/articles/476933/stop-coddlingunderworkedprofessors

9 American Association of University Professors (AAUP), "Preliminary 2022–23 Faculty Compensation Survey Results," 2023, www.aaup.org/2022-23-faculty-compensation-survey-results

10 Ibid.

11 Social Security Administration, "Average Wage Index (AWI)," 2022, accessed January 2023, www.ssa.gov/oact/cola/awidevelop.html

12 American Association of University Professors (AAUP), 2022–23 "Faculty Compensation Survey Results, Appendix 1."

13 Urban Institute, "Understanding College Affordability, State and Local Appropriations," April 2017, https://collegeaffordability.urban.org/cost-of-educating/appropriations/#/variation_across_states

14 Mary Ellen Flannery, "State Funding for Higher Education Still Lagging," *NeaToday*, National Education Association, 2023, www.nea.org/advocating-for-change/new-from-nea/state-funding-higher-education-still-lagging#:~:text=When%20state%20lawmakers%20turn%20their,down%2C%20student%20tuition%20goes%20up.

15 Ibid.

16 Vice President for Communications, "An overview of U-M's operating budget," *University of Michigan*, 2023, accessed January 2023, from https://publicaffairs.vpcomm.umich.edu/key-issues/tuition/general-fund-budget-tutorial/

NOTES

17 Moody's Investor's Service, "2019 US Higher Education Investor Outlook," December 2018, www.aascu.org/meetings/hegrc18/Shaffer.pdf

18 University of California, "Annual Financial Report 21/22," 2021–2022, https://regents.universityofcalifornia.edu/regmeet/nov22/f7attach1.pdf

19 Treasurer, "Outstanding Long-Term Obligations of the University of Colorado as of June 30, 2022," University of Colorado, 2022, accessed February 2023, from www.cu.edu/treasurer/university-debt.

20 Detailed financial data on individual nonprofit institutions can be found on IRS website https://apps.irs.gov/app/eos/

21 Sarah Holtz, "Colleges Are in Debt, but Students Pay for It," *The Nation*, September 22, 2022, www.thenation.com/article/politics/campus-debt-student-loans/

22 Jon Marcus, "Why Colleges Are Borrowing Billions," *The Atlantic*, October 10, 2017, www.theatlantic.com/education/archive/2017/10/why-colleges-are-borrowing-billions/542352/

23 Joanna Gonsalves, Rich Levy, Gayathri Raja, and Tyler Risteen, "Campus Debt Reveal, 2022, Massachusetts Public Colleges and Universities," 2022, https://massteacher.org/-/media/massteacher/files/about-us/higher-ed/mass-campus-debt-reveal.pdf

24 National Association of College and University Business Officers (NACUBO), "Moody's Rating Methodology for US Public Colleges and Universities," 2002, www.nacubo.org/-/media/Nacubo/Documents/prof_dev/Higher_Ed_Credit_Outlook_Public_University_Rating_Methodology.ashx#:~:text=Moody's%20rating%20methodology%20for%20public,elements%20of%20a%20particular%20transaction.

25 Paul Pringle, *Bad City* (New York: Celadon, 2022), 204.

26 Eleni Schirmer, "It's Not Just Students Drowning in Debt. Colleges Are Too!" *The Nation*, November 30/December 7, 2020e, www.thenation.com/article/society/student-debt-university-credit/

27 Ashlynn Warta, "Administrative Bloat Harms Teaching and Learning," *The James G. Martin Center for Academic Renewal*, August 22, 2022, www.jamesgmartin.center/2022/08/administrative-bloat-harms-teaching-and-learning/

28 Richard Vedder, "Who Is Ruining Our Universities? Administrators!" *Forbes*, August 3, 2020, www.forbes.com/sites/richardvedder/2020/08/03/who-is-ruining-our-universities--administrators/?sh=34ec3ea714df

29 Greg Murphy, "College administrative bloat is robbing our children of their futures," *Washington Examiner*, December 9, 2020, www.washingtonexaminer.com/opinion/op-eds/college-administrative-bloat-is-robbing-our-children-of-their-futures

30 rpk GROUP, 2023, accessed August 2023, https://rpkgroup.com/
31 West Virginia University, "WVU Procurement Contract and Payment Services," April 18, 2023, https://transformation.wvu.edu/files/d/c25b20f3-cf7a-43b0-a4aa-1fe7cca3ace7/rpk-contract.pdf
32 Emmy Cho, "The Consulting Conundrum," *Harvard Political Review*, August 16, 2021, https://harvardpolitics.com/consulting-conundrum/
33 rpk GROUP, ca. 2023.
34 L. E. K. Consulting, 2023, accessed August 2023, https://www.lek.com/about/who-we-are. Bain & Company, 2023, accessed August 2023, www.bain.com/. Deloitte, 2023, accessed August. 2023, www2.deloitte.com/us/en/services/consulting.html?icid=bottom_consulting. McKinsey & Company, 2023, accessed August 2023, from www.mckinsey.com/about-us/overview/our-purpose-mission-and-values. Boston Consulting Group, 2023, accessed August 2023, www.bcg.com/about/commitments
35 Credo, 2023, accessed August 2023, www.credohighered.com/about/what-we-do
36 Heads Up Educational Consulting, Background & Fees, 2023, accessed August 2023, https://headsuped.com/background-fees-2/
37 Ian MacDougall, "How McKinsey Is Making $100 Million (and Counting)," *ProPublica*, July 15, 2020, www.propublica.org/article/how-mckinsey-is-making-100-million-and-counting-advising-on-the-governments-bumbling-coronavirus-response
38 Garrett Shanley, "UF signs $4.7 million contract with global consulting firm," *The Independent Florida Alligator*, August 23, 2023, www.alligator.org/article/2023/08/uf-signs-4-7-million-contract-with-global-consulting-firm-mckinsey
39 Ibid.
40 Matt Pearce, "A corporation won't let Pete Buttigieg talk about three years of his life," *Los Angeles Times*, December 6, 2019, www.latimes.com/politics/story/2019-12-06/pete-buttigieg-has-a-nondisclosure-agreement
41 Carol Ann Alaimo & Justin Sayers, "UA's $14-million gamble: Consultant gave pricey advice to devise strategic plan," *Arizona Daily Star*, November 9, 2019, www.azcentral.com/story/news/local/arizona-education/2019/11/09/ua-paid-14-million-mckinsey-company-planning-advice/2550135001/
42 Ibid.
43 Walt Bogdanich & Michael Forsythe, *When McKinsey Comes to Town* (New York: Doubleday, 2022)

44 Ian MacDougall, "How McKinsey Makes Its Own Rules," *The New York Times*, December 14, 2019, www.nytimes.com/2019/12/14/sunday-review/mckinsey-ice-buttigieg.html
45 Ibid.
46 MacDougall, "How McKinsey Is Making $100 Million (and Counting)."
47 Bogdanich & Forsythe, *When McKinsey Comes to Town*.
48 Ibid.
49 Ibid.
50 Megan Menchaca, "UT looks to pay $20M to consultant to cut procurement costs, improve campus diversity," *Austin American-Statesman*, November 12, 2012, www.statesman.com/story/news/2021/11/12/ut-20-million-bain-company-texas-university-austin-dversity/6390513001/. Beth Timmins, "Bain consultancy banned from government work over 'misconduct,'" *BBC News*, August 3, 2022, www.bbc.com/news/business-62408116
51 Institute for Health Metrics and Evaluation, "Bill & Melinda Gates Foundation boosts vital work of the University of Washington's Institute for Health Metrics and Evaluation," January 25, 2017, https://www.gatesfoundation.org/ideas/media-center/press-releases/2017/01/ihme-announcement
52 Christopher Newfield, *The Great Mistake* (Baltimore: Johns Hopkins University Press, 2016).
53 Miranda Spivack, "Public colleges hide donors who seek to influence students," *USA TODAY*, August 13, 2020, www.usatoday.com/story/news/investigations/2020/08/13/covid-college-donations-fall-semester-2020/3314262001/
54 Lia Eustachewich, "Jeffrey Epstein 'facilitated' construction of Harvard-linked building," *New York Post*, September 13, 2019, https://nypost.com/2019/09/13/jeffrey-epstein-facilitated-construction-of-harvard-university-building/
55 *Inside Higher Ed.*, Capital Campaigns, 2023, accessed January 2023, www.insidehighered.com/capital_campaigns
56 Kevin Wallace, "Budgeting for a Capital Campaign," *Campaign Counsel*, August 16, 2023, www.campaigncounsel.org/blog/budgeting-capital-campaign#:~:text=DIRECT%20COSTS%20OF%20A%20CAPITAL,2%2D3%2Dyear%20investments.
57 Penelope Burk, *Donor-Centered Fundraising* (Chicago: Cygnus Applied Research, 2018).
58 Sarah Wood, "10 National Universities with the Biggest Endowments," *US News & World Report*, September 13, 2022, www.

usnews.com/education/best-colleges/the-short-list-college/articles/10-universities-with-the-biggest-endowments

59 *The Economist*, "America's elite universities are bloated, complacent and illiberal," March 4, 2024.

60 Douglas Belkin, "Legacy Preference Gets Fresh Look Following College-Admissions Scandal," *The Wall Street Journal*, February 22, 2020, www.wsj.com/articles/legacy-preference-gets-fresh-look-following-college-admissions-scandal-11582387200

61 Michael Kinsley, "How affirmative action helped George W.," *CNN*, January 20, 2003, https://edition.cnn.com/2003/ALLPOLITICS/01/20/timep.affirm.action.tm/

62 "Budget in Brief," *University of Wisconsin-Madison*, 2022, accessed January 2023, https://budget.wisc.edu/content/uploads/Budget-in-Brief_2021-22_V15-1.pdf

63 Board of Trustees Administration and Finance Committee, "FY23 Budget," *University of Massachusetts*, June 1, 2022, accessed February 2023, www.umassp.edu/budget-office/reports-and-initiatives/annual-operating-budget-and-financial-forecast

64 Office of the President, "Budget for Current Operations, 2022–2023," *University of California*, 2022, www.ucop.edu/operating-budget/_files/rbudget/2022-23-budget-detail.pdf

65 John McCarthy, "How UQ created a $700 million market for 'overnight successes'," *INQueensland*, December 23, 2020, https://inqld.com.au/news/2020/12/23/how-uq-created-a-700-million-market-for-overnight-successes/

66 Maria Zuber, "A primer on indirect costs and why they are important to MIT," *MIT Faculty* Newsletter, May/June 2017, https://web.mit.edu/fnl/volume/295/zuber.html

67 Karen Holbrook & Paul Sanberg, "Understanding the high cost of success in university research," *Technology and Innovation* 15 (2013): 269–80.

68 Pringle, *Bad City*, 143.

69 ALZFORUM, "Settlement Reached between UCSD and USC, Paul Aisen," July 5, 2019, www.alzforum.org/news/community-news/settlement-reached-between-ucsd-and-usc-paul-aisen

70 Beryl Lieff Benderly, "Recruiting or academic poaching?" *Science*, August 3, 2015, www.science.org/content/article/recruiting-or-academic-poaching

71 Sophie Quinton, "Why universities charge extra for engineering, business and nursing degrees," *Stateline*, Pew Charitable Trust, June 1, 2017, www.pewtrusts.org/en/research-and-analysis/blogs/

stateline/2017/06/01/why-universities-charge-extra-for-engineering-business-and-nursing-degrees

72 Jonathan Glater, "Certain Degrees Now Cost More at Public Universities," *The New York Times*, July 29, 2007, www.nytimes.com/2007/07/29/education/29tuition.html?searchResultPosition=1

73 Quinton, "Why universities charge extra."

74 National Association of College and University Business Officers (NACUBO), "Tuition Discount Rates at Private Colleges and Universities Hit All-Time Highs," May 19, 2022, www.nacubo.org/Press-Releases/2022/Tuition-Discount-Rates-at-Private-Colleges-and-Universities-Hit-All-Time-Highs

75 Jill Barshay, "Proof Points: Surprising patterns in who gets merit and need-based aid from colleges," *The Hechinger Report*, July 31, 2023, https://hechingerreport.org/proof-points-surprising-patterns-in-who-gets-merit-and-need-based-aid-from-colleges.

76 Ibid.

77 Emily Aronson, "Princeton will enhance its groundbreaking financial aid program," *Princeton Office of Communications*, September 8, 2022, www.princeton.edu/news/2022/09/08/princeton-will-enhance-its-groundbreaking-financial-aid-program#:~:text=The%20new%20financial%20aid%20policies,previous%20%2465%2C000%20annual%20income%20level

78 University of Michigan, "Go Blue Guarantee Eligibility," 2023, accessed February 2023, https://finaid.umich.edu/apply-aid/new-undergraduates/michigan-residents/go-blue-guarantee-eligibility#:~:text=U%2DM%20will%20pay%20full%20undergraduate,for%20some%20families%20earning%20more

79 Anemona Hartocollis, "Colleges Are Resetting Tuition after Applicants Balk at Costs," *The New York Times*, December 14, 2022, A: 1.

80 Hawaii Pacific University, "New Undergraduate," 2023, accessed February 2023, www.hpu.edu/financial-aid/scholarships/new-undergraduate/index.html

81 National Center for Education Statistics (NCES), "2019–20 National Postsecondary Student Aid Study (NPSAS)," NCES, June 16, 2021, https://nces.ed.gov/pubsearch/pubsinfo.asp?pubid=2021456

82 Board of Trustees Administration and Finance Committee, "FY23 Budget."

83 Josh Moody, "Tuition Discounts Hit Another Record High," *Inside Higher Ed*, May 20, 2022, www.insidehighered.com/news/2022/05/20/tuition-discounts-hit-all-time-high-nacubo-study-finds

84 Ibid.

85 Kathryn Randolph, "Colleges Announce Tuition Freeze and Resets for 2023," fastweb, January 10, 2023, accessed February 2023, www.fastweb.com/student-news/articles/colleges-announce-tuition-freeze-and-resets-for-2023

86 U.S. Government Accountability Office, "What Financial Aid Offers Don't Tell You about the Cost of College," April 4, 2023, www.gao.gov/blog/what-financial-aid-offers-dont-tell-you-about-cost-college

87 Liam Knox, "Legislating an Honest Look at College Cost," *Inside Higher Education*, June 7, 2023, www.insidehighered.com/news/government/state-policy/2023/06/07/college-financial-transparency-legislation-gains-ground

88 Ibid.

89 College Simply, "New York Public Colleges Ranked by Smallest Enrollment," 2022, accessed August 2023, www.collegesimply.com/colleges/rank/public-colleges/smallest-enrollment/state/new-york/?page=2

90 Ibid.

91 Council on Social Work Education, "Directory of Accredited Programs," 2023, accessed August 2023, www.cswe.org/accreditation/about/directory/?pg=&program_level=Baccalaureate

92 American Bar Association, "Schools by State," 2023, accessed August 2023, www.americanbar.org/groups/center-pro-bono/resources/directory_of_law_school_public_interest_pro_bono_programs/schools_by_state/

93 CEPH, "Accreditation Statistics," 2023, accessed August 2023, https://ceph.org/constituents/schools/faqs/general/accreditation-statistics/

94 Study Portals, "Bachelor's Degrees in Public Health in United Kingdom," 2023, accessed August 2023, www.bachelorsportal.com/study-options/268927066/public-health-united-kingdom.html

Chapter 4

1 Queensland University of Technology. "Our University." *QUT*, March 2023, https://www.qut.edu.au/about/our-university.

2 *The Princeton Review*, "College Administrator," 2023 accessed February 2023, www.princetonreview.com/careers/40/college-administrator

3 Caroline Simon, "Bureaucrats and Buildings: The Case for Why College Is So Expensive," *Forbes*, September 5, 2017, www.

forbes.com/sites/carolinesimon/2017/09/05/bureaucrats-and-buildings-the-case-for-why-college-is-so-expensive/. The Economist, "America's elite universities are bloated, complacent and illiberal," *The Economist*, March 4, 2024, https://www.economist.com/international/2024/03/04/americas-elite-universities-are-bloated-complacent-and-illiberal?utm_medium=cpc.adword.pd&utm_source=google&ppccampaignID=17210591673&ppcadID=&utm_campaign=a.22brand_pmax&utm_content=conversion.direct-response.anonymous&gad_source=1&gclid=CjwKCAjwtevBhBFEiwAQSv_xbFBSp4ZtiFvvx8dAI4_d4X62Ee1AErCiqNf_XDYeFG9A9lqxqGjchoCsLgQAvD_BwE&gclsrc=aw.ds

4 Rutgers AAUP-AFT, "The Rutgers Budget Swindle: Everything You Need to Know about RCM," September 9, 2021, https://rutgersaaup.org/the-rutgers-budget-swindle-everything-you-need-to-know-about-rcm/

5 American Association of University Professors (AAUP), "2022–23 Faculty Compensation Survey Results, Survey Report Table 11 (Presidential salary), by AAUP category and affiliation, 2022–23 (dollars)," June 2023, www.aaup.org/sites/default/files/AAUP-2023-SurveyTables.pdf

6 Douglas Belkin, "Big Perks for College Presidents," *The Wall Street Journal*, June 16, 2016, www.wsj.com/articles/big-perks-for-college-presidents-1466101531

7 James Finkelstein & Judith Wilde, "Bonuses and Benefits," *Inside Higher Education*, May 24, 2017, www.insidehighered.com/advice/2017/05/25/examination-growing-number-perks-and-bonuses-college-presidents-essay

8 Ibid.

9 Richard Vedder, "Are University Presidents Paid Too Little or Too Much?" *Forbes*, January 3, 2019, www.forbes.com/sites/richardvedder/2019/01/03/are-university-presidents-paid-too-little-or-too-much-how-would-one-know/?sh=7b53602b6fb8

10 Ibid.

11 Richard Vedder, "College Presidential Pay Makes No Sense: Little Relation to Excellence," *Forbes*, September 8, 2021, www.forbes.com/sites/richardvedder/2021/09/08/college-presidential-pay-makes-no-sense-little-relation-to-excellence/?sh=26dc4208de7c

12 Chris Quintana, "Ousted USC president received $7.7M payout in wake of sex-abuse, drug scandals," *USA TODAY*, July 16, 2020, www.usatoday.com/story/news/education/2020/07/16/usc-president-salary-scandal-sexual-assault/5451355002/

13 Olivia Pulsinelli & Dallas Business Journal staff, "University leaders' paychecks: Kenneth Starr No. 1 thanks to Baylor severance," *Houston*

Business Journal, December 12, 2018, www.bizjournals.com/houston/news/2018/12/12/university-leaders-paychecks-kenneth-starr-no-1.html

14 Stewart Whittingham, "Anger at £400k pay for chiefs at top UK universities," *Express*, January 2, 2023, www.express.co.uk/news/uk/1715968/university-vice-chancellors-salaries-pay-rise-lecturers-strike

15 University and College Union, "HE single pay spine," 2023, www.ucu.org.uk/he_singlepayspine

16 Lucy Carroll & Daniella White, "Top vice chancellors rake in million-dollar pay as student satisfaction recovers," *The Sydney Morning Herald*, August 25, 2022, www.smh.com.au/national/nsw/top-vice-chancellors-rake-in-million-dollar-pay-as-student-satisfaction-recovers-20220824-p5bcc9.html. James Guthrie, "Accounting for vice chancellor's salaries," *Campus Morning Mail*, August 28, 2022, https://campusmorningmail.com.au/news/accounting-for-vice-chancellors-salaries/

17 American Council on Education, "American College President Study 2017," 2023, www.aceacps.org/summary-profile/#path-to-the-presidency.

18 Tressie McMillan Cottom, Sally Hunnicutt, & Jennifer Johnson, "The Ties That Corporatize: A Social Network Analysis of University Presidents as Vectors of Higher Education Corporatization," *SocArXiv*, May 22, 2018, https://osf.io/preprints/socarxiv/wpcfq/

19 Laura McKenna, "Why Are Fewer College Presidents Academics?" *The Atlantic*, December 3, 2015, www.theatlantic.com/education/archive/2015/12/college-president-mizzou-tim-wolfe/418599/

20 Ibid.

21 Alta Spells, Leyla Santiago, & Sara Weisfeldt, "University of Florida faculty passes symbolic vote against possible selection of Sen. Ben Sasse as president," *CNN*, October 28, 2022, www.cnn.com/2022/10/28/us/ben-sasse-university-of-florida-president-no-confidence-vote/index.html. Nathan Crabbe, Gershon Harrell & Andrew Caplan, "Gainesville community reacts to Ben Sasse being secretly tapped to be UF's next president," *The Gainesville Sun*, October 7, 2022, www.gainesville.com/story/news/local/2022/10/07/uf-community-activists-react-senator-ben-sasse-being-picked-next-president/8205548001/

22 Judith Wilde & James Finkelstein, "Ben Sasse hit the jackpot with his University of Florida contract," *Higher Ed Dive*, November 28, 2022, www.highereddive.com/news/ben-sasse-jackpot-UF-contract-president/637256/#:~:text=Sasse's%20base%20salary%20begins%20at,retention%20bonus%20of%20%241%20million.

23 McKenna, "Why Are Fewer College Presidents Academics?"

NOTES

24. Teresa Watanabe, "UC chief Janet Napolitano leaving office with a mended legacy," *Los Angeles Times*, June 11, 2020, www.latimes.com/california/story/2020-06-11/uc-president-janet-napolitano-steps-down-mended-legacy-after-scandal
25. Associated Press, cmaadmin (EDU), "Highlands University Regents Vote to End Manny Aragon's Tenure as President," *Diverse: Issues in Higher Education*, July 24, 2006, www.diverseeducation.com/faculty-staff/article/15082298/highlands-university-regents-vote-to-end-manny-aragons-tenure-as-president
26. Albuquerque Journal Staff, "Breaking: Aragon Sentenced," *Albuquerque Journal* March 17, 2009, www.abqjournal.com/16581/breaking-aragon-sentenced.html
27. Kate Mcgee, "Two-thirds of board members overseeing Texas public universities are Abbott donors," *The Texas Tribune*, October 18, 2022, www.texastribune.org/2022/10/18/greg-abbott-texas-universities-donors/
28. Office of Student Involvement, University of Central Florida, "What is House Bill 233?" 2022, https://osi.ucf.edu/faq/what-is-house-bill-233/
29. Benjamin Ginsberg, *The Fall of the Faculty* (New York: Oxford University Press, 2013).
30. Christopher Beam, "Finishing school," *Slate*, August 11, 2010, https://slate.com/news-and-politics/2010/08/the-case-for-getting-rid-of-tenure.html
31. Divya Kumar, "DeSantis signs bill limiting tenure at Florida public universities," *Tampa Bay Times*, April 19, 2022, www.tampabay.com/news/education/2022/04/19/desantis-signs-bill-limiting-tenure-at-florida-public-universities/
32. Heather Hollingsworth, "Conservatives take aim at tenure for university professors," *AP News*, January 8, 2023, https://apnews.com/article/politics-colleges-and-universities-florida-state-government-texas-education-4f0fe0c5c18ed227fabae3744e8ff51d
33. American Association of University Professors (AAUP), "The Annual Report on the Economic Status of the Profession, 2021–22," November 2, 2023, www.aaup.org/report/annual-report-economic-status-profession-2021-22
34. Hans-Joerg Tiede, "The 2021 AAUP Shared Governance Survey," *AAUP*, 2021, www.aaup.org/report/2021-aaup-shared-governance-survey-findings-faculty-roles-decision-making-areas
35. Ibid.
36. William Herbert, Jacob Apkarian, & Joseph van der Naald, "2020 Supplementary Directory of New Bargaining Agents and Contracts in

Institutions of Higher Education, 2013–2019," *Hunter College National Center for the Study of Collective Bargaining in Higher Education and the Professions*, November 2020, www.hunter.cuny.edu/ncscbhep/assets/files/SupplementalDirectory-2020-FINAL.pdf

37 Johanna Foster & Marina Vujnovic, "Shared Governance Unionism and the Fight against Austerity in the Age of COVID-19," *AAUP*, Winter 2022, www.aaup.org/article/shared-governance-unionism-and-fight-against-austerity-age-covid-19

38 Maggie Levantovskaya, "Organizing Against Precarity in Higher Education," *Current Affairs*, April 6, 2022, www.currentaffairs.org/2022/04/organizing-against-precarity-in-higher-education

39 Ibid.

40 Foster & Vujnovic, "Shared Governance Unionism."

41 John Gotanda, J. 2017. Emails, April 13. In author's possession.

42 American Association of University Professors (AAUP), "The Annual Report on the Economic Status of the Profession, 2021–22."

43 Guy Standing, *The Precariat: The New Dangerous Class* (London: Bloomsbury Academic, 2016).

44 Miami University, University Policy Library, "Other Instructional Staff Titles: Policy, Instructor," accessed March 2023, from www.miamioh.edu/policy-library/employees/faculty/evaluation-promotion-tenure-faculty/other-instructional-staff.html#instructor

45 Hannah Appel, "Tenant, Debtor, Worker, Student," *New York Review*, February 8, 2023, www.nybooks.com/online/2023/02/08/tenant-debtor-worker-student/

46 Bianca Quilantan & Blake Jones, 'It's about damn time': College workers organize amid nationwide labor unrest," *Politico*, February 24, 2023, www.politico.com/news/2023/02/04/college-workers-organize-labor-unrest-00081182

47 Danielle Douglas-Gabriel, "Temple University withholds tuition assistance from striking grad students," *The Washington Post*, February 8, 2023, www.washingtonpost.com/education/2023/02/08/temple-university-strike-tuition-graduate-workers

48 Derek Newton, "College Tuition Is Actually Higher for Online Programs," *Forbes*, June 25, 2018, www.forbes.com/sites/forbesdigitalcovers/2018/07/30/the-backsies-billionaire-texan-builds-second-fortune-from-wreckage-of-real-estate-empire-hed-sold/?

49 HolonIQ, "The Anatomy of an OPM and a $7.7B Market in 2025," HolonIQ," February 13, 2019, www.holoniq.com/notes/the-anatomy-of-an-opm-and-a-7-7b-market-in-2025

50 2U, "Meet Our Partners, 2023," accessed August 2023, www.2U.edu

51. Edward Maloney & Joshua Kim, "How Universities Should Think about the Warren OPM Letter," *Inside Higher Education*, January 23, 2022, www.insidehighered.com/blogs/learning-innovation/how-universities-should-think-about-warren-opm-letter

52. Stephanie Hall & Taela Dudley, "Dear Colleges: Take Control of Your Online Courses," *The Century Foundation*, September 12, 2019, https://tcf.org/content/report/dear-colleges-take-control-online-courses/

53. Laura Spitalniak, "USC graduates sue over online social work program, alleging false advertising," *Higher Ed Dive*, May 17, 2023, www.highereddive.com/news/graduates-of-uscs-online-social-work-masters-sue-alleging-misrepresentat/649509/?utm_source=Sailthru&utm_medium=email&utm_campaign=Newsletter%20Weekly%20Roundup:%20Higher%20Ed%20Dive:%20Daily%20Dive%2005-06-2023&utm_term=Higher%20Ed%20Dive%20Weekender

54. Harriett Ryan and Matt Hamilton, "Online Degrees Made USC the World's Biggest Social Work School. Then Things Went Terribly Wrong," *Los Angeles Times*, June 6, 2019, https://www.latimes.com/local/lanow/la-me-usc-social-work-20190606-story.html.

55. Cailyn Nagle & Kaitlyn Vitez, "Fixing the Broken Textbook Market" (2nd ed.), U.S. PIRG Education Fund, June 2020, https://pirg.org/sites/pirg/files/reports/Fixing-the-Broken-Textbook-Market_June-2020_v2.pdf

56. Melanie Hanson, "Average Cost of College Textbooks, Education Data," *Education Data Initiative*, July 15, 2022 update, accessed March 2023, https://educationdata.org/average-cost-of-college-textbooks#:~:text=The%20average%20postsecondary%20student%20spends,the%202021%2D2022%20academic%20year.

57. Matthew Adarichev, "Let's call college textbooks what they are: A scam," *The Hofstra Chronicle*, September 27, 2022, www.thehofstrachronicle.com/category/editorials/2022/9/27/lets-call-college-textbooks-what-they-are-a-scam

58. Nagle & Vitez, "Fixing the Broken Textbook Market," 3.

59. Ibid.

60. Sheila Liming, "How Textbook Rentals Undercut Students," *Inside Higher Ed*, June 5, 2018, www.insidehighered.com/digital-learning/views/2018/06/06/textbook-rentals-undercut-students-we-can-do-better-opinion

61. Hanson, "Average Cost of College Textbooks."

62. Lyss Welding, "Average Cost of College Textbooks," *Best Colleges*, March 27, 2023, www.bestcolleges.com/research/average-cost-of-college-textbooks-statistics/#:~:text=In%202020%2D2021%2C%20the%20average,on%20course%20materials%20including%20books

63 SPARC, "Open Textbook Pilot Grant Program," February 5, 2019, https://sparcopen.org/our-work/open-textbook-pilot/#:~:text=Background,for%20college%20completion%20and%20affordability

64 Nicole Allen, "$1 Billion in Savings through Open Educational Resources," *SPARC*, October 12, 2018, https://sparcopen.org/news/2018/1-billion-in-savings-through-open-educational-resources/

Chapter 5

1 NCAA, "History," 2023, accessed April 2023, www.ncaa.org/sports/2021/5/4/history.aspx
2 Ibid.
3 Mitch Sherman, "Everything you need to know about the college basketball scandal," *ESPN*, February 23, 2018, www.espn.com/mens-college-basketball/story/_/id/22555512/explaining-NCAA-college-basketball-scandal-players-coaches-agents
4 John I. Jenkins & Jack Swarbrick, "College Sports Are a Treasure. Don't Turn Them into the Minor Leagues," *The New York Times*, March 23, 2023, www.nytimes.com/2023/03/23/opinion/college-sports-student-athletes-education.html
5 NCAA, "Finances," 2023, accessed April 2023, www.ncaa.org/sports/2021/5/4/finances.aspx
6 Andrew Zimbalist, "Who Wins with College Sports?" *ECONOFACT*, January 22, 2023, https://econofact.org/who-wins-with-college-sports
7 Senator Chris Murphy, "Madness, Inc. How Everyone Is Getting Rich Off College Sports—Except the Players," *Chris Murphy*, 2022, www.murphy.senate.gov/download/madness-inc
8 Education Statistics (NCES), "Characteristics of Postsecondary Faculty," May 2022, https://nces.ed.gov/programs/coe/indicator/csc/postsecondary-faculty
9 Department of the Treasury, "Form 990, National Collegiate Athletic Association for fiscal year ending," August 2020, accessed April 2023, https://projects.propublica.org/nonprofits/organizations/440567264/202141969349302369/full
10 Billy Witz, "N.C.A.A. Proposes Uncapping Compensation for Athletes," *The New York Times*, December 5, 2023, www.nytimes.com/2023/12/05/us/ncaa-athlete-compensation-cap-

proposal.html#:~:text=N.C.A.A.-,Proposes%20Uncapping%20 Compensation%20for%20Athletes,comply%20with%20Title%20 IX%20laws

11 Michael McCann, "Year in Sports Law: The NCAA Amateurism Meltdown," *Sportico*, December 27, 2023, www.sportico.com/law/analysis/2023/biggest-sports-law-controversies-2023-ncaa-amateurism-1234760591/

12 "Hawaii Pacific University Sharks," accessed March 2024, https://hpusharks.com/index.aspx

13 U.S. Department of Education, Office of Postsecondary Education, "Equity in Athletics Data Analysis (EADA)," *Equity in Athletics Data Analysis*, 2023, accessed April 2023, https://ope.ed.gov/athletics/Trend/public/#/answer/6/601/trend/-1/-1/-1/-1

14 Ibid.

15 U.S. Bureau of Labor Statistics, "Occupational Employment and Wages, May 22 English Language and Literature Teachers, Postsecondary," April 25, 2023, www.bls.gov/oes/current/oes251123.htm

16 U.S. Bureau of Labor Statistics, "Occupational Employment, and Wages, Occupational Employment and Wages, May 2022, Engineering Teachers, Postsecondary," April 25, 2023, www.bls.gov/oes/current/oes251032.htm

17 ProPublica, "Full text of 'Full Filing' for fiscal year ending June 2022," *ProPublica*, accessed August 2023, https://projects.propublica.org/nonprofits/organizations/580652518/202330529349300133/full

18 University of Georgia, "2023 Football Roster," accessed August 2023, https://georgiadogs.com/sports/football/roster

19 Ibid.

20 Ralph Russo & The Associated Press, "Big Ten signs historic TV deal for college football and basketball, raking in $1 billion a year," *Fortune*, August 18, 2022, https://fortune.com/2022/08/18/big-ten-historic-tv-deal-college-football-basketball-1-billion-a-year/

21 Michael Smith, "Big Ten officially agrees to new media deals with CBS, Fox, NBC," *Sports Business Journal*, August 18, 2022, www.sportsbusinessjournal.com/Daily/Issues/2022/08/18/Media/Big-Ten-Media-Deal.aspx

22 On3 Staff Report, "Here's a look at all the current conference TV deals," August 8, 2021, www.on3.com/news/conference-tv-deals-current-status-college-football/

23 Learfield website, 2023, accessed April 2023, from www.learfield.com/

24 Cork Gaines, "Chart Shows How Little of College Sports Revenues Goes to the Athletes," *Business Insider*, September 24, 2014, www.businessinsider.com/college-sports-revenue-athlete-scholarships-2014-9

25 Quoted in Tim Sullivan, "NCAA is not above the law:' Supreme Court finds NCAA on wrong side of antitrust argument," *Louisville Courier Journal*, 2023, https://eu.courier-journal.com/story/sports/college/louisville/2021/06/21/supreme-court-ruling-ncaa-antitrust-argument-paying-college-athletes/7770185002/

26 American Gaming Association, "68 Million Americans to Wager on March Madness," *American Gaming Association Press Release*, March 12, 2023, www.americangaming.org/new/68-million-americans-to-wager-on-march-madness/

27 Paul Myerberg, "Alabama baseball gambling scandal reflects a new reality in college athletics," *USA TODAY*, May 12, 2023, www.usatoday.com/story/sports/college/2023/05/12/alabama-baseball-gambling-scandal-college-sports-new-reality/70200887007/#:~:text=On percent20May percent201 percent2C percent20the percent20executive,Crimson percent20Tide's percent20matchup percent20against percent20LSU

28 Cole Claybourn, "Sports Betting on College Campuses: What to Know," *U.S. News & World Report*, April 18, 2023, www.usnews.com/education/best-colleges/articles/sports-betting-on-college-campuses-what-to-know#:~:text=April percent2018 percent2C percent202023 percent2C percent20at percent203 percent3A00 percent20p.m.&text=Sports percent20betting percent2C percent20now percent20legal percent20in,directly percent20and percent20indirectly percent20to percent20students.

29 Erin Bowling, "Controversy surrounds MSU's partnership with Caesars Sports Book," *WILX News*, April 7, 2023, www.wilx.com/2023/04/07/controversy-surrounds-msus-partnership-with-caesars-sports-book/

30 Anna Betts et al., "How Colleges and Sports-Betting Companies 'Caesarized' Campus Life," *The New York Times*, November 21, 2022, www.nytimes.com/2022/11/20/business/caesars-sports-betting-universities-colleges.html

31 Izzy Fincher, "CU Boulder ends sports betting partnership with PointsBet," *CU Independent*, March 31, 2023, www.cuindependent.com/2023/03/31/cu-boulder-ends-sports-betting-partnership-with-pointsbet/

32 Betts et al., "How Colleges and Sports-Betting Companies 'Caesarized.'"

33 Myerberg, "Alabama baseball gambling scandal reflects a new reality in college athletics."

34 Kevin Draper & Eric Lipton, "First Came the Sports Betting Boom. Now Comes the Backlash," *The New York Times*, May 13, 2023, www.nytimes.com/2023/05/13/sports/online-sports-gambling-regulations.html

35 American Gaming Association, "New Updates to AGA Responsible Marketing Code for Sports Wagering Prohibit 'Risk Free,' Enhance College-Aged Protections," *Press Release*, March 28, 2023, https://www.americangaming.org/new/new-updates-to-aga-responsible-marketing-code-for-sports-wagering-prohibit-risk-free-enhance-college-aged-protections/

36 Mary Sugden, "'Ignorance isn't a defense': Sports analyst weighs in on alleged sports betting by Iowa, Iowa State student athletes," *We are Iowa, 2023 WOI-TV*, May 9, 2023, www.weareiowa.com/article/news/local/iowa-state-university-of-iowa-sports-betting-allegations-student-athletes-investigation/524-623fd236-e51d-4463-8604-9866f5c0ec91#:~:text=DES percent20MOINES percent2C percent20Iowa percent20 percentE2 percent80 percent94 percent20The percent20University,been percent20linked percent20to percent20an percent20investigation

37 Rick Maese & Danny Funt, "In Iowa and Alabama, Betting Scandals Raise Red Flags for College Sports," *Washington Post*, May 12, 2023, www.washingtonpost.com/sports/2023/05/12/alabama-iowa-ncaa-sports-betting. See also Draper & Lipton, "First Came the Sports Betting Boom. Now Comes the Backlash."

38 QS Top Universities, "Clemson University," 2023, accessed August 2023, www.topuniversities.com/universities/clemson-university#:~:text=Rankings percent20 percent26 percent20ratings,-RANKINGS&text=Clemson percent20University percent20is percent20one percent20of,QS percent20World percent20University percent20Rankings percent202024.

39 Senator Chris Murphy, "Madness, Inc."

40 Brad Crawford, "College football's 25 best facilities in 2022, ranked," *24/7 Sports*, February 8, 2022, https://247sports.com/longformarticle/college-footballs-25-best-facilities-in-2022-ranked-182436036/#1830400

41 Craig Garthwaite et al., "Revenue Redistribution in Big-Time College Sports," National Bureau of Economic Research, *The Digest*, 11 (November 2020), www.nber.org/digest/202011/revenue-redistribution-big-time-college-sports

42 McCann, "Year in Sports Law: The NCAA Amateurism Meltdown."

43 Craig Garthwaite et al., "Who Profits from Amateurism? Rent-Sharing in Modern College Sports," National Bureau of Economic Research, Working Paper 27734, November 2020, www.nber.org/papers/w27734

44 Ibid.

45 PBS NewsHour, "What did Michigan State know about Larry Nassar's abuse?" January 29, 2018, www.pbs.org/newshour/show/what-did-michigan-state-know-about-larry-nassars-abuse#:~:text=They percent20said percent20very percent20little percent20initially,the percent20first percent20Indy percent20Star percent20story.

46 Ibid.

47 Jack Nissen, "Michigan AG renews request for Larry Nassar files unreleased by MSU Board," *Fox News 2*, Detroit, April 17, 2023, www.fox2detroit.com/news/michigan-ag-renews-request-for-larry-nassar-files-unreleased-by-msu-board

48 Jennifer Smola Shaffer, "What to know about Ohio State University athletic doctor Richard Strauss' career, abuse and death," *The Columbus Dispatch*, March 10, 2021, www.dispatch.com/story/news/education/2021/03/10/osu-sex-abuse-scandal-richard-strauss-career-abuse-death/6947149002/

49 Ben Jones, "Penn State Athletics: All-Time Highs Have Department Eyeing $1 Billion in Football Revenue Since James Franklin Hire," *Statecollege.com*, February 2, 2023, www.statecollege.com/articles/penn-state-sports/penn-state-athletics-all-time-highs-have-department-eying-a-billion-in-football-revenue-since-james-franklin-hire/#:~:text=Penn percent20State percent20athletics percent20reported percent20 percent24181.2,report percent20released percent20on percent20Wednesday percent20evening.

50 CNN Editorial Research, "Penn State Scandal Fast Facts," *CNN*, April 13, 2023, www.cnn.com/2013/10/28/us/penn-state-scandal-fast-facts/index.html

51 Ibid.

52 Shaffer, "What to know about Ohio State University athletic doctor."

53 Sarah Szilagy, "More Strauss lawsuits against Ohio State can proceed, but judge need not recuse himself, appeals court rules," *NBC4i*, February 15, 2023, www.nbc4i.com/news/local-news/ohio-state-university/more-strauss-lawsuits-against-ohio-state-can-proceed-but-judge-need-not-recuse-himself-appeals-court-rules/#:~:text=Strauss percent20was percent20an percent20Ohio percent20State,died percent20by percent20suicide percent20in percent202005

54 Laura Wagner, "Baylor Regents Describe Gang Rape, Other Alleged Assault by Football Players," *NPR*, October 29, 2016, www.npr.org/sections/thetwo-way/2016/10/29/499882576/baylor-regents-describe-gang-rape-other-alleged-assault-by-football-players

55 Associated Press, "Key dates and developments in the Baylor assault scandal," *Associated Press*, August 11, 2021, https://apnews.com/article/sports-college-football-violence-lawsuits-sexual-assault-9fe035761dc3d1f3d42c714a87c78a10

56 ESPN, "The timeline of Art Briles' downfall at Baylor before his hire at Grambling State," *ESPN*, February 24, 2022, www.espn.com/college-football/story/_/id/33365146/the-line-art-briles-downfall-baylor-hire-grambling-state

57 Ibid.

58 Baylor University, Baylor University Board of Regents, "Findings of Fact," 2016, accessed April 2023, https://thefacts.web.baylor.edu/

59 Wagner, "Baylor Regents Describe Gang Rape."

60 Tom Schad, "New lawsuit provides most detailed account to date of alleged Northwestern football hazing," *USA TODAY*, July 24, 2023, www.usatoday.com/story/sports/ncaaf/bigten/2023/07/24/northwestern-football-hazing-lloyd-yates-lawsuit-details-ben-crump/70454975007/

61 Matt Masterson, "The Northwestern Hazing Scandal: A Timeline of Allegations, Investigations and Lawsuits," *WTTW (Chicago Public Radio)*, July 28, 2023, https://news.wttw.com/2023/07/28/northwestern-hazing-scandal-timeline-allegations-investigations-and-lawsuits

62 Schad, "New lawsuit provides most detailed account to date of alleged Northwestern football hazing."

63 NCAA, "Recruiting Facts," 2014, www.nfhs.org/media/886012/recruiting-fact-sheet-web.pdf

64 NCAA Research, "Trends in NCAA Division I Graduation Rates," November 2022, https://ncaaorg.s3.amazonaws.com/research/gradrates/2022/2022D1RES_GSRTrends.pdf

65 Zimbalist, "Who Wins with College Sports?"

66 The Drake Group, "Why the NCAA Academic Progress Rate (APR) and the Graduation Success Rate (GSR) should be Abandoned and Replaced with More Effective Academic Metrics," July 2021, www.thedrakegroup.org/2015/06/07/why-the-ncaa-academic-progress-rate-apr-and-the-graduation-success-rate-gsr-should-be-abandoned-and-replaced-with-more-effective-academic-metrics/

67 Jordan Acker, "The Only Way College Sports Can Begin to Make Sense Again," *The New York Times*, September 21, 2023, www.nytimes.com/2023/09/21/opinion/college-sports-broken.html

68 Galanty Miller, "Here's My Advice to College Professors Being Pressured to Change Student-Athletes' Grades," *Huffpost*, September 29, 2016, www.huffpost.com/entry/heres-my-advice-to-colleg_b_8208302

69 Justin Byers, "College Athletes Could Earn $1.5B This Year," *Front Office Sports*, October 6, 2021, https://frontofficesports.com/college-athletes-could-earn-1b-this-year/#:~:text=The percent20U.S. percent20Department percent20of percent20Education, percent2C percent20merchandise percent2C percent20and percent20ticket percent20sales.

70 Cole Claybourn, "Name, Image, Likeness: What College Athletes Should Know About NCAA Rules," *U.S. News & World Report*, March 23, 2023, www.usnews.com/education/best-colleges/articles/name-image-likeness-what-college-athletes-should-know-about-ncaa-rules

71 See https://www.inflcr.com/

72 Opendorse website, 2023. https://opendorse.com

73 Carly Wanna & Bloomberg, "NCAA athletes are receiving millions of dollars from collectives created by rich college sports fans," *Fortune*, May 16, 2022, https://fortune.com/2022/05/16/ncaa-athletes-millions-compensation-funds-wealthy-college-sports-fans/

74 Ibid.

75 Nicholas Auerbach, "Federal judge blocks NCAA from enforcing NIL rules," *The Atlantic*, February 24, 2024, https://theathletic.com/5295907/2024/02/23/tennessee-ncaa-nil-lawsuit-injunction/

76 George Will, "At last, college football admits it is an unembarrassable money machine," *The Washington Post*, August 18, 2023, www.washingtonpost.com/opinions/2023/08/18/college-football-realignment-money-machine/?wpisrc=nl-georgefwill

77 On3 Transfer Protocol, "2023 College Football Transfer Portal," accessed October 2023, www.on3.com/transfer-portal/wire/football/2023/

78 Gary Shaw, *Meat on the hoof: The hidden world of Texas football* (NY: St. Martin's Press, 1972).

79 Senator Chris Murphy, "Madness, Inc."

80 Ibid.

81 Julia Elbaba, "Looking at the top college football head coach salaries in 2022," *NBC Sport*s, September 8, 2022, www.nbcsports.com/chicago/college-football-head-coach-salaries-kirby-smart-2022-new-contract. Scott Fujita, "How Much Do NFL Coaches Make? The Highest-paid NFL Coaches in 2023," *Scott Fujita*, April 11, 2023,www.scottfujita.com/how-much-do-nfl-coaches-make/#:~:text=The percent20average percent20NFL percent20coach percent20salary,the percent20average percent20is percent20 percent245.5 percent20million. See also Brent Schrotenboer, Steve Berkowitz & Christopher Schnaars, "Hiring a college football coach is expensive. Firing one is, too," *USA TODAY*, October 26, 2016, www.usatoday.com/story/sports/ncaaf/2016/10/26/college-football-coach-salary-database-buyouts-kirk-ferentz-iowa-charlie-strong-texas/92417648/

82 Babu Tendu, "NBA coaches' salaries: Who is the highest paid coach in basketball?" *Sports Brief*, March 18, 2023, https://sportsbrief.com/nba/36262-nba-coaches-salaries-highest-paid-coach-basketball/. "Highest-Paid College Basketball Coaches: Top Salaries for 2022–23 Season," *Betmgm*, 2022, https://sports.betmgm.com/en/blog/ncaab/top-college-basketball-head-coach-salaries-bm10/

83 Taylor Branch, "The Shame of College Sports," *The Atlantic*, October 2011, www.theatlantic.com/magazine/archive/2011/10/the-shame-of-college-sports/308643/

84 Ibid.

85 Richard Johnson, "A history of skyrocketing college football coach salaries, from Camp to Dabo," *Banner Society*, August 15, 2019, www.bannersociety.com/2019/8/15/20732192/coach-salaries-history-highestLet's go back to the beginning and adjust everything for inflation along the way.

86 Brett Weisband, "What would Bear Bryant be worth today?" *Saturday Down South*, 2015, www.saturdaydownsouth.com/alabama-football/bear-bryant-worth-today/

87 Candid, "University of Oregon Receives $100 Million for Athletics Programs," August 22, 2007, https://philanthropynewsdigest.org/news/university-of-oregon-receives-100-million-for-athletics-programs. See also *The Oregonian*, "Phil Knight's University of Oregon donations push $1 billion mark with new Hayward field project," March 9, 2021, https://www.oregonlive.com/news/2021/03/knights-university-of-oregon-donations-push-1-billion-mark-with-new-hayward-field-project.html

88 William Deresiewicz, "How to Overhaul Higher Education: A few modest proposals for fixing a broken system," *Persuasion*, July 31, 2023, www.persuasion.community/p/how-to-overhaul-higher-education

89 Scott Hirko, "I found 18 profitable & 211 money-losing NCAA Division-I public athletic programs in 2020," September 3, 2022, www.linkedin.com/pulse/i-found-18-profitable-211-money-losing-ncaa-public-scott-hirko-ph-d-#:~:text=Of percent20available percent20data percent2C percent20a percent20total,deficit percent20at percent20James percent20Madison percent20University

90 NCAA, "15-Year Trends in Division I Athletics Finances," 2020, https://ncaaorg.s3.amazonaws.com/committees/d1/presforum/sustain/2020D1RES_15YrTrendsD1AthFinances.pdf

91 Merritt Enright, Andrew Lehren & Jaime Longoria, "Hidden figures: College students may be paying thousands in athletic fees and not know it," *NBC News*, March 8, 2020, www.nbcnews.com/news/education/hidden-figures-college-students-may-be-paying-thousands-athletic-fees-n1145171

92 Ibid.

93 Gerald Gurney, Donna Lopiano & Andrew Zimbalist, *Unwinding Madness: What Went Wrong with College Sports?* (Washington, DC: Brookings Institution Press, 2017).

94 Benjamin Baumer & Andrew Zimbalist, "The Impact of College Athletic Success on Donations and Applicant Quality," *International Journal of Financial Studies* 7, no. 2 (April, 2019): 1–23, www.mdpi.com/2227-7072/7/2/19

95 Will, "At last, college football admits it is an unembarrassable money machine."

Chapter 6

1 Michael Crow & William Dabars, *The Fifth Wave* (Baltimore, MD: Johns Hopkins University, 2020), 3, 19.

2 Robert Gordon, *The Rise and Fall of American Growth* (Princeton, NJ: Princeton University Press, 2016).

3 *Inside Higher Education*, www.insidehighered.com/opinion/views/2023/05/09/launch-long-game

4 Louis Menand applied this concept to higher education in *The Marketplace of Ideas* (New York: W.W. Norton, 2010).

5 Michael Young, *The Rise of the Meritocracy* (London: Thames and Hudson, 1958), 103.

6 Ibid., 94.

7 Daniel Markovitz, *The Meritocracy Trap* (New York: Penguin, 2020).

8 Richard Reeves, *Dream Hoarders* (Washington, DC: Brookings Institution, 2017).

9 Branko Milanovic, *Capitalism Alone* (Cambridge, MA: Harvard University Press, 2019), 66.

10 Wikipedia, https://en.wikipedia.org/wiki/Varsity_Blues_scandal

11 Raj Chetty, David Deming, & John Friedman, "Diversifying Society's Leaders? The Determinants and Causal Effects of Admission to Highly Selective Private Colleges," *Opportunity Insights*, July 2023, https://opportunityinsights.org/wp-content/uploads/2023/07/CollegeAdmissions_Paper.pdf

12 David Leonhardt & Ashley WU, "The Top U.S. Colleges with the Greatest Economic Diversity," *The New York Times*, September 7, 2023, www.nytimes.com/interactive/2023/09/11/upshot/college-income-lookup.html. Aatish Bhatia & Claire Miller, "Explore How Income Influences Attendance at 139 Top Colleges," *The New York Times*, September 11, 2023, www.nytimes.com/interactive/2023/09/11/upshot/college-income-lookup.html

13 Paul Tough, *The Years That Matter Most* (New York: Houghton Mifflin Harcourt, 2019), 219.

14 Bhatia & Miller, "Explore How Income Influences Attendance at 139 Top Colleges."

15 Frank Bruni, *Where You Go Is Not Who You'll Be* (New York: Grand Central Publishing, 2015).

16 Mark Bovens & Anchrit Wille, *Diploma Democracies* (New York: Oxford University Press, 2017).

17 Abraham Jack, *The Privileged Poor* (Cambridge, MA: Harvard University Press, 2019), 4.

18 Jennifer Rubin, "'I don't write about polls. You shouldn't bother with them, either," *The Washington Post*, September 10, 2023, www.washingtonpost.com/opinions/2023/09/10/pollings-unrealistic-coverage/

19 Peter Coy, "The Unfinished Pursuit of a Better Poverty Measure," *The New York Times*, September 11, 2023, www.nytimes.com/2023/09/11/opinion/poverty-measure.html?action=click&module=Well&pgtype=Homepage§ion=Opinion

20 Tom Nichols, *The Death of Expertise* (New York: Oxford University Press, 2017), 35.

21 David Gaebler, *Bullshit Jobs* (New York: Penguin, 2018), 55.

22 Paul Weinstein, "Administrative Bloat in U.S. Colleges Has Skyrocketed," *Forbes*, August 28, 2023.

23 David Goodhart, *The Road to Somewhere* (London: Hurst & Company, 2017), 167–8.

24 Megan Brenner, "Americans' Confidence in Higher Education Down Sharply," *Gallup*, July 17, 2023, https://news.gallup.com/poll/508352/americans-confidence-higher-education-down-sharply.aspx

25 Frank Newport & Brandon Busteed, "Why Are Republicans Down on Higher Ed?" *Gallup*, August 16, 2017, https://news.gallup.com/poll/216278/why-republicans-down-higher.aspx

26 Joan Williams, *White Working Class* (Cambridge, MA: Harvard Business School, 2017), 104.

27 James Koch, *The Impoverishment of the American College Student* (Washington, DC: Brookings Institution, 2019).

28 Community College Daily, www.ccdaily.com/2019/02/good-news-charitable-donations/

29 Jack, *The Privileged Poor*, 22.

30 David Kirp, *The College Dropout Scandal* (New York: Oxford University Press, 2019).

31 Menand, *The Marketplace of Ideas*, 80.

32 Richard Arum & Josipa Roksa, *Academically Adrift* (Chicago, IL: University of Chicago, 2011).

33 Mark Bauerlein, *The Dumbest Generation* (New York: Penguin, 2008).

34 Kevin Carey, *The End of College* (New York: Riverhead Books, 2015).

35 Derek Bok, *Our Underachieving Colleges* (Princeton, NJ: Princeton University Press, 2006).

36 The ratio of liberal to conservative faculty varies with the discipline and the institution but probably is on the order of 5:1 overall. See Menand, *The Marketplace of Ideas*, 136–7.

37 Greg Lukianoff & Jonathan Haidt, *The Coddling of the American Mind* (New York: Penguin, 2018), 48, 80.

38 Clayton Christensen, *Disrupting Class* (New York: McGraw Hill, 2008).

Conclusion

1 Evan Castillo & Lyss Welding, "Closed Colleges: List, Statistics, and Major Closures," *Best Colleges*, August 28, 2023, www.bestcolleges.com/research/closed-colleges-list-statistics-major-closures/

2 "News Release: State Secures Private Debt Relief for Former Argosy University," *State of Hawaii, Department of Commerce and Consumer Affairs*, March 1, 2022, https://cca.hawaii.gov/blog/news-release-state-secures-private-debt-relief-for-former-argosy-university/#:~:text=Mismanagement%20by%20Dream%20Center%20ultimately,of%20Argosy%20students%20in%20Hawaii

NOTES

3   National Center for Education Statistics, "Undergraduate graduation rates," *Fast Facts*, 2022, accessed August 2023, https://nces.ed.gov/fastfacts/display.asp?id=40

4   Preston Cooper, "What's in a New Regulation Targeting For-Profit Colleges, Trade Schools," *Forbes*, May 19, 2023, www.forbes.com/sites/prestoncooper2/2023/05/19/whats-in-a-new-regulation-targeting-for-profit-colleges-trade-schools/?sh=602f9134388a

5   American Council of Trustees and Alumni (ACTA), "What Will They Learn? 2022–2023," 2024, www.goacta.org/resource/what-will-they-learn-2022-2023/

6   Ibid.

7   College Board, *Trends in College Pricing: Highlights*, 2024, https://research.collegeboard.org/trends/college-pricing/highlights#

8   Philip Levine, "The economic case for doubling the Pell Grant," *Brooking*, February 17, 2021, www.brookings.edu/articles/the-economic-case-for-doubling-the-pell-grant/

9   Up$tart website, 2019, accessed August 2023, https://www.upstartbenefits.com/

10 Amelia Josephson, "The Average Salary by Age in the U.S.—Are You Making What You Should Be?" *SmartAsset*, March 13, 2023, www.nasdaq.com/articles/the-average-salary-by-age-in-the-u.s.-are-you-making-what-you-should-be#:~:text=According%20to%20BLS%20data%2C%20the,races%2C%20genders%20and%20education%20levels.&text=Earnings%20increase%20beginning%20in%20one's,includes%20some%20new%20college%20graduates

11 United States Government Accountability Office, "Higher Education: Students Need More Information to Help Reduce Challenges in Transferring College Credits," August 2017, www.gao.gov/assets/gao-17-574.pdf

12 National Center for Education Statistics, "Table 330.20 Average undergraduate tuition, fees, room, and board charges for full-time students in degree-granting postsecondary institutions," *Digest of Education Statistics*, 2022, accessed August 2023, https://nces.ed.gov/programs/digest/d21/tables/dt21_330.20.asp

13 Lyss Welding, "Student Loan Default Rate: Facts and Statistics," *Best Colleges*, February 6, 2023, www.bestcolleges.com/research/student-loan-default-rate-facts-statistics/#:~:text=At%202.3%25%20the%20federal%20student%20loan%20default,default%20rates%2C%20the%20total%20defaulted%20loan%20balance%2C

14 Organisation for Economic Cooperation and Development (OECD), "Indicator C1. How much is spent per student on educational

institutions?" 2023, www.oecd-ilibrary.org/sites/b25ab7e2-en/index.html?itemId=/content/component/b25ab7e2-en#:~:text=In%202019%2C%20OECD%20countries%20spent,Kingdom%20and%20the%20United%20States.

15 Ibid.
16 QS Top Universities, 2023, accessed August 2023, www.topuniversities.com/student-info/choosing-university/worlds-top-100-universities
17 Paul Tough, "Americans Are Losing Faith in the Value of College. Whose Fault Is That?" *The New York Times*, September 5, 2023, www.nytimes.com/2023/09/05/magazine/college-worth-price.html
18 Ibid.
19 Council of Europe, "The Democratic Mission of Higher Education," 2024, www.coe.int/en/web/higher-education-and-research/democratic-mission-of-higher-education

Index

2U Corporation 102

Abbott, Greg 34, 95–6
academic program duplication 77
   role of accrediting bodies 78, 168
accountability, higher education 124, 150
Acker, Jordan 126
ACTA (American Council of Trustees and Alumni) 56, 165
adjunct faculty 41, 121, 156, 166–9
   exploited 100, 108
   low-paid 50, 100, 108–9, 159–60
   used to cut costs 55, 71, 92, 177
administrative bloat 56–8, 81–3, 94–5, 150, 166
affirmative action 35–6, 155
amateur sports 112, 117, 119, 139–40
American Association of University Professors (AAUP) 50–3
American Enterprise Institute 145
American exceptionalism 1
antisemitism 164
   Department of Education 35
Aragon, Manny 93–4
artificial intelligence (AI) 26, 104
athletics-based student fees 134–5
Atlas, Scott 33

Bain & Company 59
   scandal 62
Baker, Charlie 113
Bauerlein, Mark 155
Baumol's cost disease 50
Baylor University sex abuse scandal 124–5
Biden, Joe 32
Bill and Melinda Gates Foundation 47
Black, Lewis 79
Bloomberg, Michael 153
Boards of Trustees 55, 95–6, 98–9
   financial links 123, 156
   isolated from the university 169, 173
   role of 95, 150
   supporting administration 33, 38, 99
Boyer, Ernest 155
Briles, Art 124–5
Brookings 145
Brooks, David 48
Byers, Justin 127
Byers, Walter 111–2

Carey, Kevin 155
Cato Institute 145
Center on Budget and Policy Priorities 145
Center on Education and the Workforce (Georgetown University) 5, 47, 148
Chetty, Raj 1

Chicago Statement (University of Chicago) 164
Classic Learning Test (CLT) 33–4
coaching salaries 120, 130–3
  comparison with college presidents 132–3
college alternatives 27
College Board 169
college choice 13–15
college endowments 55, 71, 137, 154, 162
  Bipartisan Budget Act 168
  financial networking 92, 144, 148
  value of 65–6, 168
college enrollment declines 41, 150
college presidents, salaries 85–91
  non-traditional presidents 92–4, 167
college resentment, skepticism 32, 46, 151–2, 153
college sports industry 114–16
  broadcasting, advertising revenues 116–17
college transfer credits 172
Collegiate Learning Assessment (CLA) 29, 155
commodification 28, 46, 48, 69, 75, 160
  college sports 109, 111, 119, 121, 128, 139
  connection to corporatization and management 78–9, 96, 109
  faculty and students 40–41, 160
  institutional debt 55
  quality of education 107, 163, 180
  value of the degree 48, 81
community colleges 4, 76, 144, 154, 176
  few donations 153
  low enrollments 77, 175
  low-income students 149, 153
  ROI 15
  transition to 4-year college 172
consulting corporations 174
  cost 59–62
  impact 58–62
contract workers 55, 100
  exploitation 41, 101, 108, 160
  institutional savings 169
  no job security 101
  replace full-time faculty 71, 100, 160
core curriculum 33, 155, 164–5
  ranking 165
core values 61, 163
  free speech 164
corporatization 28, 48, 143, 145
  administrative hierarchy 79, 84–85, 109
  anti-union 108
  college sports 109, 128
  employee, faculty morale 108, 160
  increased college costs 107
  moral core 163, 180
  quality of education 107
cost-of-attendance stipend for student-athletes 127
Covid-19 49, 98, 149
  college sports 114, 134
  enrollment declines 156
  impact on college budgets 95
  suspension of student loan payments 46
Crow, Michael 143
CRT (Critical Race Theory) 32, 34, 35

Dabars, William 143
DEI (Diversity, Equity, and Inclusion) 34–5, 156
DeSantis, Ron 33, 34, 155–6
Division 1 schools 129

NCAA rules 134, 139
sports revenues and profits 129
Dunne, Olivia 127

e-sports 38
economic mobility 1
educational credentials, pushback 23–4
eliminating NCAA college sports 135–7, 177–8
European sports clubs 138

Faculty salaries 50–3
FEMA Corps 171
Fitzgerald, Pat 125
for-profit colleges and universities 1, 2, 4, 98, 144, 149
  legitimacy issues 163
  low educational standards and selectivity 21, 104, 163
  low graduation rates 21, 23
  low-income students 21, 162–3
  poor ROI 15
  predatory practices 104, 162
  shaky finances 161, 163
Freeh, Louis 123
Friedman, Milton 146

GI Bill 146
gig economy in academia 100, 160
Goodhart, David 151
Graeber, David 150
Gurney, Gerald 136

Hawaii Pacific University 99
Heritage Foundation 145
Higher Education Act of 1965 146
higher education expenditures 78
  international comparison 178–9
Hirko, Scott 129, 134

History of college sports 143–6
housing bubble and student loans 42

income inequality 1
institutional debt 54–6
Iowa House of representatives CRT ban 34
ivies 3, 148, 149, 161

Jack, Abraham 149, 154
job satisfaction, professionals 46–7
Jordan, Jim (US House Representative) 124

Kavanaugh, Brett 117
Khator, Renu 34
Knight, Phil 133–4

labor market outcomes, college graduates 7–10, 25
legacy admissions 36, 148
Levy, David 50
liberal arts cuts 37, 38
lifetime earnings, college graduates 5–7
  by race and gender 10–1
low-income students 15–18, 21–3, 143, 153, 173–4

managerialism in higher education 82, 96, 150, 167
  salaries and perks 84–5
master's degrees, growth 39–40
McCaw, Ian 124–5
McKinsey and Company 58–9
  scandals 61–2
McWilliams, James 46
median wage, professions 12–13
meritocracy 146, 147, 148–9, 150, 156
Michigan State University sex abuse scandal 122–3

Milanovic, Branko 147
Morrill Act (1862) 144
Murphy v. NCAA 117–18
Musk, Elon 47

Nader, Ralph 145
Napolitano, Janet 93
Nassar, Larry 122–3
National Labor Relations Board v. Yeshiva University 99
NBA (National Basketball Association) 131, 138, 140
NCAA (National Collegiate Athletic Association) history and scandals 111–2
athlete salaries 113–14
revenues, expenditures 112–13
salaries 113
NCAA GSR (athlete graduation success rates) 126
for minority athletes 126
problems with 126
NCAA transfer portal 128–9
NCAA v. Alston 127
Neems, Johan 47
neoliberalism 30–1, 36
New College (Florida) 33
NFL (National Football League) 131, 138, 140
Nichols, Tom 34–5, 149
NILS (name, image and likeness), 127–9
NCAA rules 128
Northwestern University hazing scandal 125

Obama administration 151, 154
OER (open educational resources) 106–8
Ohio State University sex abuse scandal 123
online education 41, 102, 108, 163, 175

Open Textbook Pilot Act 106–7
OpenStax 106
OPM (online program managers) 101–4
ending 175
market saturation 103, 108, 109, 156
Oppenheimer, Robert 48
opportunity costs, college 10, 154, 156

Paterno, Joe 123
Peace Corps 171
Pell grants 23, 146, 151, 154, 170–1
Pennsylvania State University sex abuse scandal 123
Pepper Hamilton law firm 124
politicization of higher education 31–6, 96, 97
Powell, Lewis 145

race-based admissions 36
ranking US colleges 2, 29
world ranking 4
RCM (Responsibility Centered Management) 82
Reagan, Ronald 30
research 159
funding 65, 67–8
impact on teaching 165–6
return on investment (ROI) 12, 15
Robbins, Robert 61
Rockne, Knute, Notre Dame's "Fighting Irish" 139
Rufo, Chris 33

Saban, Nick 113
Sandusky, Jerry 123
Sasse, Ben 59–60, 94
Segal AmeriCorps Education Award 171
shared governance 96–9, 104, 108

Simon Foundation 47
social welfare programs, use of 170
Spelling, Margaret 93
sports betting 117–20
 NCAA rules 119
 online campus betting 118–19
 scandals 119
sports facilities, quality and costs 120–1
 donor-funded 121, 139
Starr, Ken 124
state budget cuts, higher education 31, 32, 53, 78
Stefanik, Elise 35
STEM (science, technology, engineering, and mathematics) 38, 47
Strauss, Richard 123–4
student consumers 40–1
student loans, types 43–4
 debt trap 41
 defaults 44–5
 loan forgiveness 45–6
student poverty 20–1
student-athlete compensation 121–2
 v. professional sports 122
Summers, Jessica 61
Supreme Court ruling on affirmative action 35–6
Syracuse University, Knight Commission on Intercollegiate Athletics 130

teaching faculty 109, 166
tenure 33, 41, 92, 97, 99, 100
 anti-union 97, 160
 attacks on tenure 34, 55, 71, 96–97, 108
 costs of tenure 108
 critique of 97
 decline of tenured positions 98, 100–101, 109, 121
 replacing tenured faculty 92
 research and tenure 67, 166
Texas anti-DEI Senate Bill 34
textbooks, high cost 104–5, 106, 171
 digital and rentals 106–8
 publisher monopoly 105, 108
Thatcher, Margaret 30
Thomas, Clarence 36
Timme, Drew 127
Tough, Paul 148
transparency, higher education 72–6, 162
 manipulating costs 69–71
Trump, Donald 32, 152
tuition, increases 31, 41, 49–50, 150
 decreases 169
 transparency, hidden costs 161

university fundraising 63–5
University of Arizona 60–1
University of Arizona, consultants 60
University of Florida, consultants 60
University of Oregon's Athletics Legacy Fund 133
University of Southern California MSW program 103–4
university unions, fight against 98–9
 graduate assistants 101
Urban Institute 145

Varsity Blues scandal 147
VISTA 171
vocational focus, higher education 37, 38, 81, 109, 156

War on Poverty 149
West Virginia University 37–8, 58–9

Will, George 32–3, 140
Williams, Joan 153
woke (wokeness) 32, 35, 155–6, 164
working students 18–19

Young, Bryce 127
Young, Michael 146–7

Zimbalist, Andrew 126
zombie colleges 161